PLATO: REPUBLIC

This edition published in 2005 by
Bristol Classical Press
an imprint of
Gerald Duckworth & Co. Ltd.
90-93 Cowcross Street, London EC1M 6BF
Tel: 020 7490 7300
Fax: 020 7490 0080
inquiries@duckworth-publishers.co.uk
www.ducknet.co.uk

First published in 1957 by Bradda Books

A catalogue record for this book is available
from the British Library

ISBN 1 85399 255 0

IN PIAM MEMORIAM

M. P. C.

CONTENTS

FOREWORD

If one is to read an isolated book of the *Republic* there is much to be said for Book X. It is as near to being self-contained as a single book from a major work can be. It shows Plato as a writer both of dialogue and of myth. It introduces his views on aesthetics, metaphysics, and human destiny. Hence it seemed that there was need for an edition which would meet the requirements of the Sixth Former, the General Degree student, and the Honours student who is not a philosophy specialist. It is to these that this unpretentious edition is directed. The text is that of Burnet, with slight modifications only. The introduction, notes and appendices are designed to expound the subject-matter, to help the reader through difficult passages, and to adduce modern analogies where these seem illuminating.

The following books will be found additionally helpful. Adam's great edition is indispensable for anyone who wants to undertake a more detailed study. Cornford's translation is the best, and anyone would benefit from reading it through. Acknowledgment is due to the Oxford University Press for permission to quote from this. An inexpensive, sound, and easily accessible version has been contributed by H. D. P. Lee to the Penguin Classics. R. L. Nettleship's *Lectures on the Republic of Plato*, though more than fifty years old, remains the most brilliant assessment of the work as a whole. J. A. Stewart's *The Myths of Plato*, though a bit turgid in its writing, is a useful collocation of and commentary on the myths. G. M. A. Grube's *Plato's Thought* is the best account of its subject.

My gratitude is due to a number of people, to the General Editor of the Series, Professor W. S. Maguinness, for his advice and encouragement; to a number of friends, amongst whom must be specially named Mr J. K. Major for putting his skilled draughtsmanship at my disposal for the figures, Mr H. F. Guite for his helpful and accurate proof-reading, and Dr R. S. Bluck and Mr P. Considine for detailed criticism of the manuscript—I need hardly say that errors which remain are due to my obstinacy alone; and last but not least, to my wife for her constructive helpfulness with the typewriter and her patience with my preoccupations.

J. F.

Publisher's Note

The thanks of Methuen & Co. Ltd are due to the Syndics of the Oxford University Press for permission to reproduce the Greek text from the Oxford Classical Texts edition of *Plato's Republic*, edited by John Burnet.

INTRODUCTION

Historical Background

Greece is a land of many mountains and few extensive plains. The growth of civilized communities tended to take place in coastal lowlands shut off from one another by hill barriers which in winter might be difficult of transgress. This, combined with the effect of bright sunlight in producing sharp outlines, helps to explain the clear-cut, analytic nature of Greek thought and the Greek approach to life. A Greek temple is complete in itself, in contrast with a Gothic cathedral where generation after generation makes additions in its own style, and produces a dynamic whole. Greek thought produced the conception of *autarcy*, self-sufficiency, by contrast with the wide plains of Russia where was evolved the idea of *sobornost*, catholicity of fellowship.

There were indigenous peoples, and we can trace survivals of their practices and traditions. These were overlaid towards the end of the second millennium B.C. by waves of invaders from the north, and it was these invaders who gave to Greece her characteristic civilization of classical times. As the centuries pass we trace three significant patterns of development. The first is the fusion of the old villages into a single city-state; this development may be put in the eighth century. The second, starting at about the same time and lasting 250 or more years, is the widespread emigration to other parts of the Mediterranean, which we call colonization, due to economic distress and political discontent. This had the effect of spreading Greek culture and developing a sense of common heritage by contrast with the lands in which they settled. The third is the internal development of the city-state from monarchy through oligarchy and dictatorship to democracy. This development is to be seen most clearly and fully at Athens. At Sparta it was 'arrested'. There a form of monarchy was retained, but the power rested with a small aristocracy who used every device of censorship and violence to maintain their position. It is to be remembered that democracy meant to the Greek government by assembly, in which every citizen could share directly; in Athens even those offices (except the generalship and some priesthoods) which were necessarily limited were allocated by lot. Critics felt such a form of government was unstable and irresponsible. It is to be remembered also that all Greek politics was sustained on a foundation of degrading slavery. Athenian slaves were freer than most, but 20,000 deserted to Decelea in the last stages of the Peloponnesian War.

The fifth century began with the conjoint victory of the Greeks over Persia; it ended with the collapse of Athens and her maritime empire, before the coalition of Sparta and Corinth, substantially aided by Syracuse and Persia. The unity which had been shown against Xerxes had fallen apart. In the years which followed it was fervently preached by Isocrates, a more far-seeing statesman than the philosopher Plato or the none too scrupulous politician Demosthenes. But the fourth century showed a fresh struggle for hegemony among the city-states, weakened by war, and blind in their isolation. First Sparta was dominant after her victory, then under the genius of Conon Athens revived, then Thebes enjoyed her brief period of military splendour. Meantime in the North the state of Macedon was growing strong in a fusion of Greek and non-Greek culture, and in 338 the battle of Chaeronea saw the end of Greek liberty and the beginning of Greek unity.

In Athens the full democracy of the mid-fifth century was stabilized by the dominant personality of Pericles; it was in fact, says a writer of the time, a concealed monarchy, though he is not wholly just, for Pericles was not immune from criticism nor always secure in authority. With the death of Pericles and the passions of war, the democracy became less stable and responsible, and Cleon, who had some pretensions to statesmanship, Hyperbolus and Cleophon have become for us the type of demagogy. The disastrous expedition to Sicily brought a reaction against the democrats, and there were various movements towards an order less subject to momentary whims and ambitions; one constitution, associated with the name of Theramenes, received the tribute of praise from both Thucydides and Aristotle. With the surrender of Athens in 404, Sparta imposed the dictatorship known as 'The Thirty Tyrants'. Some of these men had been associates of Socrates. They entered on a campaign of bloodshed and proscription, and vainly attempted to implicate Socrates in their crimes. Before long a revolution brought back the democrats. They proclaimed an amnesty and behaved with signal moderation. But Socrates was a dangerous critic of democracy, too dangerous to be left. In 399 he was charged with impiety and corrupting the youth. Such charges were never preferred at Athens except as a cloak for political animosity, and this was no exception. He was condemned. His enemies no doubt only wished his banishment, but he refused to compromise and was put to death.

Against this background the *Republic* was conceived and written.

Socrates

Of all the personalities of the fifth century none is more fascinating than Socrates. He is indeed one of the three most fascinating people who have ever lived, and the only one of the three who has not been worshipped as divine. He was born in 469 and executed in 399. He was of humble origin, his father Sophroniscus being a stone-mason, and his mother Phaenarete a midwife. One story even has it that he was born a slave, but there is little to support this. He married twice, Myrto, the great-granddaughter of Aristides the Just, and Xanthippe, whose name has been handed down to posterity, without overmuch justification, as the typical shrew. A rueful remark of Socrates to a young man is however recorded, 'Marry by all means. If you marry a good wife you will be very happy. If not, you will become a philosopher, and that is good for any man.' Socrates had three sons, of no great distinction.

He himself was slow in coming into prominence; as at so many other points there is an interesting parallel with Jesus, and no doubt he followed his father's trade of masonry just as the Nazarene worked in wood. When we first come upon him it is as a speculative scientist, and as such, in his mid-forties, he was guyed by Aristophanes in *The Clouds*. But he soon became dissatisfied with the study of science. In Aristotelian language, he turned from the material to the final cause. He ceased to ask 'How?' and began instead to ask 'Why?' Further, his attention was turning from the world around to the human personality, from matter to mind, from the macrocosm to the microcosm. He was living in the age of the sophists, and as it so often happens that the most formidable opponents of a movement learn more from it than they would like to think, so Socrates was caught up in that revolution which they brought about. Cicero said that Socrates had brought Philosophy down from heaven and planted her on earth, but in truth it was sophists like Protagoras who first directed the attention of thinking men away from Ionian cosmology to human behaviour. Only the sophists on the whole were content to accept the facts of human behaviour as they found them, and to work within that accepted framework. Socrates was pestered, as he was to pester others, by this insistent 'Why?' Then someone brought to his notice a book by Anaxagoras with an opening proposition destined to become famous, 'Everything was in a state of chaos, but then Mind came and put it all in order.' Socrates was attracted. Here surely was what he was looking for, a teleological interpretation of the universe. But when he came to read the book he was dissatisfied. Anaxagoras' Mind did not provide a thread of purpose running through the whole of life. Anaxagoras was a typical Deist. His Power was transcendent but not immanent. Mind, so to say, wound up the Universe, and then left it to its own devices, and when Anaxagoras was dealing with particular events, when he in turn moved from the macrocosm to the microcosm, he spoke in purely material terms, and ignored the question 'Why?'

At this point Socrates, who was nothing if not intellectually honest, confessed himself at a loss. And at this point his friend Chaerephon asked the Delphic Oracle whether there was any wiser man in Greece than Socrates, and received the answer 'No'. Socrates was genuinely puzzled. For all the freedom of his mind he was a man of real devotion to the traditions of religion, and held the pronouncements of the oracle in respect, if not reverence. Yet he knew his own perplexity, and could not reconcile the two. So he set himself to test, indeed to refute, the oracle. He went around to those who had the highest reputation in their own fields to question them about the knowledge they possessed. He went to teachers, and found them ignorant of the very basis of the things which they professed to teach. He went to the military, and found them incapable of explaining coherently the meaning of the word 'courage'. He exposed the canting hypocrisy of much that went by the name of piety. He approached statesmen, and found in them an appalling combination of self-conceit and mental illiteracy. Life for the Athenians became one long *viva voce* examination. He took a pleasure in exposing false pretensions. One of his victims compared him to a torpedo-fish which numbs its victims before darting in to the kill. He preferred to call himself a gadfly stinging into life the noble horse of Athens. Sometimes his victims would round on him and demand that he answer his own questions. He met them with 'Socratic irony'; the word means 'self-depreciation'. They had claimed knowledge. He made no such claim, and was not bound to answer, as they were. The oracle was right. He was the wisest of men in Greece. All men know nothing; he at least knew that he knew nothing.

This is the negative aspect of his life-work. But the Socratic elenchus had its positive side too. This is expressed in his famous claim to follow his mother's profession of midwifery.[1] By a process of fruitful questioning he helped others to bring to birth the thoughts that were in them. The process was not infallible. Sometimes they came to him before they were pregnant; then, he said mischievously, he sent them off to Prodicus or some other teacher. Sometimes they went away too soon, and suffered a miscarriage. But often it was not so. He guided his associates along very different paths. Among his intimates were the hedonist Aristippus and the moralist Antisthenes. Phaedo furthered the study of logic and Euclides the science of dialectic. Plato built his metaphysical structure on Socrates' foundations, and his Academy nurtured the scientific genius of Aristotle. Stoicism took Socrates as its ideal sage; scepticism linked its tenets with his refusal of dogma. So he fostered the growth of others' souls. There is no more delightful story of Socrates than his remark to a silent youth, 'Say something, so that I may see you.'[2] There is no more significant comment than that of the Marxist Georges Sorel, who denounces him for having corrupted civilization through the false

[1] Plat., *Theaet.* 149 a ff.   [2] Apul., *Flor.* I 2.

doctrine that history moves forward through a process of intellectual inquiry and persuasion.

His peculiar vocation kept him from playing much part in the formal political life of Athens. In addition a mystical voice within vetoed any such inclinations. He accepted however the normal obligations of citizenship, served on military campaigns at Samos in 441, Potidaea in 431, Delium in 424 and Amphipolis in 422,[1] made known his opposition to his country's imperialistic designs in Sicily,[2] and took his share of duties on the Council when they fell to him. Then, and later, he showed high courage in resisting illegality and immorality, whether from democrats or oligarchs; in this he was not partisan. But his sympathies were not in doubt. He believed that politics were as skilled a profession as any other, and should thus be the province of the technical expert. Such a view ran counter to the whole theory of Athenian democracy. Worse, it was absorbed by men like Critias, Charmides and Alcibiades, who fancied themselves as the technical experts, but who lacked the moral integrity which Socrates insisted on as the first qualification of the truly successful statesman. It was because of his supposed influence on these that he was executed.[3]

His immediate contribution to philosophy may not at first sight seem substantial. Aristotle, whose real bent was scientific, was clear that the part of Socrates' work which was significant for him was his use of inductive argument and definition by generalization. If this were all he would be no more than a name in the text-books. We may stress rather his view of the soul as the part of man which really matters. Hence the need for clear and honest thinking. 'Food can poison your body; ideas can poison your soul.'

---

[1] Professor Kitto, in his lively book *The Greeks*, p. 36, strangely says that he left the city twice only.

[2] Plut., *Nic.* 13.

[3] Aeschin., *In Timarch.* 193.

B

Wickedness is worse than death; it flies faster than fate. The clear outcome of all this is the certainty of the soul's immortality. This is the conclusion of the *Phaedo*, but it shines also through the overt agnosticism of the *Apology*.

At the last the impress is of the man, not the philosopher. Aulus Gellius tells the story that, when the Megarians were forbidden entry into Athenian territory on pain of death, Euclides risked coming to Athens in disguise in order to be with Socrates, and contrasted his devotion with the attitude of contemporary students to their professors.[1] Such was Socrates' magnetism. Anatole France says that there was never any great man without a blend of contradictions. This was certainly true of Socrates. He combined rationalism with mysticism, a rationalism which could declare that 'Virtue is knowledge' with a mysticism which acknowledged within himself a divine voice circumscribing his action. He combined shrewdness with simplicity. He combined passion with purity; he never tried to deceive himself into thinking that his impulses did not exist, but he never acted from impulse alone nor allowed his impulses to be his master. He was an unusually integrated person. His highest epitaph is the often repeated words 'He was the best man I ever knew'.

Plato

Aristocles, later called Plato, from the breadth either of his figure or of his forehead or of his style, son of Ariston and Perictione, was born of aristocratic ancestry and traced his family tree back to the legendary figure of Codrus. The date of his birth, 427 B.C. and that of his death, 347, are derived from Eratosthenes and may be regarded as reasonably certain. Otherwise his life falls with suspicious convenience into periods of twenty years. He was twenty when he met Socrates, forty when he founded the Academy,

[1] vii 10.

sixty at the time of his failure at Syracuse, and eighty at his death. Despite their symmetry these dates must be 'there or thereabouts'.

In his early days he was set, like any young aristocrat, upon making his mark politically. But he was growing up in troubled times. He was only fourteen when the Athenian armies suffered irreparable disaster in Sicily. He passed his adolescence in the period when his country was fighting back against odds that ultimately proved hopeless, a period of political intrigue at home, a period dominated by the meteoric brilliance of Socrates' one-time friend Alcibiades. Plato grew up in an environment unfavourable to the sailors' democracy, but there is no evidence that he was actively associated with any of the cabals of the time. It is more likely that he lived in the spirit of critical tolerance which a right-wing conservative in a country of tolerant traditions may show towards a socialist government. During this period, though there is nothing in his writings to indicate it, he must himself have seen military service. In 404 Athens lost the war, and the democracy was replaced by the narrow oligarchy known to history as 'The Thirty Tyrants'. Among these were men Plato knew: Critias and Charmides were relatives of his. The time seemed auspicious for his entry into politics, and he had hopes that it would be in the congenial atmosphere of a wise and ordered government. But the excesses of the new government disgusted him, and their attempts to involve Socrates, whose admiring adherent by now he was, in their unjust and extortionate activities, completed the disillusion. Here again he appears as an honourable conservative rejecting out of hand the murders and concentration-camps of a Nazi or Fascist despotism. He puts principle before party. The restoration of the democracy in the early months of the following year, and their tolerance in declaring a political amnesty, led him once more to turn his mind to politics and to look hopefully to the future. But in 399, just as he was reconciled to the contemporary state of things, and ready to step forward with vigour, the democratic leaders, seeing in Socrates a dangerous critic, put him on trial and condemned him to death. Plato withdrew to Megara; if the stories of his visit to Egypt are true, they must date from this period. What is of still greater moment, he withdrew into the shell of contemplation, began to stretch out the feeler of the written word, and emerged with the assurance that good government would never be achieved until the rulers had a sure grasp of those values that are eternal and unchanging. The existence and reality of those values forms one of the major themes of the *Phaedo*, just as the greater part of the *Republic* is devoted to the method of training prospective rulers to fix their minds upon them.

A second feature of his youth was his ambition to be a writer. Later generations told of the tragedies which he had written, and which he burned when he came under the influence of Socrates. Some poems have come down to us with his name attached to them. They are exquisitely written, and come from the pen of a master of language, and hence may be authentic. One, an elegy for a lad named Aster or Star, is familiar to English readers through Shelley's version:

> Thou wert the morning-star among the living,
>   Ere thy fair light had fled;
> Now, having died, thou art as Hesperus, giving
>   New splendour to the dead.

There can be no slighting the fact that a supreme master of poetic drama was lost to the stage when Plato turned to philosophy, rather, though in reverse, as we are disposed to feel what a superb pamphleteer Euripides might have been. But Socrates was no more a poet than Bernard Shaw, of whom Chesterton once remarked that he must be the only man who had never written a line of poetry in his life.

Principal Geddes aptly quotes Wordsworth's philosophical pedlar 'with the vision and faculty divine, yet wanting the accomplishment of verse'. Further, Socrates was unsympathetic to the mimetic element in dramatic writing. He preferred at any time to deal with people, who could answer his questions, but a book might in certain circumstances draw him as a carrot draws the donkey (to modernize an expression from the opening of the *Phaedrus*). He valued books for their ideas and their power to convey ideas, not for qualities of drama or characterization. The aesthetic criticism of the *Republic* is almost certainly inherited by Plato from Socrates, and indeed much of it reads strangely from the pen of a man whose finest medium was the dramatic dialogue. Certain it is that Plato did not abandon his literary ambition. But with him literature ceased to be an end in itself. *L'art pour l'art* has no place in his philosophy. Literature is the handmaid of thought. Other qualities are incidental. But when that is said, it must be acknowledged that Plato remained a poetic dramatist, *malgré lui*, and we may thank Apollo and the Muses for his early training in a school in which Sophocles and Euripides were still teachers as he grew up.

Politics, poetry and philosophy—these are the three major influences upon his most impressionable years. Of his personal relations with Socrates we know curiously little; some have felt half a suspicion that the reverence was from a little distance. We can see the qualities of integrity and courage in the older man which attracted Plato. We can see that to a young man who was perhaps disposed too lightly to accept the familiar ideas of his environment the searching questions of Socrates would act as a stimulus and a challenge. We can see Plato's analytical faculty being developed by contagion of Socrates' ruthless dialectic, and his capacity for constructive thinking being gradually brought out into the open. Socrates was a man of deep personal insights; his

contribution was to share these rather than to construct an
intellectual system. The work of Plato was to pick up the
scattered stones the sculptor had shaped, and set them
together with a superstructure of his own in a magnificent
architectural edifice. There is a curious parallel with Paul
and Jesus. Jesus' insights, His teaching of the nature of love,
are gloriously taken up by Paul in writing to Corinth and to
Rome. He is the foundation-stone, the head of the corner.
But the metaphysical coping is Paul's. The parallel must
not be pushed too far, but it is notable that Paul's capacity
to do this arises because he stands at a little distance from
Jesus and had not in fact known Him during His life on
earth. Plato was of course an associate of Socrates, present
at his trial, and expected to be present at the final scene
in the prison. But he was not a Chaerephon or a Crito. At
any rate he set himself first to record and then to interpret
Socrates. But before we can examine his methods and
technique here we must glance briefly at the rest of his
life.

In 387 Plato went to Sicily and South Italy.[1] The visit
had two momentous consequences. In Sicily he met Dion
who was to become his closest friend and who was a member
of the royal house, and this put him again in touch with
active politics and problems of government. In Italy he
came into touch with the Pythagorean communities, was
attracted by elements in their thinking, which he began to
integrate with the lines of thought he was already developing from Socrates, and saw in their community-life and
their combination of religious philosophy with political
activity a possible basis for an educational institution. He
returned to Athens, and shortly afterwards formed the
Academy, a residential university for the training of political
leaders. The word 'academic' has come to be used dis-
paragingly of thought detached from life. Nothing was

[1] See now G. R. Levy, *Plato in Sicily* (Faber and Faber, 1956).

further from Plato's mind. He believed, it is true, that the only way to find your way through life was to detach your mind from the relativities of this world and fix it on the unchanging verities; hence the motto over the Academy door, which may be approximately rendered 'All hope abandon ye who enter here without knowledge of geometry' But this detachment was to enable you to master life, not to escape from it. It is quite wrong, with Zimmern, to describe Plato as 'despairing of the Republic and retiring into private life to wait for more Utopian times'.[1] He was following a master who asked 'Should I be doing more for politics if I merely practised as a politician than by taking care that as many people as possible should be qualified to be politicians.' [2] The philosopher returns from the sunlight into the cave and the world of shadow, and the activities of Platonists at the court of Hermias at Atarneus, and indeed the career of Dion himself, may remind us that the Academy did indeed send its students out into the hurly-burly of political actuality.

For nearly twenty years the Academy was the centre of Plato's life; its organization and teaching and research must have absorbed most of his time. Whatever detailed chronology of his writings we accept, their flow must have dwindled during this period. Then came a new opportunity for action. The old ruler of Syracuse, Dionysius I, was dead. In 367 Plato's friend, Dion, succeeded in obtaining for him an invitation to come and train the young heir in his new responsibilities. Plato saw the difficulties which lay ahead, but the opportunity was too challenging to refuse. The story of what happened is too familiar to need repetition. The basis of study on which he insisted was geometry. For a while geometry was a courtly fashion; the sanded floors of the palace became a whirl of dust as figures were drawn upon them and erased. It could not last. The young

[1] *Greek Commonwealth*, p. 158, n. 2.   [2] Xen., *Mem.* I 6 15.

Dionysius was an impatient pupil, with an arrogance under-
standable in an authoritarian ruler, but unfitted to a philosophical novice. Court intrigue played round the figure of
Dion. The experiment failed, and a last attempt to remedy
the position six years later failed also. Aristoxenus remarked
with bitter sarcasm that Plato's Sicilian venture was 'just
about as successful as that of Nicias'.[1] Plato cannot at any
time have hoped to establish an ideal commonwealth in
Syracuse; he had at least showed his readiness to enter the
lists of practical politics.

The last years of his life saw the production of the *Laws*,
a work in which the mature judgement of a great and
sensitive mind found profound religious expression, but in
which the Syracusan debacle led him to what is certainly a
greater realism but ultimately can only be called embittered
fascism. Otherwise he turned increasingly to logical studies,
to which he made some contribution, developed the esoteric
researches of the Academy, and made one notorious public
appearance to lecture on 'Truth'.

His contributions to metaphysical, aesthetic, and religious
thinking are discussed in the appendices. Here it is enough
to say that in Plato we face one of the great constructive
thinkers of all time, and one who is approached only by
Bishop Berkeley in his ability to present abstruse problems
in a lucid and winsome style.

The Platonic Socrates

A few lines need to be inserted on one of the great
academic controversies of this century. We have two major
witnesses who write of Socrates—Plato and Xenophon. In
Plato he is the mouthpiece of profound metaphysical
theory; in Xenophon he appears as a prosy commonplace
moralist. It was long assumed that the genius of the first
figure was imposed by the genius of Plato. In 1911 Burnet

[1] Lucian, *De Parasito* 34.

and Taylor, disavowing responsibility for one another's conclusions, but speaking with singular unanimity, argued that the dullness and lack of genius in the second figure might be due to the limitations of Xenophon.[1]

> Inveniat quod quisque velit: non omnibus unum est
> quod placet: hic spinas colligit, ille rosas.

Xenophon had collected the thorns. In any case he was only young, probably not a close intimate of the Socratic circle, and absent from Athens after 401. They argued therefore that his evidence is of no more than incidental importance. If we do not accept Plato's portrait of Socrates, then we have no authentic portrait of him at all, for Diogenes Laertius is hopelessly uncritical, Aristophanes gives at best a caricature of Socrates in the 420s, and Aristotle's only source of information was in fact Plato. We must accept the historical veracity of Plato's picture. So spoke Burnet and Taylor, with fervent advocacy.

We shall never return to the complete scepticism which was prevalent in some quarters regarding Plato's portrait of Socrates before Burnet and Taylor entered the lists. But it has become increasingly clear that their counter-attack has failed to win a decisive victory.[2] Four points stand out.

1. The internal evidence of the dialogues does not suggest that their purpose is historical biography. We need not make too much of occasional anachronisms. The presentation of the Theory of Forms gives a clear illustration. In the short early dialogues it does not appear; in the *Phaedo* it seems to be being presented for the first time; in the *Republic*,

---

[1] See J. Burnet, *Plato's Phaedo*; 'Socrates' in Hastings' *E.R.E.*; *Greek Philosophy—Thales to Plato*. A. E. Taylor, *Varia Socraticai* I; 'Plato's Biography of Socrates' in *P.B.A.*, 1917–18; *Socrates*. C. Ritter, *Sokrates*. I have much oversimplified a closely argued case.

[2] See especially G. C. Field, *Plato and His Contemporaries*; W. D. Ross, *Aristotle's Metaphysics*.

Phaedrus, and *Symposium* it is accepted in its maturity; in the *Parmenides* it is criticized. This makes sense if it represents a development of Plato's thought. But if it is authentic biography of Socrates it makes no sense, for then the *Parmenides* represents the first stage, and the *Phaedo* the last.

2. Plato's seventh letter, now generally accepted as genuine, contains a famous passage [1] describing how, well after Socrates' death, he came to the conviction that there was no hope for mankind until philosophers became kings or kings philosophers. It is precisely this which is put into Socrates' mouth to form the central theme of the political argument of the *Republic*, and is the strongest possible direct evidence that Plato uses the Socrates of the dialogues as his own mouthpiece.

3. The evidence of Aristotle has been unduly discounted. He had access to the unwritten traditions of the Academy, and to say that these were identical with Plato's written works is to beg the question. He clearly associates the Theory of Forms with Plato, and tells us that Socrates did not 'make the universals separable' by contrast.[2]

4. Professor Field has shown that till the time of Proclus later commentators take the views expressed by the Socrates in the dialogues as representative of the opinions of Plato, not Socrates.

The conclusion of this is not, of course, that Plato's account of Socrates is at no point to be regarded as historical; that would be abject folly. The most reasonable supposition is that Plato started, in the *Apology* and some of the shorter dialogues, giving a generally faithful picture of the historical Socrates in action. Gradually he came to develop his own metaphysic on the basis of the clues left by Socrates, combined with other influences more personal to himself, and it was natural to continue to put this logical development of Socrates' thought into the mouth of Socrates.

[1] *Ep.* VII 325c–6b.   [2] Arist., *Met.* M 1078 b 9–32.

Finally the point came when he realized that he was being led by his own mental pilgrimage further and further from his master and he could not with honesty continue the attribution. At this point we find Socrates becoming first subordinated and finally superseded in the dialogues.

The Date of the 'Republic'

The brilliant work initiated by Lewis Campbell whereby the order of Plato's dialogues has been determined by considerations of style does not help us directly to fix the date of the *Republic*, for the assumptions that this is a work of his maturity and that the *Laws* belong to his old age are the pillars which support the whole structure. The following are the principal considerations which guide us in finding the date:

1. It is unlikely that Plato began writing his philosophical dialogues much, if at all, before Socrates' death in 399.

2. It is a reasonable assumption that the shorter dialogues precede the *Republic* and lie at the beginning of Plato's career as a philosophical writer.

3. When *Rep.* X 611 b10 refers to 'other discussions' of the question of immortality the words may imply that the *Meno* and *Phaedo* are already written.

4. Aristotle tells us that the *Republic* is earlier than the *Laws*,[1] and Proclus that the *Laws* was left unfinished at Plato's death.

5. The *Timaeus* dramatically, and presumably in composition, is later than the *Republic* and is linked to it.

6. *Rep.* I 336 a and *Meno* 90 a refer to Ismenias of Thebes who only came into prominence in 395.

7. *Symp.* 193 a seems to refer to the battle of Mantinea in 385. Stylistic considerations suggest that the *Symposium* is close to the *Republic*.

8. The *Phaedo*, also close to the *Republic* stylistically, shows

[1] *Pol.* 1264 b 26.

an interest in Pythagorean ideas, which may be due to Plato's contact with Pythagoreans on his visit to Sicily and South Italy in 387.

9. Plato's seventh letter says that when he first visited Sicily in 387 he had already been driven to say 'in a eulogy of true philosophy that the salvation of mankind depends on the union of philosopher and ruler in a single person'. This must refer to *Rep.* VI 499 b.

10. Aristophanes' *Parliament of Women* performed in 392 appears to contain a parody of the principle of equal treatment for the sexes found in the *Republic*. It will not do to say that these ideas were widely current and Aristophanes is not jibing at Plato. Plato certainly thought that he was propounding something revolutionary, and the detailed verbal echoes are too close not to postulate a direct reference. Still less will it do to say with Boeckh that Plato borrowed the idea from Aristophanes!

11. On his return in 387 Plato founded the Academy and the period 387–367 would be much occupied with teaching and administration. It will not do to overstock it with writing.

12. The *Republic* is plainly a carefully planned and constructed whole.

Obviously the evidence is conflicting. I do not believe that it is possible to cram the *Republic* and all that must precede it into the period 399–388, still less 399–393. It is on the other hand easy to underestimate the writing which can be done by a teacher and administrator. The most reasonable view then would be to put the *Phaedo* as the first-fruits of his voyage of 387, and the *Republic* as written at his leisure in the years that followed. We shall have then to suppose, as we may do, that during the years before 387 he was turning over the political ideas which he incorporated in the full work, and had given expression to some of them. After all, any modern writer planning a *magnum opus* tries out his ideas in articles and lectures; this does not destroy the subsequent unity of the whole, and *mutatis mutandis* we may think that Plato did the same.

The Plan of the 'Republic'

The *Republic* is a book on moral philosophy; in this its familiar title is misleading, for we expect to find a work on political philosophy and are disconcerted by the wide range of its subject-matter, which includes problems of politics, education, aesthetics, sex, social philosophy, psychology, ethics, metaphysics, and religion. This is readily understood if we realize that Man to the Greek means Man in Society. 'Man', says Aristotle, 'is a living creature whose nature it is to live in an ordered community.' The question from which the *Republic* starts, 'What is justice?' (δικαιοσύνη), can be answered only by comprehensive reference to the destiny of man and his place in society.

The form in which Plato chose to ventilate these great issues was the dramatic dialogue. Many factors went to determine his choice. His own literary experience lay in the field of drama. In Epicharmus and Sophron, whom we know he admired, he found writers of mime who wittily purveyed philosophical ideas in rhythmic prose; the analogies are obvious. Socrates had used conversation as the means of eliciting truth, and Plato exalted this into a logical principle in his dialectical method. Basically this means that though truth is objective, the search for truth and the conviction of truth are personal, and are to be personally presented. Assent to truth is a slow process. It is like climbing a ladder, question and answer, rung by rung, not like the dogmatic sweeping discourses of the sophists.

The tenth book, then, comes at the end of a long process of intellectual inquiry, and to understand it it is necessary to survey, however summarily, what has gone before. This falls into four broad sections.

I–II 367e Introduction. The question is posed 'What is justice?' Representative answers are given and rejected. The sophist Thrasymachus puts the case for immoralism, but he is not sufficiently thoroughgoing and is without difficulty led into self-contradiction. But Plato's brothers Glaucon and Adimantus restate the case far more cogently. They can only be answered by a fundamental inquiry into the nature of justice.

II 367e–V 471c. Attention turns from the individual to society, where we may see justice 'writ large'. A complex society is logically constructed, and a radical difference drawn between those whose function is to rule and to protect (The Guardians and Auxiliaries) and the main body of the citizens. There follows a detailed analysis of the best education and way of life for the rulers, which includes censorship, equality of the sexes, absence of private property, and community of wives and children. Justice appears in a state when each class, rulers, executive and citizens, performs its own function properly; justice appears in an individual when each part of his soul, reason, temper and desire, performs its corresponding function properly.

V 471c–VII. Here is the great metaphysical exposition. There are two worlds, one permanent and unchanging, one changeful and mutable, the former the unseen world of Forms, apprehended by the intellect, the other our material environment. At the back of all, even 'beyond reality', is the Good. The good ruler will be the man who learns to fix his attention on the unseen world, and then to apply his insight into truth within the world around him.

VIII–IX. There follows an analysis of degeneracy, constitutional and psychological. The perfect state degenerates into timocracy, where the second class, which includes the military, begins to predominate. Love of honour becomes transformed to love of wealth, the characteristic feature of oligarchy. The poor rise against the rich and establish democracy, which is marked by libertarianism. The final point of degeneracy is dictatorship. Similar stages can be traced in individual psychology. In fact order, wisdom and happiness go together. The tyrant or dictator receives far less pleasure than he imagines. Real happiness derives from that inward and outward harmony whose pattern we may see in the ordered constellations of the heavens.

Book X

It remains to summarize Book X. This falls conveniently into two sections each with its own subdivisions.

595a–608b. Aesthetic theory revised. This picks up the earlier discussion from Book III:

595a–602b. The artist in any field is at two removes from reality. True reality subsists in the eternal Forms; the material world is but a representation of these; and the artist, whether painter or poet, is producing at best a representation of a representation. Further the artist does not really understand the things he represents; such understanding belongs perhaps to the craftsman, still more to the user.

602c–608b. Painting and poetry appeal to the lowest in man. Painting tries to create illusions, poetry appeals to the emotions. Both these are corrupting, for it is Reason which should be supreme in man. We cannot accept the claim of the poets to educate Greece.

608c–621d. The immortality of the soul and the destiny of man. This picks up the argument of the *Phaedo*:

608c–612a. The soul is immortal. An entity is only destroyed by its specific evil. But the specific evil of the soul, wickedness, does not destroy it. The wicked man goes on living. Therefore the soul is immortal.

612a–613e. Because the gods are just they love the

good and bless them, and punish the wicked, even in this life. In the long run the judgement of man too exalts the good and humiliates the wicked.

613e–621d. A vision of judgement. Er died in battle, but was permitted to return from the world of the dead. There he saw the judges passing judgement on the souls who came before them. He saw the grim punishment of the wicked. He caught a vision of the pattern of the Universe, ordered by Necessity. He watched the souls choosing lives for their next incarnation—the choice on which all depends—and saw how their choices were influenced by their former experiences. Finally he watched them drink the waters of Forgetfulness and sweep up to life. We would do well to contemplate the thought of the soul's immortality if all is to be well with us.

Καὶ μήν, ἦν δ' ἐγώ, πολλὰ μὲν καὶ ἄλλα περὶ αὐτῆς a
ἐννοῶ, ὡς παντὸς ἄρα μᾶλλον ὀρθῶς ᾠκίζομεν τὴν πόλιν,
οὐχ ἥκιστα δὲ ἐνθυμηθεὶς περὶ ποιήσεως λέγω.

Τὸ ποῖον; ἔφη.

Τὸ μηδαμῇ παραδέχεσθαι αὐτῆς ὅση μιμητική· παντὸς 5
γὰρ μᾶλλον οὐ παραδεκτέα νῦν καὶ ἐναργέστερον, ὡς ἐμοὶ
δοκεῖ, φαίνεται, ἐπειδὴ χωρὶς ἕκαστα διῄρηται τὰ τῆς ψυχῆς
εἴδη.   b

Πῶς λέγεις;

Ὡς μὲν πρὸς ὑμᾶς εἰρῆσθαι—οὐ γάρ μου κατερεῖτε πρὸς
τοὺς τῆς τραγῳδίας ποιητὰς καὶ τοὺς ἄλλους ἅπαντας τοὺς
μιμητικούς—λώβη ἔοικεν εἶναι πάντα τὰ τοιαῦτα τῆς τῶν 5
ἀκουόντων διανοίας, ὅσοι μὴ ἔχουσι φάρμακον τὸ εἰδέναι
αὐτὰ οἷα τυγχάνει ὄντα.

Πῇ δή, ἔφη, διανοούμενος λέγεις;

Ῥητέον, ἦν δ' ἐγώ· καίτοι φιλία γέ τίς με καὶ αἰδὼς ἐκ
παιδὸς ἔχουσα περὶ Ὁμήρου ἀποκωλύει λέγειν.   ἔοικε μὲν 10
γὰρ τῶν καλῶν ἁπάντων τούτων τῶν τραγικῶν πρῶτος διδά- c
σκαλός τε καὶ ἡγεμὼν γενέσθαι.   ἀλλ' οὐ γὰρ πρό γε τῆς
ἀληθείας τιμητέος ἀνήρ, ἀλλ', ὃ λέγω, ῥητέον.

Πάνυ μὲν οὖν, ἔφη.

Ἄκουε δή, μᾶλλον δὲ ἀποκρίνου.   5

Ἐρώτα.

Μίμησιν ὅλως ἔχοις ἄν μοι εἰπεῖν ὅτι ποτ' ἐστίν; οὐδὲ
γάρ τοι αὐτὸς πάνυ τι συννοῶ τί βούλεται εἶναι.

Ἦ που ἄρ', ἔφη, ἐγὼ συννοήσω.

10　Οὐδέν γε, ἦν δ' ἐγώ, ἄτοπον, ἐπεὶ πολλά τοι ὀξύτερον
596　βλεπόντων ἀμβλύτερον ὁρῶντες πρότεροι εἶδον.

Ἔστιν, ἔφη, οὕτως· ἀλλὰ σοῦ παρόντος οὐδ' ἂν προθυμη-
θῆναι οἷός τε εἴην εἰπεῖν, εἰ τί μοι καταφαίνεται, ἀλλ'
αὐτὸς ὅρα.

5　Βούλει οὖν ἐνθένδε ἀρξώμεθα ἐπισκοποῦντες, ἐκ τῆς
εἰωθυίας μεθόδου; εἶδος γάρ πού τι ἐν ἕκαστον εἰώθαμεν
τίθεσθαι περὶ ἕκαστα τὰ πολλά, οἷς ταὐτὸν ὄνομα ἐπιφέρομεν.
ἢ οὐ μανθάνεις;

Μανθάνω.

10　Θῶμεν δὴ καὶ νῦν ὅτι βούλει τῶν πολλῶν.　οἷον, εἰ
b　'θέλεις, πολλαί πού εἰσι κλῖναι καὶ τράπεζαι.

Πῶς δ' οὔ;

'Αλλὰ ἰδέαι γέ που περὶ ταῦτα τὰ σκεύη δύο, μία μὲν
κλίνης, μία δὲ τραπέζης.

5　Ναί.

Οὐκοῦν καὶ εἰώθαμεν λέγειν ὅτι ὁ δημιουργὸς ἑκατέρου
τοῦ σκεύους πρὸς τὴν ἰδέαν βλέπων οὕτω ποιεῖ ὁ μὲν τὰς
κλίνας, ὁ δὲ τὰς τραπέζας, αἷς ἡμεῖς χρώμεθα, καὶ τἆλλα
κατὰ ταὐτά; οὐ γάρ που τήν γε ἰδέαν αὐτὴν δημιουργεῖ
10　οὐδεὶς τῶν δημιουργῶν· πῶς γάρ;

Οὐδαμῶς.

'Αλλ' ὅρα δὴ καὶ τόνδε τίνα καλεῖς τὸν δημιουργόν.

c　Τὸν ποῖον;

Ὃς πάντα ποιεῖ, ὅσαπερ εἷς ἕκαστος τῶν χειροτεχνῶν.

Δεινόν τινα λέγεις καὶ θαυμαστὸν ἄνδρα.

Οὔπω γε, ἀλλὰ τάχα μᾶλλον φήσεις.　ὁ αὐτὸς γὰρ οὗτος
5　χειροτέχνης οὐ μόνον πάντα οἷός τε σκεύη ποιῆσαι, ἀλλὰ
καὶ τὰ ἐκ τῆς γῆς φυόμενα ἅπαντα ποιεῖ καὶ ζῷα πάντα
ἐργάζεται, τά τε ἄλλα καὶ ἑαυτόν, καὶ πρὸς τούτοις γῆν καὶ
οὐρανὸν καὶ θεοὺς καὶ πάντα τὰ ἐν οὐρανῷ καὶ τὰ ἐν "Αιδου
ὑπὸ γῆς ἅπαντα ἐργάζεται.

Πάνυ θαυμαστόν, ἔφη, λέγεις σοφιστήν. ,   d

Ἀπιστεῖς; ἦν δ' ἐγώ. καί μοι εἰπέ, τὸ παράπαν οὐκ ἂν
σοι δοκεῖ εἶναι τοιοῦτος δημιουργός, ἢ τινὶ μὲν τρόπῳ γενέσθαι ἂν τούτων ἁπάντων ποιητής, τινὶ δὲ οὐκ ἄν; ἢ οὐκ
αἰσθάνῃ ὅτι κἂν αὐτὸς οἷός τ' εἴης πάντα ταῦτα ποιῆσαι 5
τρόπῳ γέ τινι;

Καὶ τίς, ἔφη, ὁ τρόπος οὗτος;

Οὐ χαλεπός, ἦν δ' ἐγώ, ἀλλὰ πολλαχῇ καὶ ταχὺ δημιουργούμενος, τάχιστα δέ που, εἰ 'θέλεις λαβὼν κάτοπτρον
περιφέρειν πανταχῇ· ταχὺ μὲν ἥλιον ποιήσεις καὶ τὰ ἐν τῷ e
οὐρανῷ, ταχὺ δὲ γῆν, ταχὺ δὲ σαυτόν τε καὶ τἄλλα ζῷα καὶ
σκεύη καὶ φυτὰ καὶ πάντα ὅσα νυνδὴ ἐλέγετο.

Ναί, ἔφη, φαινόμενα, οὐ μέντοι ὄντα γέ που τῇ ἀληθείᾳ.

Καλῶς, ἦν δ' ἐγώ, καὶ εἰς δέον ἔρχῃ τῷ λόγῳ. τῶν 5
τοιούτων γὰρ οἶμαι δημιουργῶν καὶ ὁ ζωγράφος ἐστίν. ἢ
γάρ;

Πῶς γὰρ οὔ;

Ἀλλὰ φήσεις οὐκ ἀληθῆ οἶμαι αὐτὸν ποιεῖν ἃ ποιεῖ.
καίτοι τρόπῳ γέ τινι καὶ ὁ ζωγράφος κλίνην ποιεῖ· ἢ οὔ; 10

Ναί, ἔφη, φαινομένην γε καὶ οὗτος.

Τί δὲ ὁ κλινοποιός; οὐκ ἄρτι μέντοι ἔλεγες ὅτι οὐ τὸ 597
εἶδος ποιεῖ, ὃ δή φαμεν εἶναι ὃ ἔστι κλίνη, ἀλλὰ κλίνην τινά;

Ἔλεγον γάρ.

Οὐκοῦν εἰ μὴ ὃ ἔστιν ποιεῖ, οὐκ ἂν τὸ ὂν ποιοῖ, ἀλλά τι
τοιοῦτον οἷον τὸ ὄν, ὂν δὲ οὔ· τελέως δὲ εἶναι ὂν τὸ τοῦ 5
κλινουργοῦ ἔργον ἢ ἄλλου τινὸς χειροτέχνου εἴ τις φαίη,
κινδυνεύει οὐκ ἂν ἀληθῆ λέγειν;

Οὔκουν, ἔφη, ὥς γ' ἂν δόξειεν τοῖς περὶ τοὺς τοιούσδε
λόγους διατρίβουσιν.

Μηδὲν ἄρα θαυμάζωμεν εἰ καὶ τοῦτο ἀμυδρόν τι τυγχάνει 10
ὂν πρὸς ἀλήθειαν.

Μὴ γάρ.   b

Βούλει οὖν, ἔφην, ἐπ' αὐτῶν τούτων ζητήσωμεν τὸν μιμητὴν τοῦτον, τίς ποτ' ἐστίν;

Εἰ βούλει, ἔφη.

5 Οὐκοῦν τρτταί τινες κλῖναι αὗται γίγνονται· μία μὲν ἡ ἐν τῇ φύσει οὖσα, ἣν φαῖμεν ἄν, ὡς ἐγῷμαι, θεὸν ἐργάσασθαι. ἢ τίν' ἄλλον;

Οὐδένα, οἶμαι.

Μία δέ γε ἦν ὁ τέκτων.

10 Ναί, ἔφη.

Μία δὲ ἦν ὁ ζωγράφος. ἢ γάρ;

Ἔστω.

Ζωγράφος δή, κλινοποιός, θεός, τρεῖς οὗτοι ἐπιστάται τρισὶν εἴδεσι κλινῶν.

15 Ναὶ τρεῖς.

c Ὁ μὲν δὴ θεός, εἴτε οὐκ ἐβούλετο, εἴτε τις ἀνάγκη ἐπῆν μὴ πλέον ἢ μίαν ἐν τῇ φύσει ἀπεργάσασθαι αὐτὸν κλίνην, οὕτως ἐποίησεν μίαν μόνον αὐτὴν ἐκείνην ὃ ἔστιν κλίνη· δύο δὲ τοιαῦται ἢ πλείους οὔτε ἐφυτεύθησαν ὑπὸ τοῦ θεοῦ 5 οὔτε μὴ φυῶσιν.

Πῶς δή; ἔφη.

Ὅτι, ἦν δ' ἐγώ, εἰ δύο μόνας ποιήσειεν, πάλιν ἂν μία ἀναφανείη ἧς ἐκεῖναι ἂν αὖ ἀμφότεραι τὸ εἶδος ἔχοιεν, καὶ εἴη ἂν ὃ ἔστιν κλίνη ἐκείνη ἀλλ' οὐχ αἱ δύο.

10 Ὀρθῶς, ἔφη.

d Ταῦτα δὴ οἶμαι εἰδὼς ὁ θεός, βουλόμενος εἶναι ὄντως κλίνης ποιητὴς ὄντως οὔσης, ἀλλὰ μὴ κλίνης τινὸς μηδὲ κλινοποιός τις, μίαν φύσει αὐτὴν ἔφυσεν.

Ἔοικεν.

5 Βούλει οὖν τοῦτον μὲν φυτουργὸν τούτου προσαγορεύωμεν, ἤ τι τοιοῦτον;

Δίκαιον γοῦν, ἔφη, ἐπειδήπερ φύσει γε καὶ τοῦτο καὶ τἆλλα πάντα πεποίηκεν.

Τί δὲ τὸν τέκτονα; ἆρ' οὐ δημιουργὸν κλίνης;

Ναί.   10

Ἦ καὶ τὸν ζωγράφον δημιουργὸν καὶ ποιητὴν τοῦ τοιούτου;

Οὐδαμῶς.

Ἀλλὰ τί αὐτὸν κλίνης φήσεις εἶναι;

Τοῦτο, ἦ δ' ὅς, ἔμοιγε δοκεῖ μετριώτατ' ἂν προσαγορεύ- e
εσθαι, μιμητὴς οὗ ἐκεῖνοι δημιουργοί.

Εἶεν, ἦν δ' ἐγώ· τὸν τοῦ τρίτου ἄρα γεννήματος ἀπὸ τῆς
φύσεως μιμητὴν καλεῖς;

Πάνυ μὲν οὖν, ἔφη.   5

Τοῦτ' ἄρα ἔσται καὶ ὁ τραγῳδοποιός, εἴπερ μιμητής ἐστι,
τρίτος τις ἀπὸ βασιλέως καὶ τῆς ἀληθείας πεφυκώς, καὶ
πάντες οἱ ἄλλοι μιμηταί.

Κινδυνεύει.

Τὸν μὲν δὴ μιμητὴν ὡμολογήκαμεν. εἰπὲ δέ μοι περὶ   10
τοῦ ζωγράφου τόδε· πότερα ἐκεῖνο αὐτὸ τὸ ἐν τῇ φύσει 598
ἕκαστον δοκεῖ σοι ἐπιχειρεῖν μιμεῖσθαι ἢ τὰ τῶν δημιουργῶν
ἔργα;

Τὰ τῶν δημιουργῶν, ἔφη.

Ἆρα οἷά ἐστιν ἢ οἷα φαίνεται; τοῦτο γὰρ ἔτι διόρισον.   5

Πῶς λέγεις; ἔφη.

Ὧδε· κλίνη, ἐάντε ἐκ πλαγίου αὐτὴν θεᾷ ἐάντε καταντικρὺ
ἢ ὁπῃοῦν, μή τι διαφέρει αὐτὴ ἑαυτῆς, ἢ διαφέρει μὲν οὐδέν,
φαίνεται δὲ ἀλλοία; καὶ τἆλλα ὡσαύτως;

Οὕτως, ἔφη· φαίνεται, διαφέρει δ' οὐδέν.   10

Τοῦτο δὴ αὐτὸ σκόπει· πρὸς πότερον ἡ γραφικὴ πεποίηται b
περὶ ἕκαστον; πότερα πρὸς τὸ ὄν, ὡς ἔχει, μιμήσασθαι, ἢ
πρὸς τὸ φαινόμενον, ὡς φαίνεται, φαντάσματος ἢ ἀληθείας
οὖσα μίμησις;

Φαντάσματος, ἔφη.   5

Πόρρω ἄρα που τοῦ ἀληθοῦς ἡ μιμητική ἐστιν καί, ὡς
ἔοικεν, διὰ τοῦτο πάντα ἀπεργάζεται, ὅτι σμικρόν τι ἑκάστου

ἐφάπτεται, καὶ τοῦτο εἴδωλον. οἶον ὁ ζωγράφος, φαμέν, ζωγραφήσει ἡμῖν σκυτοτόμον, τέκτονα, τοὺς ἄλλους δημιουρ-
c γούς, περὶ οὐδενὸς τούτων ἐπαΐων τῶν τεχνῶν· ἀλλ' ὅμως παῖδάς γε καὶ ἄφρονας ἀνθρώπους, εἰ ἀγαθὸς εἴη ζωγράφος, γράψας ἂν τέκτονα καὶ πόρρωθεν ἐπιδεικνὺς ἐξαπατῷ ἂν τῷ δοκεῖν ὡς ἀληθῶς τέκτονα εἶναι.
5   Τί δ' οὔ;
      Ἀλλὰ γὰρ οἶμαι ὦ φίλε, τόδε δεῖ περὶ πάντων τῶν τοι-ούτων διανοεῖσθαι· ἐπειδάν τις ἡμῖν ἀπαγγέλλῃ περί του, ὡς ἐνέτυχεν ἀνθρώπῳ πάσας ἐπισταμένῳ τὰς δημιουργίας καὶ τἄλλα πάντα ὅσα εἶς ἕκαστος οἶδεν, οὐδὲν ὅτι οὐχὶ
d ἀκριβέστερον· ὁτουοῦν ἐπισταμένῳ, ὑπολαμβάνειν δεῖ τῷ τοιούτῳ ὅτι εὐήθης τις ἄνθρωπος, καί, ὡς ἔοικεν, ἐντυχὼν γόητί τινι καὶ μιμητῇ ἐξηπατήθη, ὥστε ἔδοξεν αὐτῷ πάσ-σοφος εἶναι, διὰ τὸ αὐτὸς μὴ οἶός τ' εἶναι ἐπιστήμην καὶ
5 ἀνεπιστημοσύνην καὶ μίμησιν ἐξετάσαι.
      Ἀληθέστατα, ἔφη.
      Οὐκοῦν, ἦν δ' ἐγώ, μετὰ τοῦτο ἐπισκεπτέον τήν τε τραγῳδίαν καὶ τὸν ἡγεμόνα αὐτῆς Ὅμηρον, ἐπειδή τινων
e ἀκούομεν ὅτι οὗτοι πάσας μὲν τέχνας ἐπίστανται, πάντα δὲ τὰ ἀνθρώπεια τὰ πρὸς ἀρετὴν καὶ κακίαν, καὶ τά γε θεῖα· ἀνάγκη γὰρ τὸν ἀγαθὸν ποιητήν, εἰ μέλλει περὶ ὧν ἂν ποιῇ καλῶς ποιήσειν, εἰδότα ἄρα ποιεῖν, ἢ μὴ οἶόν τε εἶναι
5 ποιεῖν. δεῖ δὴ ἐπισκέψασθαι πότερον μιμηταῖς τούτοις οὗτοι ἐντυχόντες ἐξηπάτηνται καὶ τὰ ἔργα αὐτῶν ὁρῶντες
599 οὐκ αἰσθάνονται τριττὰ ἀπέχοντα τοῦ ὄντος καὶ ῥᾴδια ποιεῖν μὴ εἰδότι τὴν ἀλήθειαν—φαντάσματα γὰρ ἀλλ' οὐκ ὄντα ποιοῦσιν—ἤ τι καὶ λέγουσιν καὶ τῷ ὄντι οἱ ἀγαθοὶ ποιηταὶ ἴσασιν περὶ ὧν δοκοῦσιν τοῖς πολλοῖς εὖ λέγειν.
5   Πάνυ μὲν οὖν, ἔφη, ἐξεταστέον.
      Οἴει οὖν, εἴ τις ἀμφότερα δύναιτο ποιεῖν, τό τε μιμηθη-σόμενον καὶ τὸ εἴδωλον, ἐπὶ τῇ τῶν εἰδώλων δημιουργίᾳ

ἑαυτὸν ἀφεῖναι ἂν σπουδάζειν καὶ τοῦτο προστήσασθαι τοῦ
ἑαυτοῦ βίου ὡς βέλτιστον ἔχοντα;   b
Οὐκ ἔγωγε.

'Αλλ' εἴπερ γε οἶμαι ἐπιστήμων εἴη τῇ ἀληθείᾳ τούτων
πέρι ἅπερ καὶ μιμεῖται, πολὺ πρότερον ἐν τοῖς ἔργοις ἂν
σπουδάσειεν ἢ ἐπὶ τοῖς μιμήμασι, καὶ πε οῷτο ἂν πολλὰ καὶ 5
καλὰ ἔργα ἑαυτοῦ καταλιπεῖν μνημεῖα, καὶ εἶναι προθυμοῖτ'
ἂν μᾶλλον ὁ ἐγκωμιαζόμενος ἢ ὁ ἐγκωμιάζων.
Οἶμαι, ἔφη· οὐ γὰρ ἐξ ἴσου ἥ τε τιμὴ καὶ ἡ ὠφελία.

Τῶν μὲν τοίνυν ἄλλων πέρι μὴ ἀπαιτῶμεν λόγον ῞Ομη-
ρον ἢ ἄλλον ὁντινοῦν τῶν ποιητῶν, ἐρωτῶντες εἰ ἰατρικὸς c
ἦν τις αὐτῶν ἀλλὰ μὴ μιμητὴς μόνον ἰατρικῶν λόγων, τίνας
ὑγιεῖς ποιητής τις τῶν παλαιῶν ἢ τῶν νέων λέγεται πεποιηκέναι, ὥσπερ 'Ασκληπιός, ἢ τίνας μαθητὰς ἰατρικῆς κατε-
λίπετο, ὥσπερ ἐκεῖνος τοὺς ἐκγόνους, μηδ' αὖ περὶ τὰς 5
ἄλλας τέχνας αὐτοὺς ἐρωτῶμεν, ἀλλ' ἐῶμεν· περὶ δὲ ὧν
μεγίστων τε καὶ καλλίστων ἐπιχειρεῖ λέγειν ῞Ομηρος, πολέ-
μων τε πέρι καὶ στρατηγιῶν καὶ διοικήσεων πόλεων, καὶ
παιδείας πέρι ἀνθρώπου, δίκαιόν που ἐρωτᾶν αὐτὸν πυνθα- d
νομένους· ᾿Ω φίλε ῞Ομηρε, εἴπερ μὴ τρίτος ἀπὸ τῆς ἀληθείας
εἶ ἀρετῆς πέρι, εἰδώλου δημιουργός, ὃν δὴ μιμητὴν ὡρισά-
μεθα, ἀλλὰ καὶ δεύτερος, καὶ οἷός τε ἦσθα γιγνώσκειν ποῖα
ἐπιτηδεύματα βελτίους ἢ χείρους ἀνθρώπους ποιεῖ ἰδίᾳ καὶ 5
δημοσίᾳ, λέγε ἡμῖν τίς τῶν πόλεων διὰ σὲ βέλτιον ᾠκησεν,
ὥσπερ διὰ Λυκοῦργον Λακεδαίμων καὶ δι' ἄλλους πολλοὺς
πολλαὶ μεγάλαι τε καὶ σμικραί· σὲ δὲ τίς αἰτιᾶται πόλις e
νομοθέτην ἀγαθὸν γεγονέναι καὶ σφᾶς ὠφελητέναι; Χαρώνδαν μὲν γὰρ 'Ιταλία καὶ Σικελία, καὶ ἡμεῖς Σόλωνα· σὲ δὲ
τίς; ἕξει τινὰ εἰπεῖν;
Οὐκ οἶμαι, ἔφη ὁ Γλαύκων· οὔκουν λέγεταί γε οὐδ' ὑπ' 5
αὐτῶν 'Ομηριδῶν.

'Αλλὰ δή τις πόλεμος ἐπὶ 'Ομήρου ὑπ' ἐκείνου ἄρχοντος 600

ἢ συμβουλεύοντος εὖ πολεμηθεὶς μνημονεύεται;
Οὐδείς.

Ἀλλ᾽ οἷα δὴ εἰς τὰ ἔργα σοφοῦ ἀνδρός, πολλαὶ ἐπίνοιαι
5 καὶ εὐμήχανοι εἰς τέχνας ἤ τινας ἄλλας πράξεις λέγονται,
ὥσπερ αὖ Θάλεώ τε πέρι τοῦ Μιλησίου καὶ Ἀναχάρσιος
τοῦ Σκύθου;
Οὐδαμῶς τοιοῦτον οὐδέν.

Ἀλλὰ δὴ εἰ μὴ δημοσίᾳ, ἰδίᾳ τισὶν ἡγεμὼν παιδείας
10 αὐτὸς ζῶν λέγεται Ὅμηρος γενέσθαι, οἳ ἐκεῖνον ἠγάπων ἐπὶ
b συνουσίᾳ καὶ τοῖς ὑστέροις ὁδόν τινα παρέδοσαν βίου
Ὁμηρικήν, ὥσπερ Πυθαγόρας αὐτός τε διαφερόντως ἐπὶ
τούτῳ ἠγαπήθη, καὶ οἱ ὕστεροι ἔτι καὶ νῦν Πυθαγόρειον
τρόπον ἐπονομάζοντες τοῦ βίου διαφανεῖς πῃ δοκοῦσιν εἶναι
5 ἐν τοῖς ἄλλοις;
Οὐδ᾽ αὖ, ἔφη, τοιοῦτον οὐδὲν λέγεται. ὁ γὰρ Κρεώφιλος,
ὦ Σώκρατες, ἴσως, ὁ τοῦ Ὁμήρου ἑταῖρος, τοῦ ὀνόματος ἂν
γελοιότερος ἔτι πρὸς παιδείαν φανείη, εἰ τὰ λεγόμενα περὶ
Ὁμήρου ἀληθῆ. λέγεται γὰρ ὡς πολλή τις ἀμέλεια περὶ
c αὐτὸν ἦν ὑπ᾽ αὐτοῦ ἐκείνου, ὅτε ἔζη.

Λέγεται γὰρ οὖν, ἦν δ᾽ ἐγώ. ἀλλ᾽ οἴει, ὦ Γλαύκων, εἰ
τῷ ὄντι οἷός τ᾽ ἦν παιδεύειν ἀνθρώπους καὶ βελτίους ἀπεργάζεσθαι Ὅμηρος, ἅτε περὶ τούτων οὐ μιμεῖσθαι ἀλλὰ
5 γιγνώσκειν δυνάμενος, οὐκ ἄρ᾽ ἂν πολλοὺς ἑταίρους ἐποιή-
σατο καὶ ἐτιμᾶτο καὶ ἠγαπᾶτο ὑπ᾽ αὐτῶν, ἀλλὰ Πρωταγόρας
μὲν ἄρα ὁ Ἀβδηρίτης καὶ Πρόδικος ὁ Κεῖος καὶ ἄλλοι πάμ-
πολλοι δύνανται τοῖς ἐφ᾽ ἑαυτῶν παριστάναι ἰδίᾳ συγγιγνό-
d μενοι ὡς οὔτε οἰκίαν οὔτε πόλιν τὴν αὑτῶν διοικεῖν οἷοί τ᾽
ἔσονται, ἐὰν μὴ σφεῖς αὐτῶν ἐπιστατήσωσιν τῆς παιδείας,
καὶ ἐπὶ ταύτῃ τῇ σοφίᾳ οὕτω σφόδρα φιλοῦνται, ὥστε μόνον
οὐκ ἐπὶ ταῖς κεφαλαῖς περιφέρουσιν αὐτοὺς οἱ ἑταῖροι·
5 Ὅμηρον δ᾽ ἄρα οἱ ἐπ᾽ ἐκείνου, εἴπερ οἷός τ᾽ ἦν πρὸς ἀρετὴν
ὀνῆσαι ἀνθρώπους, ἢ Ἡσίοδον ῥαψῳδεῖν ἂν περιιόντας εἴων,

a 4 O.C.T. no comma   b 6 O.C.T. Κρεώφυλος   c 1 O.C.T. ἐπ᾽

καὶ οὐχὶ μᾶλλον ἂν αὐτῶν ἀντείχοντο ἢ τοῦ χρυσοῦ καὶ
ἠνάγκαζον παρὰ σφίσιν οἴκοι εἶναι, ἢ εἰ μὴ ἔπειθον, αὐτοὶ ἂν e
ἐπαιδαγώγουν ὅπῃ ἦσαν, ἕως ἱκανῶς παιδείας μεταλάβοιεν;
Παντάπασιν, ἔφη, δοκεῖς μοι, ὦ Σώκρατες, ἀληθῆ λέγειν.
Οὐκοῦν τιθῶμεν ἀπὸ Ὁμήρου ἀρξαμένους πάντας τοὺς
ποιητικοὺς μιμητὰς εἰδώλων ἀρετῆς εἶναι καὶ τῶν ἄλλων 5
περὶ ὧν ποιοῦσιν, τῆς δὲ ἀληθείας οὐχ ἅπτεσθαι, ἀλλ' ὥσπερ
νυνδὴ ἐλέγομεν, ὁ ζωγράφος σκυτοτόμον ποιήσει δοκοῦντα
εἶναι, αὐτός τε οὐκ ἐπαΐων περὶ σκυτοτομίας καὶ τοῖς μὴ 601
ἐπαΐουσιν, ἐκ τῶν χρωμάτων δὲ καὶ σχημάτων θεωροῦσιν;
Πάνυ μὲν οὖν.
Οὕτω δὴ οἶμαι καὶ τὸν ποιητικὸν φήσομεν χρώματα ἄττα
ἑκάστων τῶν τεχνῶν τοῖς ὀνόμασι καὶ ῥήμασιν ἐπιχρωματί- 5
ζειν αὐτὸν οὐκ ἐπαΐοντα ἀλλ' ἢ μιμεῖσθαι, ὥστε ἑτέροις
τοιούτοις ἐκ τῶν λόγων θεωροῦσι δοκεῖν, ἐάντε περὶ σκυτοτομίας τις λέγῃ ἐν μέτρῳ καὶ ῥυθμῷ καὶ ἁρμονίᾳ, πάνυ εὖ
δοκεῖν λέγεσθαι, ἐάντε περὶ στρατηγίας ἐάντε περὶ ἄλλου
ὁτουοῦν· οὕτω φύσει αὐτὰ ταῦτα μεγάλην τινὰ κήλησιν b
ἔχειν. ἐπεὶ γυμνωθέντα γε τῶν τῆς μουσικῆς χρωμάτων
τὰ τῶν ποιητῶν, αὐτὰ ἐφ' αὐτῶν λεγόμενα, οἶμαί σε εἰδέναι
οἷα φαίνεται. τεθέασαι γάρ που.
Ἔγωγ', ἔφη. 5
Οὐκοῦν, ἦν δ' ἐγώ, ἔοικεν τοῖς τῶν ὡραίων προσώποις,
καλῶν δὲ μή, οἷα γίγνεται ἰδεῖν ὅταν αὐτὰ τὸ ἄνθος προλίπῃ;
Παντάπασιν, ἦ δ' ὅς.
Ἴθι δή, τόδε ἄθρει· ὁ τοῦ εἰδώλου ποιητής, ὁ μιμητής,
φαμέν, τοῦ μὲν ὄντος οὐδὲν ἐπαΐει, τοῦ δὲ φαινομένου· οὐχ 10
οὕτως; c
Ναί.
Μὴ τοίνυν ἐφ' ἡμίσεως αὐτὸ καταλίπωμεν ῥηθέν, ἀλλ'
ἱκανῶς ἴδωμεν.
Λέγε, ἔφη. 5

Ζωγράφος, φαμέν, ἡνίας τε γράψει καὶ χαλινόν;
Ναί.
Ποιήσει δέ γε σκυτοτόμος καὶ χαλκεύς;
Πάνυ γε.

10 Ἆρ' οὖν ἐπαίει οἵας δεῖ τὰς ἡνίας εἶναι καὶ τὸν χαλινὸν
ὁ γραφεύς; ἢ οὐδ' ὁ ποιήσας, ὅ τε χαλκεὺς καὶ ὁ σκυτεύς,
ἀλλ' ἐκεῖνος ὅσπερ τούτοις ἐπίσταται χρῆσθαι, μόνος ὁ
ἱππικός;
Ἀληθέστατα.

15 Ἆρ' οὖν οὐ περὶ πάντα οὕτω φήσομεν ἔχειν;
Πῶς;

d Περὶ ἕκαστον ταύτας τινὰς τρεῖς τέχνας εἶναι, χρησομένην,
ποιήσουσαν, μιμησομένην;
Ναί.

Οὐκοῦν ἀρετὴ καὶ κάλλος καὶ ὀρθότης ἑκάστου σκεύους
5 καὶ ζῴου καὶ πράξεως οὐ πρὸς ἄλλο τι ἢ τὴν χρείαν ἐστίν,
πρὸς ἣν ἂν ἕκαστον ᾖ πεποιημένον ἢ πεφυκός;
Οὕτως.

Πολλὴ ἄρα ἀνάγκη τὸν χρώμενον ἑκάστῳ ἐμπειρότατόν
τε εἶναι καὶ ἄγγελον γίγνεσθαι τῷ ποιητῇ οἷα ἀγαθὰ ἢ κακὰ
10 ποιεῖ ἐν τῇ χρείᾳ ᾧ χρῆται· οἷον αὐλητής πού αὐλοποιῷ
e ἐξαγγέλλει περὶ τῶν αὐλῶν, οἳ ἂν ὑπηρετῶσιν ἐν τῷ αὐλεῖν,
καὶ ἐπιτάξει οἵους δεῖ ποιεῖν, ὁ δ' ὑπηρετήσει.
Πῶς δ' οὔ;

Οὐκοῦν ὁ μὲν εἰδὼς ἐξαγγέλλει περὶ χρηστῶν καὶ πονηρῶν
5 αὐλῶν, ὁ δὲ πιστεύων ποιήσει;
Ναί.

Τοῦ αὐτοῦ ἄρα σκεύους ὁ μὲν ποιητὴς πίστιν ὀρθὴν ἕξει
περὶ κάλλους τε καὶ πονηρίας, συνὼν τῷ εἰδότι καὶ ἀναγκα-
602 ζόμενος ἀκούειν παρὰ τοῦ εἰδότος, ὁ δὲ χρώμενος ἐπιστήμην.
Πάνυ γε.

Ὁ δὲ μιμητὴς πότερον ἐκ τοῦ χρῆσθαι ἐπιστήμην ἕξει

περὶ ὧν ἂν γράφῃ, εἴτε καλὰ καὶ ὀρθὰ εἴτε μή, ἢ δόξαν
ὀρθὴν διὰ τὸ ἐξ ἀνάγκης συνεῖναι τῷ εἰδότι καὶ ἐπιτάττεσθαι 5
οἷα χρὴ γράφειν;
Οὐδέτερα.
Οὔτε ἄρα εἴσεται οὔτε ὀρθὰ δοξάσει ὁ μιμητὴς περὶ ὧν
ἂν μιμῆται πρὸς κάλλος ἢ πονηρίαν.
Οὐκ ἔοικεν.   10
Χαρίεις ἂν εἴη ὁ ἐν τῇ ποιήσει μιμητικὸς πρὸς σοφίαν
περὶ ὧν ἂν ποιῇ.
Οὐ πάνυ.
Ἀλλ' οὖν δὴ ὅμως γε μιμήσεται, οὐκ εἰδὼς περὶ ἑκάστου b
ὅπῃ πονηρὸν ἢ χρηστόν· ἀλλ', ὡς ἔοικεν, οἷον φαίνεται
καλὸν εἶναι τοῖς πολλοῖς τε καὶ μηδὲν εἰδόσιν, τοῦτο
μιμήσεται.
Τί γὰρ ἄλλο;   5
Ταῦτα μὲν δή, ὥς γε φαίνεται, ἐπιεικῶς ἡμῖν διωμολόγηται,
τόν τε μιμητικὸν μηδὲν εἰδέναι ἄξιον λόγου περὶ ὧν μιμεῖται,
ἀλλ' εἶναι παιδιάν τινα καὶ οὐ σπουδὴν τὴν μίμησιν, τούς
τε τῆς τραγικῆς ποιήσεως ἀπτομένους ἐν ἰαμβείοις καὶ ἐν
ἔπεσι πάντας εἶναι μιμητικοὺς ὡς οἷόν τε μάλιστα.   10
Πάνυ μὲν οὖν.
Πρὸς Διός, ἦν δ' ἐγώ, τὸ δὲ δὴ μιμεῖσθαι τοῦτο οὐ περὶ c
τρίτον μέν τί ἐστιν ἀπὸ τῆς ἀληθείας; ἢ γάρ;
Ναί.
Πρὸς δὲ δὴ ποῖόν τί ἐστιν τῶν τοῦ ἀνθρώπου ἔχον τὴν
δύναμιν ἣν ἔχει;   5
Τοῦ ποίου τινὸς πέρι λέγεις;
Τοῦ τοιοῦδε· ταὐτόν που ἡμῖν μέγεθος ἐγγύθεν τε καὶ
πόρρωθεν διὰ τῆς ὄψεως οὐκ ἴσον φαίνεται.
Οὐ γάρ.
Καὶ ταὐτὰ καμπύλα τε καὶ εὐθέα ἐν ὕδατί τε θεωμένοις 10
καὶ ἔξω, καὶ κοῖλά τε δὴ καὶ ἐξέχοντα διὰ τὴν περὶ τὰ

χρώματα αὖ πλάνην τῆς ὄψεως, καὶ πᾶσά τις ταραχὴ δήλη
d ἡμῖν ἐνοῦσα αὕτη ἐν τῇ ψυχῇ· ᾧ δὴ ἡμῶν τῷ παθήματι
τῆς φύσεως ἡ σκιαγραφία ἐπιθεμένη γοητείας οὐδὲν ἀπολείπει, καὶ ἡ θαυματοποιία καὶ αἱ ἄλλαι πολλαὶ τοιαῦται
μηχαναί.

5   Ἀληθῆ.

Ἆρ᾽ οὖν οὐ τὸ μετρεῖν καὶ ἀριθμεῖν καὶ ἱστάναι βοήθειαι
χαριέσταται πρὸς αὐτὰ ἐφάνησαν, ὥστε μὴ ἄρχειν ἐν ἡμῖν
τὸ φαινόμενον μεῖζον ἢ ἔλαττον ἢ πλέον ἢ βαρύτερον, ἀλλὰ
τὸ λογισάμενον καὶ μετρῆσαν ἢ καὶ στῆσαν;

10   Πῶς γὰρ οὔ;

e   Ἀλλὰ μὴν τοῦτό γε τοῦ λογιστικοῦ ἂν εἴη τοῦ ἐν ψυχῇ
ἔργον.

Τούτου γὰρ οὖν.

Τούτῳ δὲ πολλάκις μετρήσαντι καὶ σημαίνοντι μείζω
5 ἄττα εἶναι ἢ ἐλάττω ἕτερα ἑτέρων ἢ ἴσα τἀναντία φαίνεται
ἅμα περὶ ταὐτά.

Ναί.

Οὐκοῦν ἔφαμεν τῷ αὐτῷ ἅμα περὶ ταὐτὰ ἐναντία δοξάζειν
ἀδύνατον εἶναι;

10   Καὶ ὀρθῶς γ᾽ ἔφαμεν.

603   Τὸ παρὰ τὰ μέτρα ἄρα δοξάζον τῆς ψυχῆς τῷ κατὰ τὰ
μέτρα οὐκ ἂν εἴη ταὐτόν.

Οὐ γὰρ οὖν.

Ἀλλὰ μὴν τὸ μέτρῳ γε καὶ λογισμῷ πιστεῦον βέλτιστον
5 ἂν εἴη τῆς ψυχῆς.

Τί μήν;

Τὸ ἄρα τούτῳ ἐναντιούμενον τῶν φαύλων ἄν τι εἴη ἐν
ἡμῖν.

Ἀνάγκη.

10   Τοῦτο τοίνυν διομολογήσασθαι βουλόμενος ἔλεγον ὅτι ἡ
γραφικὴ καὶ ὅλως ἡ μιμητικὴ πόρρω μὲν τῆς ἀληθείας ὂν τὸ

αὐτῆς ἔργον ἀπεργάζεται, πόρρω δ' αὖ φρονήσεως ὄντι τῷ ἐν ἡμῖν προσομιλεῖ τε καὶ ἑταίρα καὶ φίλη ἐστὶν ἐπ' οὐδενὶ **b** ὑγιεῖ οὐδ' ἀληθεῖ.

Παντάπασιν, ἦ δ' ὅς.

Φαύλη ἄρα φαύλῳ συγγιγνομένη φαῦλα γεννᾷ ἡ μιμητική.

Ἔοικεν. 5

Πότερον, ἦν δ' ἐγώ, ἡ κατὰ τὴν ὄψιν μόνον, ἢ καὶ κατὰ τὴν ἀκοήν, ἣν δὴ ποίησιν ὀνομάζομεν;

Εἰκός γ', ἔφη, καὶ ταύτην.

Μὴ τοίνυν, ἦν δ' ἐγώ, τῷ εἰκότι μόνον πιστεύσωμεν ἐκ τῆς γραφικῆς, ἀλλὰ καὶ ἐπ' αὐτὸ αὖ ἔλθωμεν τῆς διανοίας 10 τοῦτο ᾧ προσομιλεῖ ἡ τῆς ποιήσεως μιμητική, καὶ ἴδωμεν **c** φαῦλον ἢ σπουδαῖόν ἐστιν.

Ἀλλὰ χρή.

Ὧδε δὴ προθώμεθα· πράττοντας, φαμέν, ἀνθρώπους μιμεῖται ἡ μιμητικὴ βιαίους ἢ ἑκουσίας πράξεις, καὶ ἐκ τοῦ 5 πράττειν ἢ εὖ οἰομένους ἢ κακῶς πεπραγέναι, καὶ ἐν τούτοις δὴ πᾶσιν ἢ λυπουμένους ἢ χαίροντας. μή τι ἄλλο ἢ παρὰ ταῦτα.

Οὐδέν.

Ἆρ' οὖν ἐν ἅπασι τούτοις ὁμονοητικῶς ἄνθρωπος διάκει- 10 ται; ἢ ὥσπερ κατὰ τὴν ὄψιν ἐστασίαζεν καὶ ἐναντίας εἶχεν **d** ἐν ἑαυτῷ δόξας ἅμα περὶ τῶν αὐτῶν, οὕτω καὶ ἐν ταῖς πράξεσι στασιάζει τε καὶ μάχεται αὐτὸς αὑτῷ; ἀναμιμνῄ- σκομαι δὲ ὅτι τοῦτό γε νῦν οὐδὲν δεῖ ἡμᾶς διομολογεῖσθαι· ἐν γὰρ τοῖς ἄνω λόγοις ἱκανῶς πάντα ταῦτα διωμολογησά- 5 μεθα, ὅτι μυρίων τοιούτων ἐναντιωμάτων ἅμα γιγνομένων ἡ ψυχὴ γέμει ἡμῶν.

Ὀρθῶς, ἔφη.

Ὀρθῶς γάρ, ἦν δ' ἐγώ· ἀλλ' ὃ τότε ἀπελίπομεν, νῦν μοι δοκεῖ ἀναγκαῖον εἶναι διεξελθεῖν. **e**

Τὸ ποῖον; ἔφη.

Ἀνήρ, ἦν δ' ἐγώ, ἐπιεικὴς τοιᾶσδε τύχης μετασχών, υἱὸν
ἀπολέσας ἤ τι ἄλλο ὧν περὶ πλείστου ποιεῖται, ἐλέγομέν
5 που καὶ τότε ὅτι ῥᾷστα οἴσει τῶν ἄλλων.
Πάνυ γε.
Νῦν δέ γε τόδ' ἐπισκεψώμεθα, πότερον οὐδὲν ἀχθέσεται,
ἢ τοῦτο μὲν ἀδύνατον, μετριάσει δέ πως πρὸς λύπην.
Οὕτω μᾶλλον, ἔφη, τό γε ἀληθές.

604 Τόδε δὴ νῦν μοι περὶ αὐτοῦ εἰπέ· πότερον μᾶλλον αὐτὸν
οἴει τῇ λύπῃ μαχεῖσθαί τε καὶ ἀντιτείνειν, ὅταν ὁρᾶται ὑπὸ
τῶν ὁμοίων, ἢ ὅταν ἐν ἐρημίᾳ μόνος αὐτὸς καθ' αὑτὸν
γίγνηται;
5 Πολύ που, ἔφη, διοίσει, ὅταν ὁρᾶται.
Μονωθεὶς δέ γε οἶμαι πολλὰ μὲν τολμήσει φθέγξασθαι,
ἃ εἴ τις αὐτοῦ ἀκούοι αἰσχύνοιτ' ἄν, πολλὰ δὲ ποιήσει, ἃ οὐκ
ἂν δέξαιτό τινα ἰδεῖν δρῶντα.
Οὕτως ἔχει, ἔφη.
10 Οὐκοῦν τὸ μὲν ἀντιτείνειν διακελευόμενον λόγος καὶ νόμος
b ἐστίν, τὸ δὲ ἕλκον ἐπὶ τὰς λύπας αὐτὸ τὸ πάθος;
Ἀληθῆ.
Ἐναντίας δὲ ἀγωγῆς γιγνομένης ἐν τῷ ἀνθρώπῳ περὶ τὸ
αὐτὸ ἅμα, δύο φαμὲν αὐτῷ ἀναγκαῖον εἶναι.
5 Πῶς δ' οὔ;
Οὐκοῦν τὸ μὲν ἕτερον τῷ νόμῳ ἕτοιμον πείθεσθαι, ᾗ ὁ
νόμος ἐξηγεῖται;
Πῶς;
Λέγει που ὁ νόμος ὅτι κάλλιστον ὅτι μάλιστα ἡσυχίαν
10 ἄγειν ἐν ταῖς συμφοραῖς καὶ μὴ ἀγανακτεῖν, ὡς οὔτε δήλου
ὄντος τοῦ ἀγαθοῦ τε καὶ κακοῦ τῶν τοιούτων, οὔτε εἰς τὸ
πρόσθεν οὐδὲν προβαῖνον τῷ χαλεπῶς φέροντι, οὔτε τι τῶν
c ἀνθρωπίνων ἄξιον ὂν μεγάλης σπουδῆς, ὅ τε δεῖ ἐν αὐτοῖς
ὅτι τάχιστα παραγίγνεσθαι ἡμῖν, τούτῳ ἐμποδὼν γιγνόμενον
τὸ λυπεῖσθαι.

a 1 O.C.T. no δὴ   b 4 O.C.T. αὐτῶ

Τίνι, ἦ δ' ὅς, λέγεις;

Τῷ βουλεύεσθαι, ἦν δ' ἐγώ, περὶ τὸ γεγονὸς καὶ ὥσπερ 5
ἐν πτώσει κύβων πρὸς τὰ πεπτωκότα τίθεσθαι τὰ αὑτοῦ
πράγματα, ὅπῃ ὁ λόγος αἱρεῖ βέλτιστ' ἂν ἔχειν, ἀλλὰ μὴ
προσπταίσαντας καθάπερ παῖδας ἐχομένους τοῦ πληγέντος
ἐν τῷ βοᾶν διατρίβειν, ἀλλ' ἀεὶ ἐθίζειν τὴν ψυχὴν ὅτι
τάχιστα γίγνεσθαι πρὸς τὸ ἰᾶσθαί τε καὶ ἐπανορθοῦν τὸ d
πεσόν τε καὶ νοσῆσαν, ἰατρικῇ θρηνῳδίαν ἀφανίζοντα.

Ὀρθότατα γοῦν ἄν τις, ἔφη, πρὸς τὰς τύχας οὕτω
προσφέροιτο.

Οὐκοῦν, φαμέν, τὸ μὲν βέλτιστον τούτῳ τῷ λογισμῷ 5
ἐθέλει ἕπεσθαι.

Δῆλον δή.

Τὸ δὲ πρὸς τὰς ἀναμνήσεις τε τοῦ πάθους καὶ πρὸς τοὺς
ὀδυρμοὺς ἄγον καὶ ἀπλήστως ἔχον αὐτῶν ἆρ' οὐκ ἀλόγιστόν
τε φήσομεν εἶναι καὶ ἀργὸν καὶ δειλίας φίλον;   10

Φήσομεν μὲν οὖν.

Οὐκοῦν τὸ μὲν πολλὴν μίμησιν καὶ ποικίλην ἔχει, τὸ e
ἀγανακτητικόν, τὸ δὲ φρόνιμόν τε καὶ ἡσύχιον ἦθος, παραπλήσιον ὂν ἀεὶ αὐτὸ αὑτῷ, οὔτε ῥᾴδιον μιμήσασθαι οὔτε
μιμουμένου εὐπετὲς καταμαθεῖν, ἄλλως τε καὶ πανηγύρει καὶ
παντοδαποῖς ἀνθρώποις εἰς θέατρα συλλεγομένοις· ἀλλο- 5
τρίου γάρ που πάθους ἡ μίμησις αὐτοῖς γίγνεται.

Παντάπασι μὲν οὖν.   605

Ὁ δὴ μιμητικὸς ποιητὴς δῆλον ὅτι οὐ πρὸς τὸ τοιοῦτον
τῆς ψυχῆς πέφυκέ τε καὶ ἡ σοφία αὐτοῦ τούτῳ ἀρέσκειν
πέπηγεν, εἰ μέλλει εὐδοκιμήσειν ἐν τοῖς πολλοῖς, ἀλλὰ
πρὸς τὸ ἀγανακτητικόν τε καὶ ποικίλον ἦθος διὰ τὸ εὐμί- 5
μητον εἶναι.

Δῆλον.

Οὐκοῦν δικαίως ἂν αὐτοῦ ἤδη ἐπιλαμβανοίμεθα, καὶ
τιθεῖμεν ἀντίστροφον αὐτὸν τῷ ζωγράφῳ· καὶ γὰρ τῷ φαῦλα

10 ποιεῖν πρὸς ἀλήθειαν ἔοικεν αὐτῷ, καὶ τῷ πρὸς ἕτερον τοι-
b οῦτον ὁμιλεῖν τῆς ψυχῆς ἀλλὰ μὴ πρὸς τὸ βέλτιστον, καὶ
ταύτῃ ὡμοίωται. καὶ οὕτως ἤδη ἂν ἐν δίκῃ οὐ παραδεχοί-
μεθα εἰς μέλλουσαν εὐνομεῖσθαι πόλιν, ὅτι τοῦτο ἐγείρει
τῆς ψυχῆς καὶ τρέφει καὶ ἰσχυρὸν ποιῶν ἀπόλλυσι τὸ
5 λογιστικόν, ὥσπερ ἐν πόλει ὅταν τις μοχθηροὺς ἐγκρατεῖς
ποιῶν παραδιδῷ τὴν πόλιν, τοὺς δὲ χαριεστέρους φθείρῃ·
ταὐτὸν καὶ τὸν μιμητικὸν ποιητὴν φήσομεν κακὴν πολι-
τείαν ἰδίᾳ ἑκάστου τῇ ψυχῇ ἐμποιεῖν, τῷ ἀνοήτῳ αὐτῆς
c χαριζόμενον καὶ οὔτε τὰ μείζω οὔτε τὰ ἐλάττω διαγιγνώ-
σκοντι, ἀλλὰ τὰ αὐτὰ τοτὲ μὲν μεγάλα ἡγουμένῳ, τοτὲ δὲ
σμικρά, εἴδωλα εἰδωλοποιοῦντα, τοῦ δὲ ἀληθοῦς πόρρω πάνυ
ἀφεστῶτα.
5 Πάνυ μὲν οὖν.
Οὐ μέντοι πω τό γε μέγιστον κατηγορήκαμεν αὐτῆς. τὸ
γὰρ καὶ τοὺς ἐπιεικεῖς ἱκανὴν εἶναι λωβᾶσθαι, ἐκτὸς πάνυ
τινῶν ὀλίγων, πάνδεινόν που.
Τί δ᾽ οὐ μέλλει, εἴπερ γε δρᾷ αὐτό;
10 Ἀκούων σκόπει. οἱ γάρ που βέλτιστοι ἡμῶν ἀκροώ-
μενοι Ὁμήρου ἢ ἄλλου τινὸς τῶν τραγῳδοποιῶν μιμουμένου
d τινὰ τῶν ἡρώων ἐν πένθει ὄντα καὶ μακρὰν ῥῆσιν ἀποτεί-
νοντα ἐν τοῖς ὀδυρμοῖς ἢ καὶ ᾄδοντάς τε καὶ κοπτομένους,
οἶσθ᾽ ὅτι χαίρομέν τε καὶ ἐνδόντες ἡμᾶς αὐτοὺς ἑπόμεθα
συμπάσχοντες καὶ σπουδάζοντες ἐπαινοῦμεν ὡς ἀγαθὸν
5 ποιητήν, ὃς ἂν ἡμᾶς ὅτι μάλιστα οὕτω διαθῇ.
Οἶδα· πῶς δ᾽ οὔ;
Ὅταν δὲ οἰκεῖόν τινι ἡμῶν κῆδος γένηται, ἐννοεῖς αὖ ὅτι
ἐπὶ τῷ ἐναντίῳ καλλωπιζόμεθα, ἂν δυνώμεθα ἡσυχίαν ἄγειν
e καὶ καρτερεῖν, ὡς τοῦτο μὲν ἀνδρὸς ὄν, ἐκεῖνο δὲ γυναικός,
ὃ τότε ἐπῃνοῦμεν.
Ἐννοῶ, ἔφη.
Ἦ καλῶς οὖν, ἦν δ᾽ ἐγώ, οὗτος ὁ ἔπαινος ἔχει, τὸ ὁρῶντα

τοιοῦτον ἄνδρα, οἷον ἑαυτόν τις μὴ ἀξιοῖ εἶναι ἀλλ' αἰσχύνοιτο 5
ἄν, μὴ βδελύττεσθαι ἀλλὰ χαίρειν τε καὶ ἐπαινεῖν;
Οὐ μὰ τὸν Δί', ἔφη, οὐκ εὐλόγῳ ἔοικεν.
Ναί, ἦν δ' ἐγώ, εἰ ἐκείνῃ γ' αὐτὸ σκοποίης.   606

Πῇ;

Εἰ ἐνθυμοῖο ὅτι τὸ βίᾳ κατεχόμενον τότε ἐν ταῖς οἰκείαις
συμφοραῖς καὶ πεπεινηκὸς τοῦ δακρῦσαί τε καὶ ἀποδύρασθαι
ἱκανῶς καὶ ἀποπλησθῆναι, φύσει ὂν τοιοῦτον οἷον τούτων ἐπι- 5
θυμεῖν, τότ' ἐστὶν τοῦτο τὸ ὑπὸ τῶν ποιητῶν πιμπλάμενον
καὶ χαῖρον· τὸ δὲ φύσει βέλτιστον ἡμῶν, ἅτε οὐχ ἱκανῶς
πεπαιδευμένον λόγῳ οὐδὲ ἔθει, ἀνίησιν τὴν φυλακὴν τοῦ
θρηνώδους τούτου, ἅτε ἀλλότρια πάθη θεωροῦν καὶ ἑαυτῷ b
οὐδὲν αἰσχρὸν ὂν εἰ ἄλλος ἀνὴρ ἀγαθὸς φάσκων εἶναι ἀκαί-
ρως πενθεῖ, τοῦτον ἐπαινεῖν καὶ ἐλεεῖν, ἀλλ' ἐκεῖνο κερδαίνειν
ἡγεῖται, τὴν ἡδονήν, καὶ οὐκ ἂν δέξαιτο αὐτῆς στερηθῆναι
καταφρονήσας ὅλου τοῦ ποιήματος. λογίζεσθαι γὰρ οἶμαι 5
ὀλίγοις τισὶν μέτεστιν ὅτι ἀπολαύειν ἀνάγκη ἀπὸ τῶν ἀλλο-
τρίων εἰς τὰ οἰκεῖα· θρέψαντα γὰρ ἐν ἐκείνοις ἰσχυρὸν τὸ
ἐλεινὸν οὐ ῥᾴδιον ἐν τοῖς αὑτοῦ πάθεσι κατέχειν.

Ἀληθέστατα, ἔφη.   c

Ἀρ' οὖν οὐχ ὁ αὐτὸς λόγος καὶ περὶ τοῦ γελοίου; ὅτι,
ἂν αὐτὸς αἰσχύνοιο γελωτοποιῶν, ἐν μιμήσει δὲ κωμῳδικῇ ἢ
καὶ ἰδίᾳ ἀκούων σφόδρα χαρῇς καὶ μὴ μισῇς ὡς πονηρά,
ταὐτὸν ποιεῖς ὅπερ ἐν τοῖς ἐλέοις; ὃ γὰρ τῷ λόγῳ αὖ 5
κατεῖχες ἐν σαυτῷ βουλόμενον γελωτοποιεῖν, φοβούμενος
δόξαν βωμολοχίας, τότ' αὖ ἀνιεῖς, καὶ ἐκεῖ νεανικὸν ποιήσας
ἔλαθες πολλάκις ἐν τοῖς οἰκείοις ἐξενεχθεὶς ὥστε κωμῳδο-
ποιὸς γενέσθαι.

Καὶ μάλα, ἔφη.   10

Καὶ περὶ ἀφροδισίων δὴ καὶ θυμοῦ καὶ περὶ πάντων τῶν d
ἐπιθυμητικῶν τε καὶ λυπηρῶν καὶ ἡδέων ἐν τῇ ψυχῇ, ἃ δή
φαμεν πάσῃ πράξει ἡμῖν ἕπεσθαι, ὅτι τοιαῦτα ἡμᾶς ἡ

ποιητικὴ μίμησις ἐργάζεται· τρέφει γὰρ ταῦτα ἄρδουσα, δέον
5 αὐχμεῖν, καὶ ἄρχοντα ἡμῖν καθίστησιν, δέον ἄρχεσθαι αὐτὰ
ἵνα βελτίους τε καὶ εὐδαιμονέστεροι ἀντὶ χειρόνων καὶ
ἀθλιωτέρων γιγνώμεθα.

Οὐκ ἔχω ἄλλως φάναι, ἦ δ᾽ ὅς.

e   Οὐκοῦν, εἶπον, ὦ Γλαύκων, ὅταν Ὁμήρου ἐπαινέταις
ἐντύχῃς λέγουσιν ὡς τὴν Ἑλλάδα πεπαίδευκεν οὗτος ὁ
ποιητὴς καὶ πρὸς διοίκησίν τε καὶ παιδείαν τῶν ἀνθρωπίνων
πραγμάτων ἄξιος ἀναλαβόντι μανθάνειν τε καὶ κατὰ τοῦτον
5 τὸν ποιητὴν πάντα τὸν αὑτοῦ βίον κατασκευασάμενον ζῆν,
607 φιλεῖν μὲν χρὴ καὶ ἀσπάζεσθαι ὡς ὄντας βελτίστους εἰς
ὅσον δύνανται, καὶ συγχωρεῖν Ὅμηρον ποιητικώτατον εἶναι
καὶ πρῶτον τῶν τραγῳδοποιῶν, εἰδέναι δὲ ὅτι ὅσον μόνον
ὕμνους θεοῖς καὶ ἐγκώμια τοῖς ἀγαθοῖς ποιήσεως παραδεκτέον
5 εἰς πόλιν· εἰ δὲ τὴν ἡδυσμένην Μοῦσαν παραδέξῃ ἐν μέλεσιν
ἢ ἔπεσιν, ἡδονή σοι καὶ λύπη ἐν τῇ πόλει βασιλεύσετον
ἀντὶ νόμου τε καὶ τοῦ κοινῇ ἀεὶ δόξαντος εἶναι βελτίστου
λόγου.

Ἀληθέστατα, ἔφη.

b   Ταῦτα δή, ἔφην, ἀπολελογήσθω ἡμῖν ἀναμνησθεῖσιν περὶ
ποιήσεως, ὅτι εἰκότως ἄρα τότε αὐτὴν ἐκ τῆς πόλεως ἀπεστέλλομεν τοιαύτην οὖσαν· ὁ γὰρ λόγος ἡμᾶς ᾕρει. προσεί-
πωμεν δὲ αὐτῇ, μὴ καί τινα σκληρότητα ἡμῶν καὶ ἀγροικίαν
5 καταγνῷ, ὅτι παλαιὰ μέν τις διαφορὰ φιλοσοφίᾳ τε καὶ
ποιητικῇ· καὶ γὰρ ἡ "λακέρυζα πρὸς δεσπόταν κύων"
ἐκείνη "κραυγάζουσα" καὶ "μέγας ἐν ἀφρόνων κενε-
c ἀγορίαισι" καὶ ὁ "τῶν διασόφων ὄχλος κράτων"
καὶ οἱ "λεπτῶς μεριμνῶντες," ὅτι ἄρα "πένονται,"
καὶ ἄλλα μυρία σημεῖα παλαιᾶς ἐναντιώσεως τούτων. ὅμως
δὲ εἰρήσθω ὅτι ἡμεῖς γε, εἴ τινα ἔχοι λόγον εἰπεῖν ἡ πρὸς
5 ἡδονὴν ποιητικὴ καὶ ἡ μίμησις, ὡς χρὴ αὐτὴν εἶναι ἐν πόλει
εὐνομουμένῃ, ἄσμενοι ἂν καταδεχοίμεθα, ὡς σύνισμέν γε ἡμῖν

c 1   O.C.T. κρατῶν

αὐτοῖς κηλουμένοις ὑπ' αὐτῆς· ἀλλὰ γὰρ τὸ δοκοῦν ἀληθὲς
οὐχ ὅσιον προδιδόναι. ἢ γάρ, ὦ φίλε, οὐ κηλῇ ὑπ' αὐτῆς
καὶ σύ, καὶ μάλιστα ὅταν δι' Ὁμήρου θεωρῇς αὐτήν;   d
Πολύ γε.

Οὐκοῦν δικαία ἐστὶν οὕτω κατιέναι, ἀπολογησαμένη ἐν
μέλει ἤ τινι ἄλλῳ μέτρῳ;

Πάνυ μὲν οὖν.   5

Δοῖμεν δέ γέ που ἂν καὶ τοῖς προστάταις αὐτῆς, ὅσοι μὴ
ποιητικοί, φιλοποιηταὶ δέ, ἄνευ μέτρου λόγον ὑπὲρ αὐτῆς
εἰπεῖν, ὡς οὐ μόνον ἡδεῖα ἀλλὰ καὶ ὠφελίμη πρὸς τὰς πολιτείας καὶ τὸν βίον τὸν ἀνθρώπινόν ἐστιν· καὶ εὐμενῶς ἀκου-
σόμεθα. κερδανοῦμεν γάρ που ἐὰν μὴ μόνον ἡδεῖα φανῇ ἀλλὰ   e
καὶ ὠφελίμη.

Πῶς δ' οὐ μέλλομεν, ἔφη, κερδαίνειν;

Εἰ δέ γε μή, ὦ φίλε ἑταῖρε, ὥσπερ οἱ ποτέ του ἐρα-
σθέντες, ἐὰν ἡγήσωνται μὴ ὠφέλιμον εἶναι τὸν ἔρωτα, βίᾳ   5
μέν, ὅμως δὲ ἀπέχονται, καὶ ἡμεῖς οὕτως, διὰ τὸν ἐγγεγονότα
μὲν ἔρωτα τῆς τοιαύτης ποιήσεως ὑπὸ τῆς τῶν καλῶν πολι-
τειῶν τροφῆς, εὖνοι μὲν ἐσόμεθα φανῆναι αὐτὴν ὡς βελτί-   608
στην καὶ ἀληθεστάτην, ἕως δ' ἂν μὴ οἵα τ' ᾖ ἀπολογήσασθαι,
ἀκροασόμεθ' αὐτῆς ἐπᾴδοντες ἡμῖν αὐτοῖς τοῦτον τὸν λόγον,
ὃν λέγομεν, καὶ ταύτην τὴν ἐπῳδήν, εὐλαβούμενοι πάλιν
ἐμπεσεῖν εἰς τὸν παιδικόν τε καὶ τὸν τῶν πολλῶν ἔρωτα.   5
ᾀσόμεθα δ' οὖν ὡς οὐ σπουδαστέον ἐπὶ τῇ τοιαύτῃ ποιήσει
ὡς ἀληθείας τε ἁπτομένῃ καὶ σπουδαίᾳ, ἀλλ' εὐλαβητέον
αὐτὴν ὂν τῷ ἀκροωμένῳ, περὶ τῆς ἐν αὐτῷ πολιτείας δεδιότι,   b
καὶ νομιστέα ἅπερ εἰρήκαμεν περὶ ποιήσεως.

Παντάπασιν, ἦ δ' ὅς, σύμφημι.

Μέγας γάρ, ἔφην, ὁ ἀγών, ὦ φίλε Γλαύκων, μέγας,
οὐχ ὅσος δοκεῖ, τὸ χρηστὸν ἢ κακὸν γενέσθαι, ὥστε οὔτε   5
τιμῇ ἐπαρθέντα οὔτε χρήμασιν οὔτε ἀρχῇ οὐδεμιᾷ οὐδέ γε
ποιητικῇ ἄξιον ἀμελῆσαι δικαιοσύνης τε καὶ τῆς ἄλλης
ἀρετῆς.

Σύμφημί σοι, ἔφη, ἐξ ὧν διεληλύθαμεν· οἶμαι δὲ καὶ
10 ἄλλον ὁντινοῦν.

c Καὶ μήν, ἦν δ' ἐγώ, τά γε μέγιστα ἐπίχειρα ἀρετῆς καὶ
προκείμενα ἆθλα οὐ διεληλύθαμεν.

Ἀμήχανόν τι, ἔφη, λέγεις μέγεθος, εἰ τῶν εἰρημένων
μείζω ἐστὶν ἄλλα.

5 Τί δ' ἄν, ἦν δ' ἐγώ, ἔν γε ὀλίγῳ χρόνῳ μέγα γένοιτο;
πᾶς γὰρ οὗτός γε ὁ ἐκ παιδὸς μέχρι πρεσβύτου χρόνος πρὸς
πάντα ὀλίγος πού τις ἂν εἴη.

Οὐδὲν μὲν οὖν, ἔφη.

Τί οὖν; οἴει ἀθανάτῳ πράγματι ὑπὲρ τοσούτου δεῖν
d χρόνου ἐσπουδακέναι, ἀλλ' οὐχ ὑπὲρ τοῦ παντός;

Οἶμαι ἔγωγ', ἔφη· ἀλλὰ τί τοῦτο λέγεις;

Οὐκ ᾔσθησαι, ἦν δ' ἐγώ, ὅτι ἀθάνατος ἡμῶν ἡ ψυχὴ καὶ
οὐδέποτε ἀπόλλυται;

5 Καὶ ὃς ἐμβλέψας μοι καὶ θαυμάσας εἶπε· Μὰ Δί', οὐκ
ἔγωγε· σὺ δὲ τοῦτ' ἔχεις λέγειν;

Εἰ μὴ ἀδικῶ γ', ἔφην. οἶμαι δὲ καὶ σύ· οὐδὲν γὰρ
χαλεπόν.

Ἔμοιγ', ἔφη· σοῦ δ' ἂν ἡδέως ἀκούσαιμι τὸ οὐ χαλεπὸν
10 τοῦτο.

Ἀκούοις ἄν, ἦν δ' ἐγώ.

Λέγε μόνον, ἔφη.

Ἀγαθόν τι, εἶπον, καὶ κακὸν καλεῖς;

Ἔγωγε.

e Ἆρ' οὖν ὥσπερ ἐγὼ περὶ αὐτῶν διανοῇ;

Τὸ ποῖον;

Τὸ μὲν ἀπολλύον καὶ διαφθεῖρον πᾶν τὸ κακὸν εἶναι, τὸ
δὲ σῷζον καὶ ὠφελοῦν τὸ ἀγαθόν.

5 Ἔγωγ', ἔφη.

Τί δέ; κακὸν ἑκάστῳ τι καὶ ἀγαθὸν λέγεις; οἷον ὀφθαλ-
609 μοῖς ὀφθαλμίαν καὶ σύμπαντι τῷ σώματι νόσον, σίτῳ τε

ἐρυσίβην, σηπεδόνα τε ξύλοις, χαλκῷ δὲ καὶ σιδήρῳ ἰόν,
καί, ὅπερ λέγω, σχεδὸν πᾶσι σύμφυτον ἑκάστῳ κακόν τε καὶ
νόσημα;

Ἔγωγ᾽, ἔφη.   5

Οὐκοῦν ὅταν τῷ τι τούτων προσγένηται, πονηρόν τε ποιεῖ
ᾧ προσεγένετο, καὶ τελευτῶν ὅλον διέλυσεν καὶ ἀπώλεσεν;

Πῶς γὰρ οὔ;

Τὸ σύμφυτον ἄρα κακὸν ἑκάστου καὶ ἡ πονηρία ἕκαστον
ἀπόλλυσιν, ἢ εἰ μὴ τοῦτο ἀπολεῖ, οὐκ ἂν ἄλλο γε αὐτὸ ἔτι 10
διαφθείρειεν. οὐ γὰρ τό γε ἀγαθὸν μή ποτέ τι ἀπολέσῃ, b
οὐδὲ αὖ τὸ μήτε κακὸν μήτε ἀγαθόν.

Πῶς γὰρ ἄν; ἔφη.

Ἐὰν ἄρα τι εὑρίσκωμεν τῶν ὄντων, ᾧ ἔστι μὲν κακὸν ὃ
ποιεῖ αὐτὸ μοχθηρόν, τοῦτο μέντοι οὐχ οἷόν τε αὐτὸ λύειν 5
ἀπολλύον, οὐκ ἤδη εἰσόμεθα ὅτι τοῦ πεφυκότος οὕτως ὄλεθρος
οὐκ ἦν;

Οὕτως, ἔφη, εἰκός.

Τί οὖν; ἦν δ᾽ ἐγώ· ψυχῇ ἆρ᾽ οὐκ ἔστιν ὃ ποιεῖ αὐτὴν
κακήν;   10

Καὶ μάλα, ἔφη· ἃ νυνδὴ διῇμεν πάντα, ἀδικία τε καὶ
ἀκολασία καὶ δειλία καὶ ἀμαθία.   c

Ἡ οὖν τι τούτων αὐτὴν διαλύει τε καὶ ἀπόλλυσι; καὶ
ἐννόει μὴ ἐξαπατηθῶμεν οἰηθέντες τὸν ἄδικον ἄνθρωπον καὶ
ἀνόητον, ὅταν ληφθῇ ἀδικῶν, τότε ἀπολωλέναι ὑπὸ τῆς
ἀδικίας, πονηρίας οὔσης ψυχῆς. ἀλλ᾽ ὧδε ποίει· ὥσπερ 5
σῶμα ἡ σώματος πονηρία νόσος οὖσα τήκει καὶ διόλλυσι
καὶ ἄγει εἰς τὸ μηδὲ σῶμα εἶναι, καὶ ἃ νυνδὴ ἐλέγομεν
ἅπαντα ὑπὸ τῆς οἰκείας κακίας, τῷ προσκαθῆσθαι καὶ ἐνεῖναι d
διαφθειρούσης, εἰς τὸ μὴ εἶναι ἀφικνεῖται—οὐχ οὕτω;

Ναί.

Ἴθι δή, καὶ ψυχὴν κατὰ τὸν αὐτὸν τρόπον σκόπει. ἆρα
ἐνοῦσα ἐν αὐτῇ ἀδικία καὶ ἡ ἄλλη κακία τῷ ἐνεῖναι καὶ 5

προσκαθῆσθαι φθείρει αὐτὴν καὶ μαραίνει, ἕως ἂν εἰς θάνατον
ἀγαγοῦσα τοῦ σώματος χωρίσῃ;
Οὐδαμῶς, ἔφη, τοῦτό γε.
Ἀλλὰ μέντοι ἐκεῖνό γε ἄλογον, ἦν δ' ἐγώ, τὴν μὲν ἄλλου
10 πονηρίαν ἀπολλύναι τι, τὴν δὲ αὐτοῦ μή.
Ἄλογον.

e   Ἐννόει γάρ, ἦν δ' ἐγώ, ὦ Γλαύκων, ὅτι οὐδ' ὑπὸ τῆς
τῶν σιτίων πονηρίας, ἢ ἂν ᾖ αὐτῶν ἐκείνων, εἴτε παλαιότης
εἴτε σαπρότης εἴτε ἡτισοῦν οὖσα, οὐκ οἰόμεθα δεῖν σῶμα
ἀπόλλυσθαι· ἀλλ' ἐὰν μὲν ἐμποιῇ ἡ αὐτῶν πονηρία τῶν
5 σιτίων τῷ σώματι σώματος μοχθηρίαν, φήσομεν αὐτὸ δι'
ἐκεῖνα ὑπὸ τῆς αὐτοῦ κακίας νόσου οὔσης ἀπολωλέναι· ὑπὸ
610 δὲ σιτίων πονηρίας ἄλλων ὄντων ἄλλο ὂν τὸ σῶμα, ὑπ'
ἀλλοτρίου κακοῦ μὴ ἐμποιήσαντος τὸ ἔμφυτον κακόν, οὐδέποτε
ἀξιώσομεν διαφθείρεσθαι.
Ὀρθότατα, ἔφη, λέγεις.

5   Κατὰ τὸν αὐτὸν τοίνυν λόγον, ἦν δ' ἐγώ, ἐὰν μὴ σώματος
πονηρία ψυχῇ ψυχῆς πονηρίαν ἐμποιῇ, μή ποτε ἀξιῶμεν ὑπὸ
ἀλλοτρίου κακοῦ ἄνευ τῆς ἰδίας πονηρίας ψυχὴν ἀπόλλυσθαι,
τῷ ἑτέρου κακῷ ἕτερον.
Ἔχει γάρ, ἔφη, λόγον.

10   Ἢ τοίνυν ταῦτα ἐξελέγξωμεν ὅτι οὐ καλῶς λέγομεν, ἢ
b ἕως ἂν ᾖ ἀνέλεγκτα, μή ποτε φῶμεν ὑπὸ πυρετοῦ μηδ' αὖ
ὑπ' ἄλλης νόσου μηδ' αὖ ὑπὸ σφαγῆς, μηδ' εἴ τις ὅτι
σμικρότατα ὅλον τὸ σῶμα κατατέμοι, ἕνεκα τούτων μηδὲν
μᾶλλόν ποτε ψυχὴν ἀπόλλυσθαι, πρὶν ἄν τις ἀποδείξῃ
5 ὡς διὰ ταῦτα τὰ παθήματα τοῦ σώματος αὐτὴ ἐκείνη
ἀδικωτέρα καὶ ἀνοσιωτέρα γίγνεται· ἀλλοτρίου δὲ κακοῦ
ἐν ἄλλῳ γιγνομένου, τοῦ δὲ ἰδίου ἑκάστῳ μὴ ἐγγιγνο-
c μένου, μήτε ψυχὴν μήτε ἄλλο μηδὲν ἐῶμεν φάναι τινὰ
ἀπόλλυσθαι.
Ἀλλὰ μέντοι, ἔφη, τοῦτό γε οὐδείς ποτε δείξει, ὡς τῶν

ἀποθνησκόντων ἀδικώτεραι αἱ ψυχαὶ διὰ τὸν θάνατον
γίγνονται.   5

Ἐὰν δέ γέ τις, ἔφην ἐγώ, ὁμόσε τῷ λόγῳ τολμᾷ ἰέναι
καὶ λέγειν ὡς πονηρότερος καὶ ἀδικώτερος γίγνεται ὁ ἀπο-
θνῄσκων, ἵνα δὴ μὴ ἀναγκάζηται ἀθανάτους τὰς ψυχὰς ὁμολογεῖν, ἀξιώσομέν που, εἰ ἀληθῆ λέγει ὁ ταῦτα λέγων, τὴν
ἀδικίαν εἶναι θανάσιμον τῷ ἔχοντι ὥσπερ νόσον, καὶ ὑπ᾽ 10
αὐτοῦ, τοῦ ἀποκτεινύντος τῇ ἑαυτοῦ φύσει, ἀποθνήσκειν d
τοὺς λαμβάνοντας αὐτό, τοὺς μὲν μάλιστα θᾶττον, τοὺς δ᾽
ἧττον σχολαίτερον, ἀλλὰ μὴ ὥσπερ νῦν διὰ τοῦτο ὑπ᾽ ἄλλων
δίκην ἐπιτιθέντων ἀποθνῄσκουσιν οἱ ἄδικοι.

Μὰ Δί᾽, ἦ δ᾽ ὅς, οὐκ ἄρα πάνδεινον φανεῖται ἡ ἀδικία, 5
εἰ θανάσιμον ἔσται τῷ λαμβάνοντι—ἀπαλλαγὴ γὰρ ἂν εἴη
κακῶν—ἀλλὰ μᾶλλον οἶμαι αὐτὴν φανήσεσθαι πᾶν τοὐναντίον τοὺς ἄλλους ἀποκτεινῦσαν, εἴπερ οἷόν τε, τὸν δ᾽ ἔχοντα e
καὶ μάλα ζωτικὸν παρέχουσαν, καὶ πρός γ᾽ ἔτι τῷ ζωτικῷ
ἄγρυπνον· οὕτω πόρρω που, ὡς ἔοικεν, ἐσκήνηται τοῦ
θανάσιμος εἶναι.

Καλῶς, ἦν δ᾽ ἐγώ, λέγεις. ὁπότε γὰρ δὴ μὴ ἱκανὴ ᾖ γε 5
οἰκεία πονηρία καὶ τὸ οἰκεῖον κακὸν ἀποκτεῖναι καὶ ἀπολέσαι
ψυχήν, σχολῇ τό γε ἐπ᾽ ἄλλου ὀλέθρῳ τεταγμένον κακὸν
ψυχὴν ἤ τι ἄλλο ἀπολεῖ, πλὴν ἐφ᾽ ᾧ τέτακται.

Σχολῇ γ᾽, ἔφη, ὥς γε τὸ εἰκός.

Οὐκοῦν ὁπότε μηδ᾽ ὑφ᾽ ἑνὸς ἀπόλλυται κακοῦ, μήτε 10
οἰκείου μήτε ἀλλοτρίου, δῆλον ὅτι ἀνάγκη αὐτὸ ἀεὶ ὂν εἶναι· 611
εἰ δ᾽ ἀεὶ ὄν, ἀθάνατον.

Ἀνάγκη, ἔφη.

Τοῦτο μὲν τοίνυν, ἦν δ᾽ ἐγώ, οὕτως ἐχέτω· εἰ δ᾽ ἔχει,
ἐννοεῖς ὅτι ἀεὶ ἂν εἶεν αἱ αὐταί. οὔτε γὰρ ἄν που ἐλάττους 5
γένοιντο μηδεμιᾶς ἀπολλυμένης, οὔτε αὖ πλείους· εἰ γὰρ
ὁτιοῦν τῶν ἀθανάτων πλέον γίγνοιτο, οἶσθ᾽ ὅτι ἐκ τοῦ θνητοῦ
ἂν γίγνοιτο καὶ πάντα ἂν εἴη τελευτῶντα ἀθάνατα.

Ἀληθῆ λέγεις.

10 Ἀλλ᾽, ἦν δ᾽ ἐγώ, μήτε τοῦτο οἰώμεθα—ὁ γὰρ λόγος οὐκ
b ἐάσει—μήτε γε αὖ τῇ ἀληθεστάτῃ φύσει τοιοῦτον εἶναι
ψυχήν, ὥστε πολλῆς ποικιλίας καὶ ἀνομοιότητός τε καὶ
διαφορᾶς γέμειν αὐτὸ πρὸς αὐτό.

Πῶς λέγεις; ἔφη.

5   Οὐ ῥᾴδιον, ἦν δ᾽ ἐγώ, ἀίδιον εἶναι σύνθετόν τε ἐκ πολλῶν καὶ μὴ τῇ καλλίστῃ κεχρημένον συνθέσει, ὡς νῦν ἡμῖν
ἐφάνη ἡ ψυχή.·

Οὔκουν εἰκός γε.

Ὅτι μὲν τοίνυν ἀθάνατον ψυχή, καὶ ὁ ἄρτι λόγος καὶ οἱ
10 ἄλλοι ἀναγκάσειαν ἄν· οἷον δ᾽ ἐστὶν τῇ ἀληθείᾳ, οὐ λελω-
c βημένον δεῖ αὐτὸ θεάσασθαι ὑπό τε τῆς τοῦ σώματος κοινω-
νίας καὶ ἄλλων κακῶν, ὥσπερ νῦν ἡμεῖς θεώμεθα, ἀλλ᾽ οἷόν
ἐστιν καθαρὸν γιγνόμενον, τοιοῦτον ἱκανῶς λογισμῷ δια-
θεατέον, καὶ πολύ γε κάλλιον αὐτὸ εὑρήσει καὶ ἐναργέστερον
5 δικαιοσύνας τε καὶ ἀδικίας διόψεται καὶ πάντα ἃ νῦν διήλθομεν.
νῦν δὲ εἴπομεν μὲν ἀληθῆ περὶ αὐτοῦ, οἷον ἐν τῷ παρόντι
φαίνεται· τεθεάμεθα μέντοι διακείμενον αὐτό, ὥσπερ οἱ τὸν
d θαλάττιον Γλαῦκον ὁρῶντες οὐκ ἂν ἔτι ῥᾳδίως αὐτοῦ ἴδοιεν
τὴν ἀρχαίαν φύσιν, ὑπὸ τοῦ τά τε παλαιὰ τοῦ σώματος
μέρη τὰ μὲν ἐκκεκλάσθαι, τὰ δὲ συντετρῖφθαι καὶ πάντως
λελωβῆσθαι ὑπὸ τῶν κυμάτων, ἄλλα δὲ προσπεφυκέναι,
5 ὄστρεά τε καὶ φυκία καὶ πέτρας, ὥστε παντὶ μᾶλλον θηρίῳ
ἐοικέναι ἢ οἷος ἦν φύσει, οὕτω καὶ τὴν ψυχὴν ἡμεῖς θεώμεθα
διακειμένην ὑπὸ μυρίων κακῶν. ἀλλὰ δεῖ, ὦ Γλαύκων, ἐκεῖσε
βλέπειν.

Ποῖ; ἦ δ᾽ ὅς.

e   Εἰς τὴν φιλοσοφίαν αὐτῆς, καὶ ἐννοεῖν ὧν ἅπτεται καὶ
οἵων ἐφίεται ·ὁμιλιῶν, ὡς συγγενὴς οὖσα τῷ τε θείῳ καὶ
ἀθανάτῳ καὶ τῷ ἀεὶ ὄντι, καὶ οἷα ἂν γένοιτο τῷ τοιούτῳ
πᾶσα ἐπισπομένη καὶ ὑπὸ ταύτης τῆς ὁρμῆς ἐκκομισθεῖσα

ἐκ τοῦ πόντου ἐν ᾧ νῦν ἐστίν, καὶ περικρουσθεῖσα πέτρας 5
τε καὶ ὄστρεα ἃ νῦν αὐτῇ, ἅτε γῆν ἐστιωμένη, γεηρὰ καὶ 612
πετρώδη πολλὰ καὶ ἄγρια περιπέφυκεν ὑπὸ τῶν εὐδαιμόνων
λεγομένων ἑστιάσεων. καὶ τότ' ἄν τις ἴδοι αὐτῆς τὴν ἀληθῆ
φύσιν, εἴτε πολυειδὴς εἴτε μονοειδής, εἴτε ὅπη ἔχει καὶ
ὅπως· νῦν δὲ τὰ ἐν τῷ ἀνθρωπίνῳ βίῳ πάθη τε καὶ εἴδη, 5
ὡς ἐγᾦμαι, ἐπιεικῶς αὐτῆς διεληλύθαμεν.

Παντάπασι μὲν οὖν, ἔφη.

Οὐκοῦν, ἦν δ' ἐγώ, τά τε ἄλλα ἀπελυσάμεθα ἐν τῷ λόγῳ,
καὶ οὐ τοὺς μισθοὺς οὐδὲ τὰς δόξας δικαιοσύνης ἐπῃνέκαμεν, b
ὥσπερ Ἡσίοδόν τε καὶ Ὅμηρον ὑμεῖς ἔφατε, ἀλλ' αὐτὸ
δικαιοσύνην αὐτῇ ψυχῇ ἄριστον ηὕρομεν, καὶ ποιητέον εἶναι
αὐτῇ τὰ δίκαια, ἐάντ' ἔχῃ τὸν Γύγου δακτύλιον, ἐάντε μή,
καὶ πρὸς τοιούτῳ δακτυλίῳ τὴν Ἄιδος κυνῆν; 5

Ἀληθέστατα, ἔφη, λέγεις.

Ἆρ' οὖν, ἦν δ' ἐγώ, ὦ Γλαύκων, νῦν ἤδη ἀνεπίφθονόν
ἐστιν πρὸς ἐκείνοις καὶ τοὺς μισθοὺς τῇ δικαιοσύνῃ καὶ τῇ
ἄλλῃ ἀρετῇ ἀποδοῦναι, ὅσους τε καὶ οἵους τῇ ψυχῇ παρέχει c
παρ' ἀνθρώπων τε καὶ θεῶν, ζῶντός τε ἔτι τοῦ ἀνθρώπου
καὶ ἐπειδὰν τελευτήσῃ;

Παντάπασι μὲν οὖν, ἦ δ' ὅς.

Ἆρ' οὖν ἀποδώσετέ μοι ἃ ἐδανείσασθε ἐν τῷ λόγῳ; 5

Τί μάλιστα;

Ἔδωκα ὑμῖν τὸν δίκαιον δοκεῖν ἄδικον εἶναι καὶ τὸν
ἄδικον δίκαιον· ὑμεῖς γὰρ ᾐτεῖσθε, κἂν εἰ μὴ δυνατὸν εἴη
ταῦτα λανθάνειν καὶ θεοὺς καὶ ἀνθρώπους, ὅμως δοτέον εἶναι
τοῦ λόγου ἕνεκα, ἵνα αὐτὴ δικαιοσύνη πρὸς ἀδικίαν αὐτὴν 10
κριθείη. ἢ οὐ μνημονεύεις; d

Ἀδικοίην μεντἄν, ἔφη, εἰ μή.

Ἐπειδὴ τοίνυν, ἦν δ' ἐγώ, κεκριμέναι εἰσί, πάλιν ἀπαιτῶ
ὑπὲρ δικαιοσύνης, ὥσπερ ἔχει δόξης καὶ παρὰ θεῶν καὶ παρ'
ἀνθρώπων, καὶ ἡμᾶς ὁμολογεῖν περὶ αὐτῆς δοκεῖσθαι οὕτω, 5

ἵνα καὶ τὰ νικητήρια κομίσηται, ἀπὸ τοῦ δοκεῖν κτωμένη ἃ
δίδωσι τοῖς ἔχουσιν αὐτήν, ἐπειδὴ καὶ τὰ ἀπὸ τοῦ εἶναι
ἀγαθὰ διδοῦσα ἐφάνη καὶ οὐκ ἐξαπατῶσα τοὺς τῷ ὄντι
λαμβάνοντας αὐτήν.

e   Δίκαια, ἔφη, αἰτῇ.

Οὐκοῦν, ἦν δ' ἐγώ, πρῶτον μὲν τοῦτο ἀποδώσετε, ὅτι
θεούς γε οὐ λανθάνει ἑκάτερος αὐτῶν οἷός ἐστιν;
Ἀποδώσομεν, ἔφη.

5   Εἰ δὲ μὴ λανθάνετον, ὁ μὲν θεοφιλὴς ἂν εἴη, ὁ δὲ
θεομισής, ὥσπερ καὶ κατ' ἀρχὰς ὡμολογοῦμεν.
Ἔστι ταῦτα.

Τῷ δὲ θεοφιλεῖ οὐχ ὁμολογήσομεν, ὅσα γε ἀπὸ θεῶν
613 γίγνεται, πάντα γίγνεσθαι ὡς οἷόν τε ἄριστα, εἰ μή τι
ἀναγκαῖον αὐτῷ κακὸν ἐκ προτέρας ἁμαρτίας ὑπῆρχεν;
Πάνυ μὲν οὖν.

Οὕτως ἄρα ὑποληπτέον περὶ τοῦ δικαίου ἀνδρός, ἐάντ'
5 ἐν πενίᾳ γίγνηται ἐάντ' ἐν νόσοις ἤ τινι ἄλλῳ τῶν δοκούν-
των κακῶν, ὡς τούτῳ ταῦτα εἰς ἀγαθόν τι τελευτήσει ζῶντι
ἢ καὶ ἀποθανόντι. οὐ γὰρ δὴ ὑπό γε θεῶν ποτε ἀμελεῖται
ὃς ἂν προθυμεῖσθαι ἐθέλῃ δίκαιος γίγνεσθαι καὶ ἐπιτηδεύων
b ἀρετὴν εἰς ὅσον δυνατὸν ἀνθρώπῳ ὁμοιοῦσθαι θεῷ.

Εἰκός γ', ἔφη, τὸν τοιοῦτον μὴ ἀμελεῖσθαι ὑπὸ τοῦ
ὁμοίου.

Οὐκοῦν περὶ τοῦ ἀδίκου τἀναντία τούτων δεῖ διανοεῖσθαι;
5   Σφόδρα γε.

Τὰ μὲν δὴ παρὰ θεῶν τοιαῦτ' ἄττ' ἂν εἴη νικητήρια τῷ
δικαίῳ.

Κατὰ γοῦν ἐμὴν δόξαν, ἔφη.

Τί δέ, ἦν δ' ἐγώ, παρ' ἀνθρώπων; ἆρ' οὐχ ὧδε ἔχει, εἰ
10 δεῖ τὸ ὂν τιθέναι; οὐχ οἱ μὲν δεινοί τε καὶ ἄδικοι δρῶσιν
ὅπερ οἱ δρομῆς ὅσοι ἂν θέωσιν εὖ ἀπὸ τῶν κάτω, ἀπὸ δὲ
τῶν ἄνω μή; τὸ μὲν πρῶτον ὀξέως ἀποπηδῶσιν, τελευτῶντες

δὲ καταγέλαστοι γίγνονται, τὰ ὦτα ἐπὶ τῶν ὤμων ἔχοντες c
καὶ ἀστεφάνωτοι ἀποτρέχοντες· οἱ δὲ τῇ ἀληθείᾳ δρομικοὶ
εἰς τέλος ἐλθόντες τά τε ἆθλα λαμβάνουσιν καὶ στεφανοῦν-
ται. οὐχ οὕτω καὶ περὶ τῶν δικαίων τὸ πολὺ συμβαίνει;
πρὸς τὸ τέλος ἑκάστης πράξεως καὶ ὁμιλίας καὶ τοῦ βίου 5
εὐδοκιμοῦσί τε καὶ τὰ ἆθλα παρὰ τῶν ἀνθρώπων φέρονται;
Καὶ μάλα.

Ἀνέξῃ ἄρα λέγοντος ἐμοῦ περὶ τούτων ἅπερ αὐτὸς ἔλεγες
περὶ τῶν ἀδίκων; ἐρῶ γὰρ δὴ ὅτι οἱ μὲν δίκαιοι, ἐπειδὰν d
πρεσβύτεροι γένωνται, ἐν τῇ αὐτῶν πόλει ἄρχουσί τε ἂν
βούλωνται τὰς ἀρχάς, γαμοῦσί τε ὁπόθεν ἂν βούλωνται,
ἐκδιδόασί τε εἰς οὓς ἂν ἐθέλωσι· καὶ πάντα ἃ σὺ περὶ
ἐκείνων, ἐγὼ νῦν λέγω περὶ τῶνδε. καὶ αὖ καὶ περὶ τῶν 5
ἀδίκων, ὅτι οἱ πολλοὶ αὐτῶν, καὶ ἐὰν νέοι ὄντες λάθωσιν,
ἐπὶ τέλους τοῦ δρόμου αἱρεθέντες καταγέλαστοί εἰσιν καὶ
γέροντες γιγνόμενοι ἄθλιοι προπηλακίζονται ὑπὸ ξένων τε
καὶ ἀστῶν, μαστιγούμενοι καὶ ἃ ἄγροικα ἔφησθα σὺ εἶναι, e
ἀληθῆ λέγων—εἶτα στρεβλώσονται καὶ ἐκκαυθήσονται—
πάντα ἐκεῖνα οἷον καὶ ἐμοῦ ἀκηκοέναι ὡς πάσχουσιν. ἀλλ᾽
ὃ λέγω, ὅρα εἰ ἀνέξῃ.

Καὶ πάνυ, ἔφη· δίκαια γὰρ λέγεις. 5

Ἃ μὲν τοίνυν, ἦν δ᾽ ἐγώ, ζῶντι τῷ δικαίῳ παρὰ θεῶν τε
καὶ ἀνθρώπων ἆθλά τε καὶ μισθοὶ καὶ δῶρα γίγνεται πρὸς 614
ἐκείνοις τοῖς ἀγαθοῖς οἷς αὐτὴ παρείχετο ἡ δικαιοσύνη, τοιαῦτ᾽
ἂν εἴη.

Καὶ μάλ᾽, ἔφη, καλά τε καὶ βέβαια.

Ταῦτα τοίνυν, ἦν δ᾽ ἐγώ, οὐδέν ἐστι πλήθει οὐδὲ μεγέθει 5
πρὸς ἐκεῖνα ἃ τελευτήσαντα ἑκάτερον περιμένει· χρὴ δ᾽
αὐτὰ ἀκοῦσαι, ἵνα τελέως ἑκάτερος αὐτῶν ἀπειλήφῃ τὰ ὑπὸ
τοῦ λόγου ὀφειλόμενα ἀκοῦσαι.

Λέγοις ἄν, ἔφη, ὡς οὐ πολλὰ ἄλλ᾽ ἥδιον ἀκούοντι. b

Ἀλλ᾽ οὐ μέντοι σοι, ἦν δ᾽ ἐγώ, Ἀλκίνου γε ἀπόλογον

ἐρῶ, ἀλλ᾽ ἀλκίμου μὲν ἀνδρός, Ἠρὸς τοῦ ᾽Αρμενίου, τὸ
γένος Παμφύλου· ὅς ποτε ἐν πολέμῳ τελευτήσας, ἀναιρε-
5 θέντων δεκαταίων τῶν νεκρῶν ἤδη διεφθαρμένων, ὑγιὴς μὲν
ἀνῃρέθη, κομισθεὶς δ᾽ οἴκαδε μέλλων θάπτεσθαι δωδεκαταῖος
ἐπὶ τῇ πυρᾷ κείμενος ἀνεβίω, ἀναβιοὺς δ᾽ ἔλεγεν ἃ ἐκεῖ
ἴδοι. ἔφη δέ, ἐπειδὴ οὗ ἐκβῆναι τὴν ψυχὴν, πορεύεσθαι
c μετὰ πολλῶν, καὶ ἀφικνεῖσθαι σφᾶς εἰς τόπον τινὰ δαιμόνιον,
ἐν ᾧ τῆς τε γῆς δύ᾽ εἶναι χάσματα ἐχομένω ἀλλήλοιν καὶ
τοῦ οὐρανοῦ αὖ ἐν τῷ ἄνω ἄλλα καταντικρύ. δικαστὰς δὲ
μεταξὺ τούτων καθῆσθαι, οὕς, ἐπειδὴ διαδικάσειαν, τοὺς μὲν
5 δικαίους κελεύειν πορεύεσθαι τὴν εἰς δεξιάν τε καὶ ἄνω διὰ
τοῦ οὐρανοῦ, σημεῖα περιάψαντας τῶν δεδικασμένων ἐν τῷ
πρόσθεν, τοὺς δὲ ἀδίκους τὴν εἰς ἀριστεράν τε καὶ κάτω,
ἔχοντας καὶ τούτους ἐν τῷ ὄπισθεν σημεῖα πάντων ὧν
d ἔπραξαν. ἑαυτοῦ δὲ προσελθόντος εἰπεῖν ὅτι δέοι αὐτὸν
ἄγγελον ἀνθρώποις γενέσθαι τῶν ἐκεῖ καὶ διακελεύοιτό οἱ
ἀκούειν τε καὶ θεᾶσθαι πάντα τὰ ἐν τῷ τόπῳ. ὁρᾶν δὴ
ταύτῃ μὲν καθ᾽ ἑκάτερον τὸ χάσμα τοῦ οὐρανοῦ τε καὶ τῆς
5 γῆς ἀπιούσας τὰς ψυχάς, ἐπειδὴ αὐταῖς δικασθείη, κατὰ δὲ
τὼ ἑτέρω ἐκ μὲν τοῦ ἀνιέναι ἐκ τῆς γῆς μεστὰς αὐχμοῦ τε
καὶ κόνεως, ἐκ δὲ τοῦ ἑτέρου καταβαίνειν ἑτέρας ἐκ τοῦ
e οὐρανοῦ καθαράς. καὶ τὰς ἀεὶ ἀφικνουμένας ὥσπερ ἐκ
πολλῆς πορείας φαίνεσθαι ἥκειν, καὶ ἀσμένας εἰς τὸν λειμῶνα ἀπιούσας οἷον ἐν πανηγύρει κατασκηνᾶσθαι, καὶ ἀσπά-
ζεσθαί τε ἀλλήλας ὅσαι γνώριμαι, καὶ πυνθάνεσθαι τάς τε
5 ἐκ τῆς γῆς ἡκούσας παρὰ τῶν ἑτέρων τὰ ἐκεῖ καὶ τὰς ἐκ
τοῦ οὐρανοῦ τὰ παρ᾽ ἐκείναις. διηγεῖσθαι δὲ ἀλλήλαις τὰς
615 μὲν ὀδυρομένας τε καὶ κλαούσας, ἀναμιμνῃσκομένας ὅσα τε
καὶ οἷα πάθοιεν καὶ ἴδοιεν ἐν τῇ ὑπὸ γῆς πορείᾳ——εἶναι δὲ
τὴν πορείαν χιλιέτη——τὰς δ᾽ αὖ ἐκ τοῦ οὐρανοῦ εὐπαθείας
διηγεῖσθαι καὶ θέας ἀμηχάνους τὸ κάλλος. τὰ μὲν οὖν
5 πολλά, ὦ Γλαύκων, πολλοῦ χρόνου διηγήσασθαι· τὸ δ᾽ οὖν

b 8 O.C.T. ἐκβῆναι, τὴν ψυχὴν

κεφάλαιον ἔφη τόδε εἶναι, ὅσα πώποτέ τινα ἠδίκησαν καὶ
ὅσους ἕκαστοι, ὑπὲρ ἁπάντων δίκην δεδωκέναι ἐν μέρει,
ὑπὲρ ἑκάστου δεκάκις—τοῦτο δ' εἶναι κατὰ ἑκατονταετηρίδα
ἑκάστην, ὡς βίου ὄντος τοσούτου τοῦ ἀνθρωπίνου—ἵνα δεκα- b
πλάσιον τὸ ἔκτεισμα τοῦ ἀδικήματος ἐκτίνοιεν, καὶ οἷον εἴ
τινες πολλοῖς θανάτων ἦσαν αἴτιοι, ἢ πόλεις προδόντες ἢ
στρατόπεδα, καὶ εἰς δουλείας ἐμβεβληκότες ἤ τινος ἄλλης
κακουχίας μεταίτιοι, πάντων τούτων δεκαπλασίας ἀλγηδόνας 5
ὑπὲρ ἑκάστου κομίσαιντο, καὶ αὖ εἴ τινας εὐεργεσίας εὐερ-
γετηκότες καὶ δίκαιοι καὶ ὅσιοι γεγονότες εἶεν, κατὰ ταὐτὰ
τὴν ἀξίαν κομίζοιντο. τῶν δὲ εὐθὺς γενομένων καὶ ὀλίγον c
χρόνον βιούντων πέρι ἄλλα ἔλεγεν οὐκ ἄξια μνήμης. εἰς
δὲ θεοὺς ἀσεβείας τε καὶ εὐσεβείας καὶ γονέας καὶ αὐτόχειρος
φόνου μείζους ἔτι τοὺς μισθοὺς διηγεῖτο.

Ἔφη γὰρ δὴ παραγενέσθαι ἐρωτωμένῳ ἑτέρῳ ὑπὸ ἑτέρου 5
ὅπου εἴη Ἀρδιαῖος ὁ μέγας. ὁ δὲ Ἀρδιαῖος οὗτος τῆς
Παμφυλίας ἔν τινι πόλει τύραννος ἐγεγόνει, ἤδη χιλιοστὸν
ἔτος εἰς ἐκεῖνον τὸν χρόνον, γέροντά τε πατέρα ἀποκτείνας
καὶ πρεσβύτερον ἀδελφόν, καὶ ἄλλα δὴ πολλά τε καὶ ἀνόσια d
εἰργασμένος, ὡς ἐλέγετο. ἔφη οὖν τὸν ἐρωτώμενον εἰπεῖν,
" Οὐχ ἥκει," φάναι, " οὐδ' ἂν ἥξει δεῦρο. ἐθεασάμεθα γὰρ
οὖν δὴ καὶ τοῦτο τῶν δεινῶν θεαμάτων· ἐπειδὴ ἐγγὺς τοῦ
στομίου ἦμεν μέλλοντες ἀνιέναι καὶ τἆλλα πάντα πεπονθότες, 5
ἐκεῖνόν τε κατείδομεν ἐξαίφνης καὶ ἄλλους—σχεδόν τι αὐτῶν
τοὺς πλείστους τυράννους· ἦσαν δὲ καὶ ἰδιῶταί τινες τῶν
μεγάλα ἡμαρτηκότων—οὓς οἰομένους ἤδη ἀναβήσεσθαι οὐκ e
ἐδέχετο τὸ στόμιον, ἀλλ' ἐμυκᾶτο ὁπότε τις τῶν οὕτως
ἀνιάτως ἐχόντων εἰς πονηρίαν ἢ μὴ ἱκανῶς δεδωκὼς δίκην
ἐπιχειροῖ ἀνιέναι. ἐνταῦθα δὴ ἄνδρες, ἔφη, ἄγριοι, διάπυροι
ἰδεῖν, παρεστῶτες καὶ καταμανθάνοντες τὸ φθέγμα, τοὺς μὲν 5
διαλαβόντες ἦγον, τὸν δὲ Ἀρδιαῖον καὶ ἄλλους συμποδί-
σαντες χεῖράς τε καὶ πόδας καὶ κεφαλήν, καταβαλόντες καὶ 616

ἐκδείραντες, εἷλκον παρὰ τὴν ὁδὸν ἐκτὸς ἐπ' ἀσπαλάθων κνάμπτοντες, καὶ τοῖς ἀεὶ παριοῦσι σημαίνοντες ὧν ἕνεκά τε καὶ ὅτι εἰς τὸν Τάρταρον ἐμπεσούμενοι ἄγοιντο." ἔνθα
5 δὴ φόβων, ἔφη, πολλῶν καὶ παντοδαπῶν σφίσι γεγονότων, τοῦτον ὑπερβάλλειν, μὴ γένοιτο ἑκάστῳ τὸ φθέγμα ὅτε ἀναβαίνοι, καὶ ἀσμενέστατα ἕκαστον σιγήσαντος ἀναβῆναι. καὶ τὰς μὲν δὴ δίκας τε καὶ τιμωρίας τοιαύτας τινὰς
b εἶναι, καὶ αὖ τὰς εὐεργεσίας ταύταις ἀντιστρόφους. ἐπειδὴ δὲ τοῖς ἐν τῷ λειμῶνι ἑκάστοις ἑπτὰ ἡμέραι γένοιντο, ἀναστάντας ἐντεῦθεν δεῖν τῇ ὀγδόῃ πορεύεσθαι, καὶ ἀφικνεῖσθαι τεταρταίους ὅθεν καθορᾶν ἄνωθεν διὰ παντὸς τοῦ οὐρανοῦ
5 καὶ γῆς τεταμένον φῶς εὐθύ, οἷον κίονα, μάλιστα τῇ ἴριδι προσφερῆ, λαμπρότερον δὲ καὶ καθαρώτερον· εἰς ὃ ἀφικέσθαι προελθόντες ἡμερησίαν ὁδόν, καὶ ἰδεῖν αὐτόθι κατὰ
c μέσον τὸ φῶς ἐκ τοῦ οὐρανοῦ τὰ ἄκρα αὐτοῦ τῶν δεσμῶν τεταμένα—εἶναι γὰρ τοῦτο τὸ φῶς σύνδεσμον τοῦ οὐρανοῦ, οἷον τὰ ὑποζώματα τῶν τριήρων, οὕτω πᾶσαν συνέχον τὴν περιφοράν—ἐκ δὲ τῶν ἄκρων τεταμένον Ἀνάγκης ἄτρακτον,
5 δι' οὗ πάσας ἐπιστρέφεσθαι τὰς περιφοράς· οὗ τὴν μὲν ἠλακάτην τε καὶ τὸ ἄγκιστρον εἶναι ἐξ ἀδάμαντος, τὸν δὲ σφόνδυλον μεικτὸν ἔκ τε τούτου καὶ ἄλλων γενῶν. τὴν δὲ
d τοῦ σφονδύλου φύσιν εἶναι τοιάνδε· τὸ μὲν σχῆμα οἷαπερ ἡ τοῦ ἐνθάδε, νοῆσαι δὲ δεῖ ἐξ ὧν ἔλεγεν τοιόνδε αὐτὸν εἶναι, ὥσπερ ἂν εἰ ἐν ἑνὶ μεγάλῳ σφονδύλῳ κοίλῳ καὶ ἐξεγλυμμένῳ διαμπερὲς ἄλλος τοιοῦτος ἐλάττων ἐγκέοιτο ἁρμόττων,
5 καθάπερ οἱ κάδοι οἱ εἰς ἀλλήλους ἁρμόττοντες, καὶ οὕτω δὴ τρίτον ἄλλον καὶ τέταρτον καὶ ἄλλους τέτταρας. ὀκτὼ γὰρ εἶναι τοὺς σύμπαντας σφονδύλους, ἐν ἀλλήλοις ἐγκειμένους,
e κύκλους ἄνωθεν τὰ χείλη φαίνοντας, νῶτον συνεχὲς ἑνὸς σφονδύλου ἀπεργαζομένους περὶ τὴν ἠλακάτην· ἐκείνην δὲ διὰ μέσου τοῦ ὀγδόου διαμπερὲς ἐληλάσθαι. τὸν μὲν οὖν πρῶτόν τε καὶ ἐξωτάτω σφόνδυλον πλατύτατον τὸν τοῦ
5 χείλους κύκλον ἔχειν, τὸν δὲ τοῦ ἕκτου δεύτερον, τρίτον δὲ

τὸν τοῦ τετάρτου, τέταρτον δὲ τὸν τοῦ ὀγδόου, πέμπτον δὲ
τὸν τοῦ ἑβδόμου, ἕκτον δὲ τὸν τοῦ πέμπτου, ἕβδομον δὲ τὸν
τοῦ τρίτου, ὄγδοον δὲ τὸν τοῦ δευτέρου. καὶ τὸν μὲν τοῦ
μεγίστου ποικίλον, τὸν δὲ τοῦ ἑβδόμου λαμπρότατον, τὸν δὲ
τοῦ ὀγδόου τὸ χρῶμα ἀπὸ τοῦ ἑβδόμου ἔχειν προσλάμποντος, **617**
τὸν δὲ τοῦ δευτέρου καὶ πέμπτου παραπλήσια ἀλλήλοις,
ξανθότερα ἐκείνων, τρίτον δὲ λευκότατον χρῶμα ἔχειν, τέταρτον δὲ ὑπέρυθρον, δεύτερον δὲ λευκότητι τὸν ἕκτον. κυκλεῖσθαι δὲ δὴ στρεφόμενον τὸν ἄτρακτον ὅλον μὲν τὴν αὐτὴν 5
φοράν, ἐν δὲ τῷ ὅλῳ περιφερομένῳ τοὺς μὲν ἐντὸς ἑπτὰ
κύκλους τὴν ἐναντίαν τῷ ὅλῳ ἠρέμα περιφέρεσθαι, αὐτῶν δὲ
τούτων τάχιστα μὲν ἰέναι τὸν ὄγδοον, δευτέρους δὲ καὶ ἅμα
ἀλλήλοις τόν τε ἕβδομον καὶ ἕκτον καὶ πέμπτον· τρίτον **b**
δὲ φορᾷ ἰέναι, ὡς σφίσι φαίνεσθαι, ἐπανακυκλούμενον τὸν
τέταρτον, τέταρτον δὲ τὸν τρίτον καὶ πέμπτον τὸν δεύτερον.
στρέφεσθαι δὲ αὐτὸν ἐν τοῖς τῆς Ἀνάγκης γόνασιν. ἐπὶ δὲ
τῶν κύκλων αὐτοῦ ἄνωθεν ἐφ' ἑκάστου βεβηκέναι Σειρῆνα 5
συμπεριφερομένην, φωνὴν μίαν ἱεῖσαν, ἕνα τόνον· ἐκ πασῶν
δὲ ὀκτὼ οὐσῶν μίαν ἁρμονίαν συμφωνεῖν. ἄλλας δὲ καθη-
μένας πέριξ δι' ἴσου τρεῖς, ἐν θρόνῳ ἑκάστην, θυγατέρας τῆς **c**
Ἀνάγκης, Μοίρας, λευχειμονούσας, στέμματα ἐπὶ τῶν κεφα-
λῶν ἐχούσας, Λάχεσίν τε καὶ Κλωθὼ καὶ Ἄτροπον, ὑμνεῖν
πρὸς τὴν τῶν Σειρήνων ἁρμονίαν, Λάχεσιν μὲν τὰ γεγονότα,
Κλωθὼ δὲ τὰ ὄντα, Ἄτροπον δὲ τὰ μέλλοντα. καὶ τὴν μὲν 5
Κλωθὼ τῇ δεξιᾷ χειρὶ ἐφαπτομένην συνεπιστρέφειν τοῦ
ἀτράκτου τὴν ἔξω περιφοράν, διαλείπουσαν χρόνον, τὴν δὲ
Ἄτροπον τῇ ἀριστερᾷ τὰς ἐντὸς αὖ ὡσαύτως· τὴν δὲ Λάχεσιν
ἐν μέρει ἑκατέρας ἑκατέρᾳ τῇ χειρὶ ἐφάπτεσθαι. σφᾶς οὖν, **d**
ἐπειδὴ ἀφικέσθαι, εὐθὺς δεῖν ἰέναι πρὸς τὴν Λάχεσιν. προφήτην οὖν τινα σφᾶς πρῶτον μὲν ἐν τάξει διαστῆσαι, ἔπειτα
λαβόντα ἐκ τῶν τῆς Λαχέσεως γονάτων κλήρους τε καὶ βίων
παραδείγματα, ἀναβάντα ἐπί τι βῆμα ὑψηλὸν εἰπεῖν— 5

b 1 O.C.T. [τὸν] τρίτον

"'Ανάγκης θυγατρὸς κόρης Λαχέσεως λόγος. Ψυχαὶ
ἐφήμεροι, ἀρχὴ ἄλλης περιόδου θνητοῦ γένους θανατηφόρου.
e οὐχ ὑμᾶς δαίμων λήξεται, ἀλλ' ὑμεῖς δαίμονα αἱρήσεσθε.
πρῶτος δ' ὁ λαχὼν πρῶτος αἱρείσθω βίον ᾧ συνέσται ἐξ
ἀνάγκης. ἀρετὴ δὲ ἀδέσποτον, ἣν τιμῶν καὶ ἀτιμάζων
πλέον καὶ ἔλαττον αὐτῆς ἕκαστος ἕξει. αἰτία ἑλομένου·
5 θεὸς ἀναίτιος."
   Ταῦτα εἰπόντα ῥῖψαι ἐπὶ πάντας τοὺς κλήρους, τὸν
δὲ παρ' αὑτὸν πεσόντα ἕκαστον ἀναιρεῖσθαι πλὴν οὗ, ἑ
δὲ οὐκ ἐᾶν· τῷ δὲ ἀνελομένῳ δῆλον εἶναι ὁπόστος εἰλή-
618 χει. μετὰ δὲ τοῦτο αὖθις τὰ τῶν βίων παραδείγματα εἰς
τὸ πρόσθεν σφῶν θεῖναι ἐπὶ τὴν γῆν, πολὺ πλείω τῶν
παρόντων. εἶναι δὲ παντοδαπά· ζῴων τε γὰρ πάντων βίους
καὶ δὴ καὶ τοὺς ἀνθρωπίνους ἅπαντας. τυραννίδας τε
5 γὰρ ἐν αὐτοῖς εἶναι, τὰς μὲν διατελεῖς, τὰς δὲ καὶ μεταξὺ
διαφθειρομένας καὶ εἰς πενίας τε καὶ φυγὰς καὶ εἰς πτω-
χείας τελευτώσας· εἶναι δὲ καὶ δοκίμων ἀνδρῶν βίους,
τοὺς μὲν ἐπὶ εἴδεσιν καὶ κατὰ κάλλη καὶ τὴν ἄλλην ἰσχύν
b τε καὶ ἀγωνίαν, τοὺς δ' ἐπὶ γένεσιν καὶ προγόνων ἀρεταῖς,
καὶ ἀδοκίμων κατὰ ταῦτα, ὡσαύτως δὲ καὶ γυναικῶν. ψυχῆς
δὲ τάξιν οὐκ ἐνεῖναι διὰ τὸ ἀναγκαίως ἔχειν ἄλλον ἑλομένην
βίον ἀλλοίαν γίγνεσθαι· τὰ δ' ἄλλα ἀλλήλοις τε καὶ πλού-
5 τοις καὶ πενίαις, τὰ δὲ νόσοις, τὰ δ' ὑγιείαις μεμεῖχθαι,
τὰ δὲ καὶ μεσοῦν τούτων. ἔνθα δή, ὡς ἔοικεν, ὦ φίλε
Γλαύκων, ὁ πᾶς κίνδυνος ἀνθρώπῳ, καὶ διὰ ταῦτα μάλιστα
c ἐπιμελητέον ὅπως ἕκαστος ἡμῶν τῶν ἄλλων μαθημάτων
ἀμελήσας τούτου τοῦ μαθήματος καὶ ζητητὴς καὶ μαθητὴς
ἔσται, ἐάν ποθεν οἷός τ' ᾖ μαθεῖν καὶ ἐξευρεῖν τίς αὐτὸν
ποιήσει δυνατὸν καὶ ἐπιστήμονα, βίον καὶ χρηστὸν καὶ πονη-
5 ρὸν διαγιγνώσκοντα, τὸν βελτίω ἐκ τῶν δυνατῶν ἀεὶ πανταχοῦ αἱρεῖσθαι· ἀναλογιζόμενον πάντα τὰ νυνδὴ ῥηθέντα
καὶ συντιθέμενα ἀλλήλοις καὶ διαιρούμενα πρὸς ἀρετὴν βίου

πῶς ἔχει, εἰδέναι τί κάλλος πενίᾳ ἢ πλούτῳ κραθὲν καὶ
μετὰ ποίας τινὸς ψυχῆς ἕξεως κακὸν ἢ ἀγαθὸν ἐργάζεται, d
καὶ τί εὐγένειαι καὶ δυσγένειαι καὶ ἰδιωτεῖαι καὶ ἀρχαὶ καὶ
ἰσχύες καὶ ἀσθένειαι καὶ εὐμαθίαι καὶ δυσμαθίαι καὶ πάντα
τὰ τοιαῦτα τῶν φύσει περὶ ψυχὴν ὄντων καὶ τῶν ἐπικτήτων
τί συγκεραννύμενα πρὸς ἄλληλα ἐργάζεται, ὥστε ἐξ ἁπάντων 5
αὐτῶν δυνατὸν εἶναι συλλογισάμενον αἱρεῖσθαι, πρὸς τὴν
τῆς ψυχῆς φύσιν ἀποβλέποντα, τόν τε χείρω καὶ τὸν ἀμείνω
βίον, χείρω μὲν καλοῦντα ὃς αὐτὴν ἐκεῖσε ἄξει, εἰς τὸ ἀδικω- e
τέραν γίγνεσθαι, ἀμείνω δὲ ὅστις εἰς τὸ δικαιοτέραν. τὰ δὲ
ἄλλα πάντα χαίρειν ἐάσει· ἑωράκαμεν γὰρ ὅτι ζῶντί τε
καὶ τελευτήσαντι αὕτη κρατίστη αἵρεσις. ἀδαμαντίνως δὴ
δεῖ ταύτην τὴν δόξαν ἔχοντα εἰς Ἅιδου ἰέναι, ὅπως ἂν ᾖ καὶ 619
ἐκεῖ ἀνέκπληκτος ὑπὸ πλούτων τε καὶ τῶν τοιούτων κακῶν,
καὶ μὴ ἐμπεσὼν εἰς τυραννίδας καὶ ἄλλας τοιαύτας πράξεις
πολλὰ μὲν ἐργάσηται καὶ ἀνήκεστα κακά, ἔτι δὲ αὐτὸς μείζω
πάθη, ἀλλὰ γνῷ τὸν μέσον ἀεὶ τῶν τοιούτων βίον αἱρεῖσθαι 5
καὶ φεύγειν τὰ ὑπερβάλλοντα ἑκατέρωσε καὶ ἐν τῷδε τῷ
βίῳ κατὰ τὸ δυνατὸν καὶ ἐν παντὶ τῷ ἔπειτα· οὕτω γὰρ
εὐδαιμονέστατος γίγνεται ἄνθρωπος. b

Καὶ δὴ οὖν καὶ τότε ὁ ἐκεῖθεν ἄγγελος ἤγγελλε τὸν
μὲν προφήτην οὕτως εἰπεῖν· "Καὶ τελευταίῳ ἐπιόντι, ξὺν
νῷ ἑλομένῳ, συντόνως ζῶντι κεῖται βίος ἀγαπητός, οὐ
κακός. μήτε ὁ ἄρχων αἱρέσεως ἀμελείτω μήτε ὁ τελευτῶν 5
ἀθυμείτω."

Εἰπόντος δὲ ταῦτα τὸν πρῶτον λαχόντα ἔφη εὐθὺς ἐπιόντα
τὴν μεγίστην τυραννίδα ἑλέσθαι, καὶ ὑπὸ ἀφροσύνης τε καὶ
λαιμαργίας οὐ πάντα ἱκανῶς ἀνασκεψάμενον ἑλέσθαι, ἀλλ'
αὐτὸν λαθεῖν ἐνοῦσαν εἱμαρμένην παίδων αὑτοῦ βρώσεις καὶ c
ἄλλα κακά· ἐπειδὴ δὲ κατὰ σχολὴν σκέψασθαι, κόπτεσθαί
τε καὶ ὀδύρεσθαι τὴν αἵρεσιν, οὐκ ἐμμένοντα τοῖς προρρη-
θεῖσιν ὑπὸ τοῦ προφήτου· οὐ γὰρ ἑαυτὸν αἰτιᾶσθαι τῶν

5 κακῶν, ἀλλὰ τύχην τε καὶ δαίμονας καὶ πάντα μᾶλλον ἀνθ᾽
ἑαυτοῦ. εἶναι δὲ αὐτὸν τῶν ἐκ τοῦ οὐρανοῦ ἡκόντων, ἐν
τεταγμένῃ πολιτείᾳ ἐν τῷ προτέρῳ βίῳ βεβιωκότα, ἔθει
d ἄνευ φιλοσοφίας ἀρετῆς μετειληφότα. ὡς δὲ καὶ εἰπεῖν, οὐκ
ἐλάττους εἶναι ἐν τοῖς τοιούτοις ἁλισκομένους τοὺς ἐκ τοῦ
οὐρανοῦ ἥκοντας, ἅτε πόνων ἀγυμνάστους· τῶν δ᾽ ἐκ τῆς
γῆς τοὺς πολλούς, ἅτε αὐτούς τε πεπονηκότας ἄλλους τε
5 ἑωρακότας, οὐκ ἐξ ἐπιδρομῆς τὰς αἱρέσεις ποιεῖσθαι. διὸ
δὴ καὶ μεταβολὴν τῶν κακῶν καὶ τῶν ἀγαθῶν ταῖς πολλαῖς
τῶν ψυχῶν γίγνεσθαι καὶ διὰ τὴν τοῦ κλήρου τύχην· ἐπεὶ
εἴ τις ἀεί, ὁπότε εἰς τὸν ἐνθάδε βίον ἀφικνοῖτο, ὑγιῶς φιλο-
e σοφοῖ καὶ ὁ κλῆρος αὐτῷ τῆς αἱρέσεως μὴ ἐν τελευταίοις
πίπτοι, κινδυνεύει ἐκ τῶν ἐκεῖθεν ἀπαγγελλομένων οὐ μόνον
ἐνθάδε εὐδαιμονεῖν ἄν, ἀλλὰ καὶ τὴν ἐνθένδε ἐκεῖσε καὶ δεῦρο
πάλιν πορείαν οὐκ ἂν χθονίαν καὶ τραχεῖαν πορεύεσθαι,
5 ἀλλὰ λείαν τε καὶ οὐρανίαν.

Ταύτην γὰρ δὴ ἔφη τὴν θέαν ἀξίαν εἶναι ἰδεῖν, ὡς ἕκασται
620 αἱ ψυχαὶ ᾑροῦντο τοὺς βίους· ἐλεινήν τε γὰρ ἰδεῖν εἶναι καὶ
γελοίαν καὶ θαυμασίαν. κατὰ συνήθειαν γὰρ τοῦ προτέρου
βίου τὰ πολλὰ αἱρεῖσθαι. ἰδεῖν μὲν γὰρ ψυχὴν ἔφη τήν
ποτε Ὀρφέως γενομένην κύκνου βίον αἱρουμένην, μίσει τοῦ
5 γυναικείου γένους διὰ τὸν ὑπ᾽ ἐκείνων θάνατον οὐκ ἐθέλουσαν
ἐν γυναικὶ γεννηθεῖσαν γενέσθαι· ἰδεῖν δὲ τὴν Θαμύρου
ἀηδόνος ἑλομένην· ἰδεῖν δὲ καὶ κύκνον μεταβάλλοντα εἰς
ἀνθρωπίνου βίου αἵρεσιν, καὶ ἄλλα ζῷα μουσικὰ ὡσαύτως.
b εἰκοστὴν δὲ λαχοῦσαν ψυχὴν ἑλέσθαι λέοντος βίον· εἶναι
δὲ τὴν Αἴαντος τοῦ Τελαμωνίου, φεύγουσαν ἄνθρωπον γενέσθαι, μεμνημένην τῆς τῶν ὅπλων κρίσεως. τὴν δ᾽ ἐπὶ
τούτῳ Ἀγαμέμνονος· ἔχθρᾳ δὲ καὶ ταύτην τοῦ ἀνθρωπίνου
5 γένους διὰ τὰ πάθη ἀετοῦ διαλλάξαι βίον. ἐν μέσοις δὲ
λαχοῦσαν τὴν Ἀταλάντης ψυχήν, κατιδοῦσαν μεγάλας τιμὰς
ἀθλητοῦ ἀνδρός, οὐ δύνασθαι παρελθεῖν, ἀλλὰ λαβεῖν. μετὰ

δὲ ταύτην ἰδεῖν τὴν Ἐπειοῦ τοῦ Πανοπέως εἰς τεχνικῆς c
γυναικὸς ἰοῦσαν φύσιν· πόρρω δ' ἐν ὑστάτοις ἰδεῖν τὴν τοῦ
γελωτοποιοῦ Θερσίτου πίθηκον ἐνδυομένην. κατὰ τύχην δὲ
τὴν Ὀδυσσέως λαχοῦσαν πασῶν ὑστάτην αἱρησομένην ἰέναι,
μνήμῃ δὲ τῶν προτέρων πόνων φιλοτιμίας λελωφηκυῖαν 5
ζητεῖν περιιοῦσαν χρόνον πολὺν βίον ἀνδρὸς ἰδιώτου ἀ-
πράγμονος, καὶ μόγις εὑρεῖν κείμενόν που καὶ παρημελημένον
ὑπὸ τῶν ἄλλων, καὶ εἰπεῖν ἰδοῦσαν ὅτι τὰ αὐτὰ ἂν ἔπραξεν d
καὶ πρώτη λαχοῦσα, καὶ ἀσμένην ἑλέσθαι. καὶ ἐκ τῶν
ἄλλων δὴ θηρίων ὡσαύτως εἰς ἀνθρώπους ἰέναι καὶ εἰς
ἄλληλα, τὰ μὲν ἄδικα εἰς τὰ ἄγρια, τὰ δὲ δίκαια εἰς τὰ
ἥμερα μεταβάλλοντα, καὶ πάσας μείξεις μείγνυσθαι. 5
Ἐπειδὴ δ' οὖν πάσας τὰς ψυχὰς τοὺς βίους ᾑρῆσθαι,
ὥσπερ ἔλαχον ἐν τάξει προσιέναι πρὸς τὴν Λάχεσιν·
ἐκείνην δ' ἑκάστῳ ὃν εἵλετο δαίμονα, τοῦτον φύλακα συμπέμπειν τοῦ βίου καὶ ἀποπληρωτὴν τῶν αἱρεθέντων. ὃν e
πρῶτον μὲν ἄγειν αὐτὴν πρὸς τὴν Κλωθὼ ὑπὸ τὴν ἐκείνης
χεῖρά τε καὶ ἐπιστροφὴν τῆς τοῦ ἀτράκτου δίνης, κυροῦντα
ἣν λαχὼν εἵλετο μοῖραν· ταύτης δ' ἐφαψάμενον αὖθις ἐπὶ
τὴν τῆς Ἀτρόπου ἄγειν νῆσιν, ἀμετάστροφα τὰ ἐπικλω- 5
σθέντα ποιοῦντα· ἐντεῦθεν δὲ δὴ ἀμεταστρεπτὶ ὑπὸ τὸν τῆς
Ἀνάγκης ἰέναι θρόνον, καὶ δι' ἐκείνου διεξελθόντα, ἐπειδὴ 621
καὶ οἱ ἄλλοι διῆλθον, πορεύεσθαι ἅπαντας εἰς τὸ τῆς Λήθης
πεδίον διὰ καύματός τε καὶ πνίγους δεινοῦ· καὶ γὰρ εἶναι
αὐτὸ κενὸν δένδρων τε καὶ ὅσα γῆ φύει. σκηνᾶσθαι οὖν
σφᾶς ἤδη ἑσπέρας γιγνομένης παρὰ τὸν Ἀμέλητα ποταμόν, 5
οὗ τὸ ὕδωρ ἀγγεῖον οὐδὲν στέγειν. μέτρον μὲν οὖν τι τοῦ
ὕδατος πᾶσιν ἀναγκαῖον εἶναι πιεῖν, τοὺς δὲ φρονήσει μὴ
σῳζομένους πλέον πίνειν τοῦ μέτρου· τὸν δὲ ἀεὶ πιόντα
πάντων ἐπιλανθάνεσθαι. ἐπειδὴ δὲ κοιμηθῆναι καὶ μέσας b
νύκτας γενέσθαι, βροντήν τε καὶ σεισμὸν γενέσθαι, καὶ
ἐντεῦθεν ἐξαπίνης ἄλλον ἄλλῃ φέρεσθαι ἄνω εἰς τὴν γένεσιν,

ᾄττοντας ὥσπερ ἀστέρας. αὐτὸς δὲ τοῦ μὲν ὕδατος κωλυ-
5 θῆναι πιεῖν· ὅπῃ μέντοι καὶ ὅπως εἰς τὸ σῶμα ἀφίκοιτο,
οὐκ εἰδέναι, ἀλλ᾽ ἐξαίφνης ἀναβλέψας ἰδεῖν ἕωθεν αὐτὸν
κείμενον ἐπὶ τῇ πυρᾷ.

Καὶ οὕτως, ὦ Γλαύκων, μῦθος ἐσώθη καὶ οὐκ ἀπώλετο,
c καὶ ἡμᾶς ἂν σώσειεν, ἂν πειθώμεθα αὐτῷ, καὶ τὸν τῆς Λήθης
ποταμὸν εὖ διαβησόμεθα καὶ τὴν ψυχὴν οὐ μιανθησόμεθα.
ἀλλ᾽ ἂν ἐμοὶ πειθώμεθα, νομίζοντες ἀθάνατον ψυχὴν καὶ
δυνατὴν πάντα μὲν κακὰ ἀνέχεσθαι,· πάντα δὲ ἀγαθά, τῆς
5 ἄνω ὁδοῦ ἀεὶ ἑξόμεθα καὶ δικαιοσύνην μετὰ φρονήσεως παντὶ
τρόπῳ ἐπιτηδεύσομεν, ἵνα καὶ ἡμῖν αὐτοῖς φίλοι ὦμεν καὶ
τοῖς θεοῖς, αὐτοῦ τε μένοντες ἐνθάδε, καὶ ἐπειδὰν τὰ ἆθλα
d αὐτῆς κομιζώμεθα, ὥσπερ οἱ νικηφόροι περιαγειρόμενοι, καὶ
ἐνθάδε καὶ ἐν τῇ χιλιέτει πορείᾳ, ἣν διεληλύθαμεν, εὖ
πράττωμεν.

NOTES

595 a 1 *ἦν δ' ἐγώ.* Socrates is telling an unknown interlocutor of a conversation held supposedly the previous day at Cephalus' house. Plato has earlier (III 398 a) protested against dramatic composition, where the author identifies himself with all his characters, good, bad, and indifferent. But an author may identify himself with an uplifting character, such as Socrates, and report what others have said.

ἦν from *ἠμι.* The root is the same as the Latin 'aio'. The *δέ* is not translated.

The other speaker is Plato's brother Glaucon.

αὐτῆς, i.e. the city.

a 2 *παντὸς μᾶλλον,* 'more than anything', i.e. 'without any doubt'. *ᾠκίζομεν.* Note the tense. The procedure was tentative.

a 3 *οὐχ ἥκιστα δέ κ.τ.λ.* 'I am thinking particularly of poetry as I speak.'

a 5 *τὸ μηδαμῇ παραδέχεσθαι.* The infinitive, like *τὸ ποῖον,* just before, is the object of *ἐνθυμηθείς.* 'I am thinking of our refusal to admit . . .'

αὐτῆς, partitive genitive, 'the part of it associated with drama'. *ὅση* for *ὅσον* by a very easy attraction of the sort that Greek loves. For *μίμησις,* see Appendix 2.

παντὸς γὰρ μᾶλλον . . . φαίνεται. An easy sentence to get lost in, as some of the old copyists, and even the philosopher Proclus found. *παραδεκτέα* is the predicate, *καί* 'even', *ἐναργέστερον* comparative adverb.

a 7 *τὰ τῆς ψυχῆς εἴδη.* IV 438 d ff. The soul is divided between the rational and irrational, the latter comprising the lowest part of the soul, the sensual, and the element we might call high spirit or temper. The division corresponds to, and is no doubt derived from, Hindu analysis. Tamas is the sensual element, Rajas stands for emotional energy and passion, Sattva is the element of intellectual and moral virtue. (See further notes on 600 b 2, 605 b 5, 618 a 3.)

69

The first-century writer Heraclitus tries (not very plausibly) to make Plato derive the tripartite soul from Homer. In the *Phaedrus* Plato uses the image of a chariot in which the charioteer Reason tries to control two more or less unruly horses. The word εἶδος, which sometimes represents the Universal Forms, here means little more than 'part'. We need to be reminded that we are not dealing with an age of highly sophisticated technical vocabulary.

b 2   ὡς μὲν πρὸς ὑμᾶς εἰρῆσθαι. This curious infinitive is very common with ὡς and found even without it, e.g. Hdt. I 61,4. We use the same idiom in English, 'To address myself to you'. Perhaps the infinitive, being a verb-noun, stands in apposition to the whole sentence.

b 5   λώβη. Predicate, having no article. τῆς διανοίας depends on it. πάντα τὰ τοιαῦτα is subject.

b 6   φάρμακον. Also to be taken predicatively. 'All who do not possess the knowledge of their true nature as an antidote.' The μή is generic, 'the sort of people who do not . . .'

c 1   καλῶν. Not, as is sometimes said, just sarcastic. Plato had a respect for the tragedians. They achieved beauty—of a sort. But because it had no firm moral basis it was at the last spurious.

πρῶτος διδάσκαλός τε καὶ ἡγεμών. The characterization of Homer as schoolmaster and commander-in-chief of the tragedians is interesting, and is twice repeated (598 b, 607 a). Plato is not just, as Cornford suggests, saying that the plots of tragedy were taken from epic. This is true. But as a matter of fact there is not a single extant Greek tragedy whose plot is based on Homer. Why not? Because the *Odyssey* was a romantic comedy which could lend itself to a satyr-play like Euripides' *Cyclops*, but not to high tragedy. And in the *Iliad* the theme was tragically handled with a depth and grandeur that beggared rivalry. This is not a historical judgement of literary indebtedness, but a critical judgement of quality and character. Aristotle appears to have agreed (*Poet.* 1448 b38). So did Isocrates (*Ad. Nicocl.* 24c).

c 2   ἀλλ' οὐ γὰρ πρό γε τῆς ἀληθείας τιμητέος ἀνήρ. This famous judgement derives from words which Plato puts into Socrates' mouth in prison, and which may be Socrates' own. *Phaedo* 91 b σμικρὸν φροντίσαντες Σωκράτους, τῆς δὲ ἀληθείας πολὺ μᾶλλον. So Aristotle quotes it against Plato in rejecting his Theory of Forms, N.E. I vi

1096 a16, ἄμφοιν γὰρ ὄντοιν φίλοιν ὅσιον προτιμᾶν τὴν ἀλήθειαν. Cf. [Ammonius] *Life of Aristotle*, φίλος μὲν Σωκράτης ἀλλὰ φιλτέρα ἡ ἀλήθεια. Augustine praises Porphyry for acting similarly, 'homini praeposuit veritatem' (*De C.D.* X 30). The familiar 'amicus Plato sed magis amica veritas' is found in Cervantes' *Don Quixote* II 8 and cannot be traced further back. Cf. Roger Bacon *Op. mai.* I vii, 'amicus est Socrates, magister meus, sed magis est amica veritas'. For the opposite view, see Cicero, *T.D.* I 17,39, 'errare mehercule malo cum Platone . . . quam cum istis vera sentire'.

c 5 ἀποκρίνου. Socrates always preferred to elicit truth by a process of question and answer rather than impose it by the connected exposition of the lecturer. Educationalists can still learn from this.

c 7 μίμησιν. In English we omit this from the main clause. 'Can you tell me in general what representation is?' The Greek form is 'I know thee who thou art'; the natural English, 'I know who you are.'

c 9 ἦ που ἄρα. The collocation of particles makes for sarcasm. 'I suppose I *shall* understand it.'

c 10 Socrates speaks without his customary self-depreciation (εἰρωνεία).

596 a 1 εἶδον. The aorist is originally, as the name implies, nontemporal, and used in generalized reflections.

a 3 οἷός τε εἴην. The optative depends on the conditional implicit in σοῦ παρόντος, not on the one expressed in εἰ . . . καταφαίνεται. So in English, 'if you were present I should not be able . . ., if anything did occur to me'.

a 6 μεθόδου, 'doctrine', as in *Theaet.* 183 c. For the theory, see Appendix I.

a 7 τὰ πολλά, 'groups' or 'collections of objects', almost 'genera'.

b 1 κλῖναι καὶ τράπεζαι. The fact that Plato here speaks of the Forms of manufactured objects is apparently contrary to a passage of Aristotle (*Met. Λ* 4, 1070 a 18) which praises him for limiting the Forms to natural objects, and Proclus found it impossible to take this part of the *Republic* seriously. But the *Cratylus*, apart from anything else, shows the Forms of artefacts along with others. A delightful story (D.L. VI 53) tells how Plato had been speaking of 'tableness'

table and a cup, but not tableness and cupness.' 'Precisely,' replied
Plato, 'for the eye is the instrument for the perception of a table and
cup, and you possess eyes, but the intelligence is the instrument for
the perception of tableness and cupness, and that you do not possess.'
Note that because all Forms exist φύσει a bed must do also (597 b 6).

b 6 This passage is admirably illustrated by *Cratylus* 389 a–d.
A carpenter wanting to make a weaver's comb (κερκίς) will consider
what will naturally perform the function required. If one comb
breaks, in making another he will not take as his model the broken
object, but this Form, which he discerns with the mind's eye as
naturally fitted to his purpose. In exactly the same way the Creator
in the *Timaeus* takes the eternal Forms as the pattern by which he
moulds matter into the objects of the natural universe.

b 12 τόνδε, 'the following'. ὅδε generally looks forward, οὖτος
back.

c 5 οἷός τε. Supply ἐστι.

c 8 Note the chiastic repetition, characteristic of Greek Prose;
cf. 612 c 10 and J. D. Denniston, *Greek Prose Style*, pp. 74 ff.

d 1 σοφιστήν. The word was originally not derogatory, meaning
merely an 'expert', either in a particular field, or generally: it is
applied to poets, musicians, those skilled in horsemanship, even to
cooks, and Herodotus uses it without sarcasm of the Seven Sages.
In the latter part of the fifth century growing cultural standards led
to a demand for higher education, which was met by experts willing
to purvey their knowledge for a fee. Many of these were genuinely
expert, and Protagoras, Gorgias, Hippias, and Prodicus were men of
integrity who made a genuine contribution to the advancement of
knowledge and the spread of education. Others were less scrupulous,
seeing a chance of making quick money, passing on slick techniques
of insubstantial argumentation or just enough ill-digested subject-
matter to give the appearance of cleverness. These brought odium
upon the name of 'sophist', which became associated with slick
quibbling, and the sort of cleverness that was too clever by half.
The feeling behind the word here is 'jack-of-all-trades'. Curiously,
under the Roman Empire, the word regained some of its old
dignity, and was applied to professors of rhetoric and philosophical
authors without innuendo.

L. and S. cite this passage as referring to the Creator of the
Universe: this is of course quite wrong.

d 2 'Do you think that it would be absolutely impossible for a craftsman of this sort to exist, or that in some sense a man might bring all these objects into being, but in some sense only?' Compare the idiomatic Greek for 'absolutely everyone', οὐχ οἱ μὲν οἱ δ' οὐκ ἀλλὰ πάντες. Cornford's note is strangely misleading. There is no reference to the divine Creator, who could hardly be said to manufacture himself. The only 'sense' in which such production is possible at all is the illusory sense of artistic production—and the use of mirrors.

d 8 δημιουργούμενος strictly refers to τρόπος, but the writing is conversational and the meaning clear.

d 9 κάτοπτρον. Not of course glass, but a circular piece of polished bronze, perhaps with an ornamental handle attached, and a cover for the polished face.

Emerson, *The Poet*: 'The rich poets—as Homer, Chaucer, Shakespeare, and Raphael—have no limits to their riches except the limits of their lifetime, and resemble a mirror carried through the streets ready to render an image of every created thing.'

e 4 φαινόμενα. 'Apparent to the senses', not, with L. and S., 'apparent to the mind'.

e 5 εἰς δέον, idiomatically 'opportunely'. τῷ λόγῳ, probably dative of advantage, 'for the argument'.

τῶν τοιούτων . . . δημιουργῶν, partitive genitive 'one of . . .'

597 a 2 ὃ ἔστι κλίνη, 'the real bed'. ὃ ἔστιν has become so much a technical term of the Theory of Forms that the gender is not attracted —similarly we find αὐτὸ δικαιοσύνη. There are three grades of existence. The Form, single and absolute, alone has full reality. The particular beds we use, the product of manufacturers, come next in the scale; they are imitations of the perfect Form of Bed. Third are the illusions of material beds produced by painters or those who hold mirrors. Plato does not complicate matters with paintings of reflections, such as are to be seen in some of the older Dutch artists, or reflections of paintings.

a 4 οὐκοῦν κ.τ.λ. 'Then if the thing which he makes does not really exist' (inverting the Greek arrangement), 'the object of his production could not be reality but something which resembles reality without belonging to it.' τὸ ὄν is wider than ὃ ἔστιν.

a 8 τοῖς περὶ τοὺς τοιούσδε λόγους διατρίβουσιν, 'those familiar

with arguments of this nature'. The Theory of Forms was first presented in the *Phaedo* which was probably written shortly after Plato's
first Italian journey in 387. By the time the tenth book of the
Republic was complete, it must have been widely discussed, especially within the Academy. Common sense of course attributes reality
to the material, visible, tangible bed, and regards Plato's Form as a
vacuous abstraction.

a 11   πρός, 'in face of', 'by contrast with'.

b 2   ἐπί, 'in the light of'. With people, 'in the presence of'.

b 6   θεὸν ἐργάσασθαι. A very difficult passage to fit in with the
rest of Plato's philosophy. Nowhere else is it said that God makes the
Forms, and in the *Timaeus* they are clearly the pre-existing blueprints
of creation. Further the Forms are eternal, and that which is truly
eternal has neither end nor beginning. Yet it is impossible to discount
the evidence of this passage—which is not to say that Plato's views
may not have changed later. The difficulty may have arisen from
his choice of an artefact as an illustration. Once an artefact, always
an artefact, and he may at this time have felt that just as the material
bed is the product of the human artificer, the Form of Bed must be
the product of the divine Artificer. If so, he did not, to our knowledge,
develop the view, but it would explain this passage. Such considerations would not apply to the Form of horse or dog, beauty or courage.

θεός without the article is not necessarily 'a god' and may properly be rendered 'God'.

b 14   εἴδεσι, loosely 'types', not technically.

c 1   οὐκ, very closely with ἐβούλετο, 'whether he was unwilling'.
Hence not μή.

c 3   αὐτὴν ἐκείνην ὃ ἔστιν κλίνη. Cf. 597 a 2 note. The neuter
gender is scarcely felt and the antecedent is attracted into the
feminine.

c 5   οὔτε μὴ φυῶσιν. μή with the subjunctive in Homer, and later,
expresses apprehension. Thus μὴ λάβωσί σε (Eur., *Or.* 776) means
'perhaps they may seize you'. οὐ prefixed to this negatives the μή
and expresses strong denial, 'there is no fear of their seizing you'.
Hence the general usage of οὐ μή in Attic with either the subjunctive
or (by transference) the future indicative to express strong prohibi-
tion or denial. The subjunctive was probably in origin a sort of

future. Such, at least, is the most plausible explanation yet given of a thorny subject.

c 7 ποιήσειεν, 'if he should make'. Davies and Vaughan make a rare error of translation. The single bed will appear in order to explain the common features of the two beds. Again, Socrates and Plato are both human. We must postulate the Form of Man to be the ground of their resemblance. A similar argument was later turned against the Theory of Forms. Does Socrates resemble the Form of Man or not? If not, what is its relevance? If so, does not the argument demand that we shall again postulate a third Man to explain the resemblance, and so, like Augustus de Morgan's fleas, *ad infinitum*?

d 5 φυτουργόν , 'creator of the real'. In the *Timaeus* where God appears as moulding the material world he is called the δημιουργός.

e 3 τοῦ τρίτου γεννήματος. The ancients counted inclusively. In English 'the author of that which is twice removed from full reality'. μιμητήν is predicative. In Dante, *Inferno* xi 105, Vergil calls art the grandchild of God, since art copies nature, and nature is the child of God.

e 6 τοῦτ' ἄρα ἔσται. This apparently simple sentence is in fact tricky. τοῦτο is adverbial, in general apposition to the sentence, and means 'consequently' (cf. Laws III 686e). καί is 'also', 'as well'. ὁ τραγῳδοποιός is the subject of ἔσται and τρίτος τις the predicate.

e 7 ἀπὸ βασιλέως καὶ τῆς ἀληθείας, a sort of hendiadys, 'the sovereignty of truth'. The use of the article reflects the fact that there is one truth but may be more than one king. In *Philebus* 28c Plato calls Reason king of heaven and earth.

598 a 7 The questions here raised and dismissed are of quite remarkable interest. How do we know what an object is like *in itself* when we can only know our own percepts of it? The bed, we say, *is* rectangular. But from most standpoints, perhaps from all, it appears quite different in shape. By what right, then, do we say that it *is* one of these appearances rather than another, or indeed that it *is* a shape which never appears to the eye at all? If we say that we measure the angles by a protractor and the sides by a ruler we are no better off. For why should the appearance to protractors and rulers (to speak loosely) be regarded as more valid than any other? And in any event are we not simply pushing the problem a stage farther back, for what are we to say of our percepts of the protractor and ruler? These and similar questions inspired the greatest period of British philosophy, represented by the figures of John Locke, George Berkeley and David Hume. A convenient, lucid, and lively presentation of the issues involved will be found in the first part of C. E. M. Joad's *Guide to Philosophy*. Plato can dismiss the question because he believes the real shape to be known by memory of Forms intellectually perceived before birth.

b 2 πρὸς τὸ ὄν, ὡς ἔχει, μιμήσασθαι. The whole phrase is to be taken together, 'directed to the representation of the true nature of reality'. ὡς ἔχει, as often, 'as it really is'.

b 7 διὰ τοῦτο κ.τ.λ, 'the reason why there is nothing that it cannot turn out is that . . .'

c 1 τεχνῶν. Not, as with most English renderings, 'arts', but 'crafts', 'sciences', 'skills', in modern jargon 'expertise'. Plato's point is that a man's skill in carpentry cannot be conveyed by outward appearances. A painter paints a picture and labels it 'The Carpenter'. Yet all he does is to reproduce the outward appearance of the man and does not touch the essence of carpentry in him. One wonders how Plato would have responded to the Pre-Raphaelites, who did take the trouble to understand their subject and what he was doing, and by laborious understanding and minute representation of detail conveyed so far as possible the outward manifestations of the inward essence. See, for example, Millais's *Christ at the House of his Parents* in the Tate Gallery, a painting which caused a storm in the Victorian teacup, or, in the same genre, Madox Brown's *Work* at Manchester. One wonders still more what he would have made of paintings which abjured reproductive naturalism and sought to convey the inner essence instead, like Picasso's *Three Musicians* in the Museum of Living Art, New York. Probably he would have accorded limited approval to the former. They are still at two removes from reality, but at that level have an integrity which some of their fellows lack. The others he would not have understood, and, as so many do, might have judged them by standards of naturalism. But if he could have understood them he might well have said that they were essaying something on what he would have regarded as an altogether higher plane.

c 2 παῖδας κ.τ.λ, obj. of ἐξαπατῶ ἄν. γράψας ἄν . . . ἐπιδεικνύς stands for a second conditional clause.

c 3 ἐξαπατῶ ἄν. This type of artistry was well known to the ancients. A famous story tells how Zeuxis and Parrhasius competed in friendly rivalry to see who could paint the most subtle illusion. Zeuxis painted a bunch of grapes such that the birds flew down and pecked at them. He then called on Parrhasius to pull the curtain away from his picture, and Parrhasius laughed, because his picture was a picture of a curtain. On another occasion Zeuxis is said to have painted a boy carrying a bunch of grapes, and again the birds pecked at the fruit. But Zeuxis was disappointed, for had the painting been really successful the boy would have scared away the birds. When Praxiteles' statue of Hermes was first discovered a photograph of it was sent to Germany, and a distinguished German savant, while admiring the statue, regretted that the photographer had left his old cloth in the picture. The 'old cloth' was in fact carved drapery, and part of the statue. Just so people visiting Madame Tussaud's have been known to ask the way of a wax policeman. The modern tendency is to say that it is not the function of art to ape reality, but to be true to its own medium. The cinema is not necessarily artistically better when it employs 3D and stereophonic sound. The essential quality of painting is not its ability to create a three-dimensional illusion: hence the work, in different ways, of Matisse, Klee, and Ben Nicholson. The sculptor does not impose form on the stone: he must be true to the block of stone which he is using. The point is made by Epstein in his autobiography, *Let There be Sculpture*; it is to be seen well in Henry Moore or Barbara Hepworth. It is notable that the neo-Platonist Plotinus here criticizes his master (*Enn.* V 8, 1–2): 'Art does not merely imitate the visible, but runs up to the seminal reasons from which nature springs. Phidias fashioned his Zeus on no pattern of sense, but showed him as he would and might be if revealed to mortal eye.' In fairness to Plato it should be added that he allowed the possibility of idealizing in art (*Rep.* V 472d).

d 4 αὐτός, nominative, the subject of the infinitive being the same as the subject of ἐξηπατήθη. It is possible that Plato is here girding at his older contemporary Antisthenes, a close associate of Socrates and precursor of the Cynic school of philosophy. We know that Antisthenes rejected Plato's Theory of Forms and his supernatural metaphysic; we know also that he used Homer as a basis for his moral philosophy; so that the allusion fully accords with the passage.

d 8   τινων. A verb of hearing is followed by the accusative of the thing heard and the genitive of the source from which one hears it.

e 1   οὗτοι, i.e. the poets. Cf. Dryden, *Essay on Satire*, who says of Shakespeare and Homer that in them 'we find all arts and sciences, all moral and natural philosophy without knowing that they ever studied them'.

e 3   περὶ ὧν ἂν ποιῇ, indefinite. περὶ ὧν is elliptical for περὶ τούτων περὶ ὧν.

e 6   ἐξηπάτηνται, perfect passive.

599 a 1   ῥᾴδια, sc. ὄντα.

a 2   μὴ εἰδότι, 'for a man *even if* he has no knowledge of the truth'.

a 4   περὶ ὧν, elliptical for ταῦτα περὶ ὧν.

a 8   καὶ τοῦτο . . . ὡς βέλτιστον ἔχοντα, 'and to value this more than his means of livelihood as his noblest possession'. The construction is precisely paralleled in VII 531 b, ὦτα τοῦ νοῦ προστησάμενοι. We might expect the article with βέλτιστον, but it is easily lost in the predicative position, cf. I 330 d, μέγιστον ἀγαθόν. ἔχοντα is here emphatic, 'possessing'. Plato's point is clear. The popular artist in all departments and in all ages commands lucrative rewards. The man of integrity will not be led aside by this prospect from a higher calling which he is capable of fulfilling. Throughout this discussion of art Plato has the sophists at the back of his mind, as his language from time to time reveals. They, instead of mastering one subject thoroughly, professed to teach any subject under the sun—and for money. It is difficult to know how to judge this contempt for the professionalizing of the teacher. There is in it something of the sense of superiority the man of independent means feels towards the wage-slave. But this does not apply to Socrates, and there is also something of the distaste we should feel if a minister of religion refused to give spiritual help except for a fee. Other interpretations of προστήσασθαι, e.g. 'set in the forefront of', or 'set before as an aim' are less satisfactory.

b 3   τούτων πέρι ἅπερ καί. Notice the ponderous weight of the expression. περὶ ὧν would have conveyed the general sense, but not the precise emphasis. πέρι accents paroxytone when it follows the genitive it accompanies.

b 7 μᾶλλον ὁ ἐγκωμιαζόμενος ἢ ὁ ἐγκωμιάζων. Sallust (*Cat.* 8) makes the point that the Athenians always had plenty of people to record their prowess: the Romans preferred action to words, 'optimus quisque facere quam dicere, sua ab aliis benefacta laudari quam ipse aliorum narrare malebat'. Ovid too (*Fasti* 3,103), after speaking of the Greeks as more eloquent than courageous, contrasts the Romans:

> qui bene pugnabat Romanam noverat artem,
> mittere qui poterat pila disertus erat.

The conception of poetry as purveying a second-hand account of someone's great deeds (and therefore a third-hand account of true Greatness) is to be noted: it is as limited as Plato's account of the visual arts. For a very different view of poetry, see Shelley's *Defence of Poetry*, where he defends poetry because it exercises the imagination, and the imagination is the great instrument of the moral life since it is always reaching outwards beyond the self. This Plato would hardly have accepted, but he puts a far more favourable estimate of poetry into the mouth of Diotima at *Symp.* 209 D; there attention is focused on the poet as fathering offspring of beauty. In general the classical poets defended their art as more durable than actions, cf. Pindar's ῥῆμα δ' ἐργμάτων χρονιώτερον βιοτεύει, 'words outlive actions' (*Nem.* 4, 6), or Horace's 'exegi monumentum aere perennius' (*Od.* 3, 30). Also Shakespeare:

> 'So long as men can breathe or eyes can see,
> So long lives this, and this gives life to thee.'

b 8 ὠφελία, whether to himself or others is not clear.

b 9 ἀπαιτῶμεν, with the acc. of the person asked and the thing asked for: both limit in different ways the action of the verb.

c 4 Ἀσκληπιός. In Homer a skilled doctor, who passed on his skill to his sons, Machaon and Podalirius, which made them useful members of Agamemnon's army. After that we hear little of him till towards the end of the fifth century, when he emerges into prominence as a god of healing. According to legend he was the son of Apollo and Coronis, inherited his father's healing powers, but was

killed by Zeus' thunderbolt for overstepping the mark and essaying
to raise the dead. He became one of the most popular Greek divi-
nities, with a celebrated shrine at Epidaurus. He was introduced to
Rome as a measure to counter the alarm and despondency of the
Second Punic War and took up residence on the island in mid-Tiber,
where St Bartholomew has since usurped charge of his hospital.
The Asclepiadae—the name given to his sons in Homer—were the
doctors attached to the cult; they must have combined some sound
medical knowledge with a flair for psychology. There is an interesting
account of the cult under the Roman Empire to be gleaned from
Aelius Aristides: for a convenient summary in English, see A.-J.
Festugière, *Personal Religion among the Greeks* c. vi. Also C. T. Seltman,
The Twelve Olympians and their Guests, pp. 178 ff.

d 7 Λυκοῦργον. The legendary law-giver of Sparta. In Herodotus
he appears as responsible for the Council of Elders and for the
Ephors; later writers foist almost everything in the Spartan constitution upon him. Probably he was originally a god who accumu-
lated responsibility for what was in fact a lengthy but forgotten
process of development. But Plato certainly regarded him as
historical.

e 1 αἰτιᾶται, not 'accuses' in a bad sense but 'holds responsible'.

e 2 Χαρώνδαν. Law-giver of his native city, Catana, Rhegium,
and other Chalcidic colonies in south Italy and Sicily, he lived perhaps at the beginning of the sixth century. Aristotle praises his care
for detail, but we in fact know little of the details. His laws were
aristocratic in outlook; he disapproved of credit in business trans-
actions, made perjury an indictable offence, and was concerned with
family right, but we can say little more with certainty. There is a
learned discussion of his laws in Bentley's *Dissertation upon the Epistles
of Phalaris*.

e 3 Σόλωνα. The great Athenian statesman (c. 640–560) who, perhaps in 594–593, was appointed 'archon and reconciler' in a situation
of dangerous anarchy. As so often in history, economic difficulty had
brought political disaster and serfdom to the poor. He cancelled
debts and ended borrowing on the security of the person, fostered
trade and commerce, revised the legal code, and reformed the constitution in such a way as to limit the power of the old nobility and
extend the responsibility of all free citizens. His immediate policies

failed; in the long run he was properly seen as the founder of the Athenian constitution. He appears in most lists of the Seven Sages.

e 6 Ὁμηριδῶν. Perhaps originally Homer's descendants; later a guild centring on Chios and claiming such descent; they arrogated to themselves a special authority on Homeric questions. See Strabo xiv 645; Pind., *Nem.* 2,2; Isoc., *Hel.* 218 e; Plat., *Ion.* 530c; Plat., *Phaedr.* 252b–c.

600 a 1 ἐπί, 'in the time of'.

a 4 ἀλλ' . . . λέγονται. A difficult sentence. 'Well then, are several bright ideas attributed to him in relation to applied science or other practical activities, things which characterize a man of practical ability?' I have simplified Burnet's text by placing a comma after ἀνδρός. ἐπίνοιαι are 'notions' or 'inventions'. αὐτοῦ must be supplied with λέγονται from what follows. οἷα is difficult to defend, but Plato uses the neuter very loosely, and there is no manuscript justification for οἷαι. The genitive at ἀνδρός denotes characteristic—'it is the mark of'—as commonly. εἰς τὰ ἔργα depends on σοφοῦ and is to be taken closely with it.

a 6 Θάλεω. Thales, whose maturity dates to the early part of the sixth century, like Solon, appears in most of the lists of the Seven Sages. He is best known as the man who inaugurated European philosophy by the questions he asked about the original substance from which the world was formed and the way in which material change took place. His home was Miletus on the coast of Asia Minor. He and his associates, Anaximander and Anaximenes, by reason of the train of thought they started, have an importance beyond the particular answers they gave; Thales, for example, thought the substratum was water, which produces solids by freezing and gases by boiling, and plainly ministers to life. His practical skill was shown in contributions he made to navigation and land-surveying by improved techniques of geometry and astronomy; his ability to predict an eclipse in 585 made a great impression on his contemporaries. His advocacy of confederation shows some interest in political science. To Aristophanes he is the typical practical genius (*Clouds* 180, *Birds* 1009), cf. Plautus, *Captivi* 274, *Bacch.* 122, *Rud.* 1003. An entertaining story tells how he was accused of being a 'head in the air' professor. He quietly used his knowledge of meteorology to predict a bumper crop of olives and cornered oil-presses during the off-season, thus making a small fortune for himself (Arist., *Pol.* I 11, 1259a 18). Plato keeps the Ionic form of the genitive.

'Ἀναχάρσιος. Anacharsis was a contemporary of Thales who also appears in some lists of the Seven Sages. He came from the wild country round the Black Sea, but assimilated Greek culture. His contributions to applied science were said to be the anchor and the potter's wheel (D.L. I, 105).

a 10   ἐπί, with the dat. 'for', 'by reason of'.

b 2   Πυθαγόρας. This is the only time he is named in Plato, and up to 300 B.C. there are only four other references to the name, in Xenophanes (fr. 7), Heraclitus (fr. 17), Herodotus (4,95), and Isocrates (*Bus.* 28). Yet we have two full lives of him written in the third century A.D.! This is not to say that 'there's no sich person'. But the thought of the Pythagoreans has too close affinities with Indian thought for the resemblance to be accidental, and the similarity of the name with the Indian Pitta-guru 'father-teacher' is suggestive. In the sixth century the ideas spread from Asia Minor to Sicily and S. Italy, perhaps through refugees from the political tyranny of Polycrates at Samos. There societies were established, holding community of possessions (κοινὰ τὰ φίλων), and devoted to a religious discipline, to which Plato here refers, in which the study of mathematics (to which the Pythagoreans made genuine contributions) fixed the mind on eternal truths, the observance of tabus ensured a ritual cleanliness and later fostered a deeper understanding by symbolic means, and silence, self-examination, study and purity of living exalted the soul. The soul was regarded as a fallen divinity, condemned to repeated imprisonment in the bodies of men and animals (hence the Pythagoreans were vegetarians: in Shakespeare's *Twelfth Night* the opinion of Pythagoras is cited 'that the soul of our grandam might haply inhabit a bird'). The way of life was designed to lift the soul to a higher plane in subsequent incarnations and eventually out of the gloomy cycle of birth and death altogether. Plato no doubt encountered the communities in his journey to the west in 387—he certainly met Archytas at Tarentum. The impact of these contacts is plainly discernible in the *Phaedo*, and it affected both the organization of the Academy and the substance of the *Republic*.

b 4 τοῦ βίου. The expression is loose; we might expect Πυθαγόρειον ἐπονομάζοντες τὸν τοῦ βίου τρόπον.

b 5 ἐν τοῖς ἄλλοις, personal 'against the background of the rest of mankind'.

b 6 Κρεώφιλος. One of the earliest of the Homeridae, author of an epic poem *Oechalia*, now lost, dealing with the capture of that town by Heracles. He is here described as Homer's disciple (ἑταῖρος, as in c 5 below). His authentic name was Creophylus, but we must read Κρεώφιλος on minor manuscript authority to make sense of the joke about his name. Those who cultivated a meat diet were despised by the Greeks as tending to brawn without brains. Sir Andrew Aguecheek's remark in *Twelfth Night* is apposite: 'I am a great eater of beef and I believe that does harm to my wits.' There is plainly some manuscript corruption here: see below c 1.

b 8 πρὸς παιδείαν, 'in relation to education'.

c 1 ὑπ' αὐτοῦ ἐκείνου. All the manuscripts read ἐπ'. περὶ αὐτόν must refer to Homer. The manuscript reading then means either 'Homer was much neglected in Creophilus' lifetime when Homer was alive', which is almost intolerable, or 'Homer was much neglected in his own lifetime when he was alive', which is pleonastic and very indirect as a criticism of Creophilus. Ast (not Adam—Burnet's apparatus) conjectured ὑπ' which gives excellent sense, 'Homer was much neglected in his lifetime by Creophilus'. That this is right is suggested by the parallel with ὑπ' αὐτῶν at c 6; the corruption may be associated with ἐπ' ἐκείνου at d 5. The general sense is that Homer cannot have been a good teacher if his own most intimate disciple neglected him. The scholiast says that Homer entrusted the *Iliad* to Creophylus, a curious tradition which if authentic raises many questions. Did he entrust it by teaching it orally, conveying it in writing, or (if Homer were blind) by dictating it? Why the *Iliad* and not the *Odyssey*? Does this reflect a time when Homer was known as the poet of the *Iliad*, and the *Odyssey* was from a different hand—or tongue? Or did some failure of Creophylus over the *Iliad* lead him to deposit the *Odyssey* elsewhere?

c 6 Πρωταγόρας. The most distinguished of the 'sophists' and Socrates' chief interlocutor in the dialogue named after him. He claimed to teach ἀρετή, 'how to live'. Plato treats him with respect, though feeling that his claim accorded ill with his theory of the relativity of knowledge ('Man is the measure of all things') and religious agnosticism. If what appears true to me is true for me, and what appears true to you is true for you, how can you claim to teach me? Protagoras' answer was that his view of life was not truer than the next man's, but it was better, and the fact that he continued to uphold the authority of moral standards told in his favour. The tremendous enthusiasm which attended him is well conveyed by the attitude of Hippocrates at the beginning of Plato's dialogue. His influence is to be seen in his being chosen as law-giver for the new foundation of Thurii in 444. Abdera, his home town, lay to the North on the Thracian coast: its inhabitants were proverbial for their stupidity, though it gave to Greek thought Democritus as well as Protagoras.

c 7 Πρόδικος. A contemporary of Protagoras, and another distinguished sophist, whose lecturing Socrates once attended, and whose special study of the precise connotations of words is delightfully parodied in the *Protagoras*. Like Protagoras he was a moralist and his parable *The Choice of Heracles* became a stock standby for sermon and diatribe. Like the poet Simonides, he came from the island of Ceos, not far from the coast of Attica, and impressed the Athenian public alike by his conduct of official diplomacy and by the brilliance of his educational lecturing.

d 2 σφεῖς, 'they', i.e. Protagoras, Prodicus and company.

τῆς παιδείας. Verbs of ruling are regularly accompanied by the genitive, dependent on the noun inherent in the verb.

d 3 μόνον οὐκ, 'all but'. So in Latin 'tantum non'.

d 6 'Ησίοδον. The perhaps eighth-century Boeotian poet, author of the *Works and Days*, the *Theogony*, and the *Shield*, whom Vergil followed in the *Georgics*. Apart from Homer he is the earliest poet whose work survives, and with Homer he did more than anyone to canonize the Olympian mythology in a settled pattern. Hence his appearance here as one of the poets who were regarded as religious teachers.

ῥαψῳδεῖν, lit. 'to stitch songs together', applied indifferently to original poets and to minstrels who rendered the works of others.

d 7 αὐτῶν. Verbs of grasping are accompanied by a partitive genitive, since one in fact gets hold of a portion only. So with τυγχάνειν, 'to hit'.

e 2 αὐτοὶ ἂν ἐπαιδαγώγουν, 'they would have danced attendance on them'—so Cornford, very happily. The same usage is found in *Alc.* I 135d. The παιδαγωγός was a slave who accompanied a boy to and from school.

601 a 1 αὐτός τε . . . ἐπαΐουσιν. The grammatical construction is clearer without τε and καί. 'The painter, himself ignorant of cobbling, will produce what looks like a cobbler to those who are similarly ignorant.' The whole phrase is curious since the two parts are not in any case co-ordinate. The use of τε and καί produces the effect of the English (Cornford, adapted), 'those who are as ignorant of cobbling as he is himself'. The μή is generic.

a 2 θεωροῦσιν, parallel to ἐπαΐουσιν, and likewise with τοῖς, thus adding further complexity to an already complex sentence.

a 5 ὀνόμασι καὶ ῥήμασι, 'words and phrases' rather than 'nouns and verbs'.

a 6 οὐκ ἐπαΐοντα ἀλλ' ἢ μιμεῖσθαι, a single phrase, 'with no knowledge save how to produce representations'. So in Latin 'vincere scis', 'you know how to conquer'. ἀλλά was originally the neuter plural of ἄλλος, a fact which easily explains the usage here.

a 8 ἐν μέτρῳ καὶ ῥυθμῷ καὶ ἁρμονίᾳ. At III 398d Plato says that lyrical poetry consists of words, rhythm, and musical setting. Here μέτρον is not easily to be distinguished from ῥυθμός. μέτρον is definite 'metre', ῥυθμός is a wider term denoting 'time' or 'rhythm' which prose may have as well as poetry. ἁρμονία is not our 'harmony', which is συμφωνία, but 'musical setting' generally. We are apt to forget that Greek poetry was sung, just as we are apt to forget that Greek statuary was painted.

a 9 δοκεῖν. The repetition of the word for the sake of clarity is so unobtrusively carried out as to be scarcely noticeable.

b 7 ὡραίων . . . καλῶν δὲ μή, 'of those who have had the bloom of youth without real beauty'. Cf. Spenser:

> For that same goodly hew of white and red
> With which the cheekes are sprinckled shal decay.

μή, generic.

ἰδεῖν, epexegetic (explanatory) infinitive with οἷα, 'as they are to see'.

This passage is quoted by Aristotle (*Rhet.* III 4) as an example of the rhetorical use of the simile.

c 3 ἐφ' ἡμίσεως. The reading is found as a gloss in one manuscript; if we accept ἡμίσεως on its own, we must take it as an otherwise unattested adverb.

c 12 μόνος ὁ ἱππικός. The jockey knows more about the tools required in horsemanship than the smith. It has been known to happen that the occupier finds snags in a house which the architect has failed to see. Plato is not, of course, here thinking of metaphysical knowledge of the Forms.

d 5 τὴν χρείαν. This relating of excellence to function picks up the discussion at the end of book I, though there it is expressed in terms of a naïve teleology (genuinely Socratic, as we know from Xenophon) which discovers the function of an animal or a natural object in its utility for man, a very dangerous assumption. But the linking of excellence and function is a point of some importance. It is cardinal to Aristotle's ethical system: see *N.E.* I 7. Cf. Bishop Butler, *Sermons*, Pref.: 'Every work, both of Nature and of art, is a system; and as every particular thing, both natural and artificial, is for some use or purpose out of and beyond itself, one may add to what has already been brought into the idea of a system, its conduciveness to this one or more ends.'

d 10 ποιεῖ, not connected with ποιητῇ in the previous line: the subject is the instrument (ᾧ χρῆται).

e 1 τῶν αὐλῶν. The αὐλός, often rendered 'flute', was played not like a flute, but like a recorder. It might be made of reed, wood, bone, ivory, or metal. There were different kinds—hence the plural —varying according to mode (Dorian, Phrygian, Lydian), though later inventions enabled the different modes to be rendered on a single instrument, or according to pitch (bass, treble). Sometimes two αὐλοί would be played simultaneously, as we know from vase-paintings.

e 5 πιστεύων. In the celebrated simile of the Line in VI 509d–511e, Plato divides the total extent of apprehension into four, εἰκασία and πίστις, which are contained under the general head of δόξα, and διάνοια and νόησις, both of which deal with the intelligible world, not the world of appearances. νόησις or ἐπιστήμη has as its

object the Forms, διάνοια works in the realm of mathematics and
other branches of knowledge which start from unverified axioms or
postulates, πίστις in the material world, and εἰκασία amid images
and representations. The man who makes a tool, Plato says, may
make it properly, but he does not really understand what he is doing;
he is familiar with the materials of his craft, but he has not studied
the relation of function' to excellence. And to get it right without
knowing why is to have correct belief, but not knowledge. The
representational artist, whether poet or painter, is a stage further
removed from true intelligence; in the realm of εἰκασία, he works
by guess rather than by God. At the other end of the scale Plato is
speaking more loosely, and is not to be pressed into saying that
because a man is familiar with the use of a tool he has necessarily a
philosophical knowledge of the true reality which underlies it. For
the Line, see Fig. 4, p. 133.

602 a 11 χαρίεις, ironical.   Cf. 'here's a pretty mess!'

b 1 The piling on of particles is remarkable.

b 3 μηδέν, as so often, generic.

b 7 μηδέν. After verbs of speaking the regular negative is οὐ,
but if anything is implied in the verb beyond a simple statement μή
may be found.

b 8 παιδίαν. Plato likes to play on παιδεία and παιδία. Cf. *Laws*
656c.

οὐ σπουδήν. The words must be taken closely together or the
negative would conform with μηδέν in the previous line. cf. 597 c 1.

b 9 ἐν ἰαμβείοις καὶ ἐν ἔπεσι, 'in iambics and heroic verse'.
Iambics were the regular metre of tragic dialogue. ἔπη (cf. epic)
originally dactylic hexameters, the metre of epic, as opposed to lyric,
tragic, or dithyramb; later also applied to heroic couplets. The
reference here is to Homer, who has been cited in company with
the tragedians.

b 10 ὡς οἷόν τε μάλιστα, 'to the nth degree'. Lit., perhaps 'super-
latively as far as possible', but the phrase has become an idiom.

c 1 περὶ τρίτον μέν. περί with the acc. is perhaps a little more
precise than περί with the genitive, but the usages are almost in-
distinguishable. μέν and δέ in association with prepositional phrases
sometimes follow the whole phrase, sometimes the preposition. Here
both are found; the effect is to put a stronger emphasis on τρίτον.

c 4   πρὸς δὲ δὴ ποῖόν τί ἐστιν. Lit., 'In relation to what sort of the parts of man is it in possession of the power which it possesses?' i.e. 'What is the character of that part of human nature towards which the influence it possesses is directed?' The expression is clumsy even in Greek.

c 10   Refraction is a commonplace in philosophical criticism of the reliability of sense-perception; it is used, for example, by Cicero and Sextus Empiricus in defence of Academic suspension of judgement. So Tennyson, *Higher Pantheism*, 'All we have power to see is a straight staff bent in a pool.'

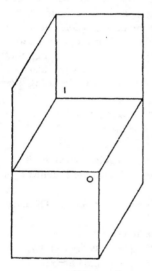

c 11   διὰ τὴν περὶ τὰ χρώματα αὖ πλάνην τῆς ὄψεως. What is Plato thinking of? Probably something like those drawings of cubes, which appear at will projecting from the paper or hollowed out from it. It is true that these do not depend on colour for their effect, but we must remember that the Greeks had no pencils; their effect would be obtained with a paintbrush. See Fig. 1.

c 12   καὶ πᾶσά τις ταραχὴ δήλη ἡμῖν ἐνοῦσα αὕτη ἐν τῇ ψυχῇ. A very difficult sentence, though the general meaning is clear. If αὕτη is the right reading it may perhaps be taken as equivalent to the English use of 'here'; 'it is clear that there is every sort of confusion here in our mind'. οὗτος was used to reinforce the gesture of pointing. The view that πᾶσα and αὕτη are to be taken together as standing for πᾶν τοῦτο is surely impossible.

FIG. 1 (602 c 11)
Whichever way up the page is held it can appear as a corner seat.

d 2   οὐδὲν ἀπολείπει, an idiom as at VII 533a, 'falls nothing short of'. ἀπολείπειν is intr.

d 6   ἱστάναι, 'weighing'. Plato has not seen the more fundamental point: our knowledge of our measuring instruments is equally obtained through the senses and is subject to the same criticisms.

See the note to 598 a 7 and C. E. M. Joad's book there mentioned.

d 8 τὸ φαινόμενον . . . τὸ λογισάμενον. The antithesis is not perfect, but that is deliberate. Plato is not saying that the lower part of the soul is liable to take over command instead of the higher; he is saying that the lower part of the soul is liable to be ruled by sense-appearances instead of reason. Note the change from pres. part. to aor.; the one denotes a state, the other an action.

e 1 λογιστικοῦ. A slight play on words has taken Plato from calculation to reason in general. ἡ λογιστική is 'arithmetic', and 'logistics' in Eng. is confined to calculation, especially as applied to military movements. But τὸ λογιστικόν is the whole reasoning faculty in man.

e 5 τἀναντία φαίνεται, 'there is an appearance of the contradictory'. Not that the highest part of the soul is directly subject to sense-impressions, but that it is presented with two sets of evidence, one from calculation, one which has come through the senses.

603 a 6 τί μήν; almost exactly our 'Well?'

b 1 ἐπ' οὐδενὶ ὑγιεῖ, 'with a view to . . .' They are 'up to no good'.

b 9 ἐκ τῆς γραφικῆς with τῷ εἰκότι. Cornford (excellently) 'instead of trusting merely to the analogy from painting'.

b 10 τῆς διανοίας. Not in Plato the lower parts of the soul, nor yet the highest (νοῦς) though more closely linked with the latter than the former. It appears a little oddly here. But (a) Plato often uses imprecisely terms which are elsewhere precise, (b) it is arguable that there is an intellectual element in the appreciation of poetry which does not exist in relation to the sort of painting Plato has been describing, (c) he does not wish wholly or too obviously to prejudge his case.

c 2 φαῦλον ἢ σπουδαῖον. More formal writing would put πότερον before φαῦλον.

c 4 πράττοντας. This shows that Plato's attention is confined to narrative and dramatic poetry. Note the assumption, echoed in Aristotle's famous definition of tragedy in the *Poetics*, that drama deals with man in action. Maeterlinck's Static Drama, Shaw's Play of Ideas were undreamed of.

c 5 βιαίους, fem. agreeing with πράξεις, in its rarer passive sense 'involuntary'.

c 7 μὴ . . .ᾖ. 'Perhaps there is something else besides these points.' Burnet, following Ast, reads ἦν and points as a question, 'there isn't anything else, is there?' but the imperfect is difficult to justify.

d 1 ἐστασίαζεν, 'he was suffering from inner dissension'. The metaphor is from political revolution, the contemporary analogy with Latin America.

d 4 τοῦτο, obj. of διομολογεῖσθαι; not to be taken with οὐδὲν δεῖ.

d 5 ἐν γὰρ τοῖς ἄνω λόγοις. IV 435 e ff. There the main conflict between desire and reason is illustrated by the man who though thirsty refuses to drink, say, because the liquid is poisoned. He is pulled in two directions, divided against himself. The third element in the soul, temper, sides now with one, now with the other. If he drinks, he is liable to say, 'What a fool I am to poison myself!' If he refrains, he is liable to say, 'What a fool I am not to quench my thirst!'

e 3 ὑόν. The usual form is υἱός, but the grammarians claim ὑός as more proper, and it is attested in inscriptions. Augustus' epigram, 'Melius est Herodis porcum esse quam filium' (Macrob., *Sat.* ii 4), must have been originally in Greek.

e 5 ῥᾷστα . . . τῶν ἄλλων. Greek idiom conflates 'more easily than the rest' and 'most easily of any' into a single expression.

e 8 μετριάσει. Perhaps directed against Antisthenes' exaltation of ἀπάθεια. Cf. Seneca (though a Stoic), *Ep.* 99, 15, 'inhumanitas est ista, non virtus'.

604 a 1 τόδε δή. The meaning is clear, the reading uncertain. Most manuscripts have τὸ δέ, where τό must be demonstrative; with νῦν following this is intolerably ambiguous. τόδε is also found, but such an abrupt opening is without parallel. The demonstrative at the beginning of the protagonist's speech is regularly followed by δή, cf. 603 c 4, and it could easily drop out. But it is strange that it is found in ĥo manuscript at all.

a 5 διοίσει, used with double meaning, 'he will behave differently' and 'he will see it through unflinchingly'.

a 10 οὐκοῦν τὸ μὲν ἀντιτείνειν διακελευόμενον κ.τ.λ. 'Then the force which impels him to resist is reason—law—the force which drags him to succumb to grief is the actual impact of sensation.' The structure is shown by the absence of the article from λόγος καὶ νόμος. (In αὐτὸ τὸ πάθος, αὐτὸ τό is a single idiom.) Note that the antithesis of 602 d 8 between reason and the external force is maintained. Note also the implication that in succumbing to grief you are succumbing to something outside yourself, and this is undesirable. From the fourth century onwards philosophy increasingly pursued αὐτάρκεια, 'self-sufficiency', roughly what Aldous Huxley in *Ends and Means* calls 'non-attachment'. Even pity was suspect, because it makes your peace of mind subject to forces outside your control—so Aristotle and the Stoics.

b 4 αὐτῷ. This has the great weight of manuscript authority and gives perfectly good sense. 'We say that, there must be two elements in his nature'. The conjecture αὐτώ would refer to λόγος and πάθος.

b 10 οὔτε δήλου ὄντος . . . οὔτε . . . προβαῖνον . . . The mixture of acc. and gen. absolute is odd, but found in Thuc. vii, 25, ὡς καί τῶν Ἀθηναίων προσδοκίμων ὄντων ἄλλη στρατιᾷ καί, ἢν φθάσωσιν αὐτοὶ πρότερον διαφθείραντες τὸ παρὸν στράτευμα αὐτῶν, διαπεπολεμησόμενον 'as the Athenians were expecting a fresh army, and, if they got in first with the annihilation of their present forces, the war would be over'. It appears that the Greek acc. and gen. absolute and the Latin abl. absolute all have different origins. The first is probably derived from an acc. which limits the verb in relation to extant or duration of time; the second from the use of the partitive gen. for the time within which an action falls; the third is an instrumental abl. corresponding to the English 'with'. The use of οὐ here shows that these are not just propositions in the mind of the man concerned, but, for Plato, firm actualities.

b 12 εἰς τὸ πρόσθεν, 'in a forward direction', 'positively'.

c 1 ἐν αὐτοῖς, i.e. τὰ ἀνθρώπινα.

c 6 ἐν πτώσει κύβων. Our knowledge of ancient games, except where they are very simple, does not enable us to reconstruct them fully. This will surprise no-one who has attempted to pick up a new card-game from instructions in a book; for ancient pastimes we have not even the book of instructions. Certainly there were ordinary dice (κύβοι), which the Greeks threw as we do, normally using three at a time. Equally certainly there were some sort of draughtsmen (πεσσοί), which were used in a game of skill, like our draughts or chess. The two are often spoken of together; Palamedes, for example, is credited with inventing both. The Romans, in their game 'latrunculi', combined chance and skill, by making the movement of the pieces depend, at least in part, on the fall of dice, and the reference here is to a similar Greek game. The nearest modern parallel is backgammon.

c 7 ὁ λόγος ωἱρεῖ, from its recurrence in Herodotus a stock phrase, sometimes with a personal object, sometimes without—'reason directs', cf. 607 b 3.

c 8 τοῦ πληγέντος. For the gen., cf. 600 d 7 note. Demosthenes says to the Athenians (*Phil.* I 40), 'your war with Philip is exactly like foreigners boxing. When one of them is hit he invariably covers the place struck'—ἀεὶ τῆς πληγῆς ἔχεται—'and if he is hit somewhere else, there go his hands.'

e 1 μίμησιν . . . ἔχει, 'contains material for imitation' or 'the possibility of being imitated'. This use of ἔχει is common in Aristotle.

e 3 παραπλήσιον ὂν ἀεὶ αὐτὸ αὑτῷ, i.e. 'fairly consistent'.

οὔτε ῥᾴδιον μιμήσασθαι. There is a *non-sequitur* here. Even if we allow that the faculty of representation is linked with the lower not the higher aspects of man's nature it does not follow that the higher aspects are not easy to represent.

e 4 μιμουμένου, gen. abs. 'if anyone does represent it'.

πανήγυρις, a religious festival, here with especial reference to Dionysus, in whose honour the tragedies were enacted.

e 5 ἀλλοτρίου γάρ. Note the emphasis, 'the representation is of an experience unfamiliar to them'. It is interesting, and a little strange, to find πάθος of the calm demeanour of the intellectual. Plato is thinking (not strictly grammatically) of the impact on the audience.

605 a 8 ἐπιλαμβανοίμεθα, a technical word, meaning to distrain property or to arrest people. The gen. is typical of verbs of taking hold, cf. 600 d 7 note, 604 c 8 note.

a 9 ἀντίστροφον, 'counterpart', 'mirror-image'. An appropriate word because of its application to Greek tragedy. The chorus would first sing a stanza weaving a dance-pattern, then a corresponding stanza weaving the same pattern in the reverse direction.

a 10 ἔοικεν αὐτῷ. The dramatist resembles the painter (*a*) in producing creations far inferior to reality (*b*) in dealing with a similar part of human nature, and not the highest. καὶ ταύτῃ ὡμοίωται is otiose, but which of us in talk does not similarly repeat himself?

b 3 μέλλουσαν εὐνομεῖσθαι. μέλλειν usually, but not invariably, is accompanied by the fut. inf. Here there is no special fut. reference. τοῦτο . . . τῆς ψυχῆς, 'this part of the soul'.

b 5 ὥσπερ ἐν πόλει. This parallelism between the individual and the community is cardinal to the argument of the Republic. The theoretical construction of the State starts from the assumption of its legitimacy (II 368 c ff.). The classes in the State correspond with the parts of the individual soul. Plato is not arguing an analogy, but a precise correspondence and dependence. This, like the actual three-fold division of the soul (see 595 e 7 note), is probably derived from Hindu philosophy where the same division is found. The Brahmins, the priest-rulers, represent Sattva, intelligence and moral integrity. The Kshattryas, soldiers and administrators represent Rajas—what the Americans call, or used to call, 'go-getting'. The Vaishyas, producers and traders, represent Tamas, desire for physical satisfaction. Hindu society had a fourth caste, the Sudras, but they were set off from the other castes as 'once-born' against 'twice-born', and correspond with Plato's slaves. This parallelism raises some interesting contemporary problems. Is a union of human beings, a nation or trade union for example, different in principle from the sum of its members? Is it subject to the same moral code?

b 7 ταὐτόν found as an alternative for ταὐτό. Here adverbial 'in the same way', an obvious extension of the cognate accusative.

d 2 ᾄδοντάς τε καὶ κοπτομένους. There is a contrast between the ῥῆσις, which was spoken, and the κομμός or choral lament. So in Synge's *Riders to the Sea* we might contrast the speeches with the keening at the end.

d 4 συμπάσχοντες. Aristotle too suggested that the pleasure we receive from tragic drama comes from the excitement of the emotions of pity and fear within us. But he seeks to give this social justification by saying that by being thus excited these undesirable emotions are purged from us, worked out of our system. For the general thought (though there applied to actor rather than audience), cf. the scene between Hamlet and the Players:

> What's Hecuba to him, or he to Hecuba,
> That he should weep for her?

e 1 ἀνδρὸς . . . γυναικός. 'Characteristic of . . .'

e 4 τὸ . . . μὴ βδελύττεσθαι. The construction is loose, for the failure to feel disgust and the actual feeling of contentment are hardly to be in apposition to ὁ ἔπαινος, but the meaning is clear, and it is helped by the fact that the whole apposed phrase is included within τὸ . . . ἐπαινεῖν.

606 a 3 εἰ ἐνθυμοῖο ὅτι κ.τ.λ. The ὅτι clause is not easy to disentangle. The subject is τὸ . . . κατεχόμενον . . . καὶ πεπεινηκός . . ., the latter being followed by the genitive of the source of the hunger ('the element that hankers after sorrow, etc.'); φύσει . . . ἐπιθυμεῖν is parenthetical; the consecutive infinitive with οἷος is common. τοῦτο picks up the subject, which was in danger of getting lost, and τὸ . . . πιμπλάμενον καὶ χαῖρον is predicate. The two τότες are in contrast with one another: the first refers to occasions of private grief, the second to dramatic performances.

b 1 θεωροῦν . . . αἰσχρὸν ὄν. The first is nom. agreeing with τὸ φύσει βέλτιστον, the second acc. absolute. By such variations Plato avoids the mannered antithesis, and approaches normal conversational practice.

b 4 τὴν ἡδονήν explains ἐκεῖνο, 'he thinks that this he has on the profit side—his entertainment'.

καὶ οὐκ ἂν δέξαιτο . . . ποιήματος, 'and he could not allow himself to forfeit his entertainment because he had scruples about the work of art as a whole'.

b 6 ἀπολαύειν. The ironical use is quite common, 'a man inevitably uses for his own life the harvest which he reaps from the lives of others'.

b 8 τὸ ἐλεινόν. For Aristotle's very different view, see note on 605 d 4.

c 3 ἂν αὐτὸς αἰσχύνοιο . . . ἐν τοῖς ἐλέοις. Another difficult sentence. ἂ (ἂν = ἂ ἄν) has no antecedent; it is the object of γελωτοποιῶν (forcing the normal meaning slightly) and ἀκούων. 'In relation to those things which (a) you would be ashamed to do personally for a laugh, but (b) you delight to hear, etc.' Both parts are virtual conditionals; Plato shows some irony in making the shame more remote than the enjoyment.

c 7 τότε . . . ἐκεῖ 'during the performance', 'at the theatre'.
νεανικὸν ποιήσας, rather as we say 'getting fresh'.

d 4 δέον, acc. absolute, as commonly with the impersonals when the gen. might be ambiguous.

d 5 ἄρχοντα, n.pl., with ταῦτα.

e 1 Ὁμήρου ἐπαινέταις. Plato may have Antisthenes specifically in mind—see note on 598 d 4. But his purview is wider; so incidentally was Antisthenes'. Xenophon (*Symp*. III 5–6) tells how Niceratus records how his father Nicias, being anxious to see him develop into a good man, made him learn the whole of Homer off by heart. Antisthenes is quick to point out that the rhapsodes, the professional reciters, who were not noted for their intelligence, could do this. Clearly, then, to Antisthenes Homer was not enough, though his respect for Homer was considerable. Clearly, too, others regarded Homer as the foundation of education; one imagines that the worthy Nicias was not original in his approach. Homer was in fact staple food from the early stages of literary studies, and Niceratus argues that from him you can learn the principles of domestic economy, public speaking or military strategy, and to emulate the great heroes of old. So too Aristophanes (*Frogs* 1035) commends Homer because he inspires the martial virtues. Often the stories were moralized or allegorized: the Stoics were to carry this to extremes, but we find Socrates himself doing it (Xen., *Mem*. I 3,7). Probably the fairest parallel is the attitude of many people today, or, better, towards the beginning of the century, to the place of the Old Testament in education.

607 a 3 ὅσον μόνον. ὅσον, ὅσον μόνον and μόνον ὅσον are used interchangeably for 'so far and no further'. Here 'nothing but'. ὅσον is adverbial.

a 4 θεοῖς . . . τοῖς ἀγαθοῖς. Dative of the person concerned. Normally one noun depends upon another in the gen. But there are exceptions. Cf. *Symp*. 194d, τοῦ ἐγκωμίου τῷ Ἔρωτι.

a 5 μέλεσιν, lyric poetry.

a 7 τοῦ κοινῇ ἀεὶ δόξαντος εἶναι βελτίστου λόγου. Hence in the *Laws* (801 c–d) Plato provides for a strict censorship of literary production, though in the *Politicus* (299 d–e) he sees the limitations of any attempt to govern life by written rules. Milton's *Areopagitica* remains the classic defence of the liberal position. The issue is a living one in the twentieth century. Is there to be freedom to publish horror comics, gangster films, and the like, or should the best judgement of the community limit such publication? And if so, how is the censorship, introduced for the highest motives, to be safeguarded against abuse and the repression of inconvenient publication? And indeed has a government the right, even the responsibility, to check the publication of political views which it genuinely deems dangerously revolutionary?

b 2 ἀπεστέλλομεν. III 398 b and the discussion leading up to it.

b 3 ὁ γὰρ λόγος ἡμᾶς ᾗρει. Cf. 604 c 7 note.

b 5 καταγνῷ, originally 'to discover something about somebody', hence 'to accuse', still, normally, with the person in the gen. and the charge in the acc.

παλαιὰ μέν τις διαφορὰ φιλοσοφίᾳ τε καὶ ποιητικῇ. The philosophers were not long in assailing the influence of Homer and Hesiod. If we may trust the tradition, such criticism was associated with the name of Pythagoras; certainly by the end of the sixth century Heraclitus and Xenophanes, and later Empedocles, were hostile. The poetic counterblast is less easy to trace. A fragment of Pindar (fr. 209) describes the natural philosophers as 'reaping an unprofitable crop of wisdom'. Aristophanes, Eupolis, Cratinus and others had made a comic butt of Socrates. The quotations which follow are untraceable; they seem to be from lyric, but one or more may be from tragedy. We know that the first was from an attack upon Anaxagoras and his followers for their rationalistic treatments of the heavenly bodies (Laws 967 c–d). The 'yelping bitch' is philosophy. Cf. also Keats, Lamia:

> Do not all charms fly
> At the mere touch of cold philosophy?

and Wordsworth, A Poet's Epitaph:

> Philosopher! a fingering slave,
> One that would peep and botanize
> Upon his mother's grave

Maximus of Tyre (XVII 3) remarks plaintively, 'It is possible to love Homer and Plato too.'

c 1 τῶν διασόφων ὄχλος κράτων. The reading is uncertain. διάσοφος is not found elsewhere, though διασοφίζεσθαι appears in Aristophanes. Adam's κράτων gives 'the gang of professorial pates' and is better than the manuscript κρατῶν which would have to be strained to mean 'the bossy gang of professors'.

c 2 ὅτι, dependent on μεριμνῶντες, 'carefully working out the fact that'.

d 1 δι' Ὁμήρου. Plato in his poetic sensibility cannot resist a tribute.

e 6 διὰ τὸν ἐγγεγονότα μὲν . . . εὖνοι μὲν . . . ἕως δ᾽ἄν. One of the μένs is pleonastic.

e 7 ὑπό with ἐγγεγονότα.

608 a 1 εὖνοι, followed by acc. and inf., by an easy extension 'delighted that . . .'

a 4 ἐπῳδήν, 'a charm', in Homer sung over a wound to heal it.

a 5 εἰς τὸν παιδικόν τε καὶ τὸν τῶν πολλῶν ἔρωτα, 'an adolescent, Bert-and-Vi love', Cornford (very cleverly), 'which most people have never outgrown'.

a 6 ᾀσόμεθα. Even in a work not concerned with textual criticism it is worth drawing attention to this brilliant emendation of Madvig's from the non-existent αἰσθόμεθα.

b 1 τῆς ἐν αὐτῷ πολιτείας. Cf. 605 b 5 and note.

b 5 ὅσος, here 'as small as'; the word is ambivalent.

τὸ χρηστὸν ἢ κακὸν γενέσθαι, in loose apposition to ὁ ἀγών.

οὔτε . . . οὔτε . . . οὐδέ γε. Cf. VI 499 b, οὔτε πόλις οὔτε πολιτεία οὐδέ γε ἀνήρ. The οὐδέ γε means 'nor even'.

c 1 ἐπίχειρα, 'the things which are put into your hand', hence 'wages'.

c 5 'The days of our years are threescore years and ten; and if by reason of strength they be fourscore years, yet is their strength labour and sorrow; for it is soon cut off, and we fly away'—Ps. xc 10. 'Life's a short summer'—Johnson, *Winter.* 'One life,—a little gleam of time between two Eternities'—Carlyle, *Heroes and Hero-Worship;* 'La vie est brève' is a commonplace in all languages and at all times. the contrast with eternity may be made in a spirit of optimism or of pessimism.

Cf. also Tennyson, *Locksley Hall Sixty Years After*:

Truth for truth, and good for good! The Good, the True, the Pure,
  the Just—
Take the charm 'For ever' from them, and they crumble into dust.

c 9 πράγματι. Most edd. take it, 'Do you think an immortal
object ought to be concerned with so short a space of time rather
than the whole of time?' This is possible, though the dat. with δεῖ is
rare. Cf. Xen. *An.* 3,4,35; *Oec.* 7,20. Perhaps it should be, 'Do you
think that one should be concerned over an immortal object for so
short a space of time', etc. For πρᾶγμα in this sense, cf. Dem. 383,4,
ἀσταθμητότατον πρᾶγμα ὁ δῆμος. χρῆμα is similarly used.

d 5 μὰ Δι', οὐκ ἔγωγε. The astonishment is very remarkable.
See further Appendix 3.

d 7 εἰ μὴ ἀδικῶ γ', ἔφην, 'I have no right to refuse' (Adam).
Cf. IV 430 d; *Charm.* 156 a; *Menex.* 236 b. The meaning is clear from
the variant at 612 d 2, ἀδικοίην μεντἄν, ἔφη, εἰ μή.

e 3 τὸ μὲν . . . ἀγαθόν. Normal, but not invariable, Greek practice
puts the article with the subject and not with the predicate. Here the
article is found with both, and this, together with the ambiguous
position of πᾶν, means that the two are co-extensive. All evil is
destructive, and everything that is destructive is evil.

609 a 3 So Ruskin, *Time and Tide.* 'Every faculty of man's soul, and
every instinct of it by which he is meant to live, is exposed to its own
special form of corruption.' This is of course consciously Platonic.

b 1 οὐ . . . μή. See 597 c 5 note.

b 2 τὸ μήτε κακὸν μήτε ἀγαθόν. The μή is generic.

b 6 οὕτως with τοῦ πεφυκότος, 'the object thus constituted'.

b 7 ἦν. The imperfect expresses a fact which was true all along,
but whose truth has only just been recognized, ef. Hor. *Od.* i 37, 2-4.

> Nunc Saliaribus
>   ornare pulvinar deorum
>   tempus erat dapibus, sodales.

'Now all along was the real time. . . .'

b 11 ἃ νυνδὴ διῇμεν πάντα. He has argued this at IV 444 c.

c 4 ὑπό, common in Attic with nouns that are not strictly personal,
and accompanying verbs that are not strictly passive.

c 5 ὧδε, looking forward as usual, 'as follows'.

d 1 τῷ προσκαθῆσθαι, instrumental, 'by settling in'.

d 6 εἰς θάνατον. Of the soul's death.

d 7 τοῦ σώματος χωρίσῃ. Life in this world consists of the union of body and soul. In the *Phaedo* Plato has defined death as the separation of soul from body. When the soul is taken away from the body, the body dies. But when the body is taken away from the soul the soul does not die, and the soul's peculiar afflictions do not take the body away from it.

The gen. is of course a gen. of separation.

e 1 ἐννόει γάρ κ.τ.λ. The argument is involved. The body does not perish because the food is mouldy with age or has gone bad, because these are peculiar afflictions of food, not of bodies. There must be an intermediate point when the body becomes infected through the food with its own peculiar affliction, disease. He proceeds to argue that disease does not touch the soul, for the soul's peculiar affliction is injustice. Injury to the body does not infect the soul with injustice, and in any case injustice does not cause death.

e 2 ᾗ ἂν ᾖ, indef.

e 3 δεῖν, a little strange, 'we do not imagine that a body cannot avoid being destroyed'.

610 a 1 ἄλλων ὄντων ἄλλο ὂν τὸ σῶμα. Make this a separate sentence. 'The body is one thing and food something different.'

a 6 μή ποτε ἀξιῶμεν, 'let us never claim'.

a 8 τῷ ἑτέρου κακῷ ἕτερον, 'i.e. that one thing is destroyed by the affliction peculiar to another'. The neuter is easy to justify, the dat. picking up ὑπό less easy, but Plato cultivates variety.

a 10 ἢ τοίνυν ταῦτα ἐξελέγξωμεν κ.τ.λ. 'Either we should demonstrate that this statement of ours is unsound, or, as long as this is not done . . .'—jussive subj.

b 2 ὅτι σμικρότατα, 'as minutely as possible', like the Latin quam + superlative. So too ὅσον τάχιστα.

b 3 ἕνεκα τούτων. ἕνεκα usually but not invariably follows the word it accompanies.

b 7 μή. The gen. absolute stands for a conditional.

c 6   This paragraph shows the fallacy in Plato's argument. ψυχή is for him (a) the principle of life (b) the moral personality. The identity of these is uncritically assumed. This is the true fallacy, and the ambiguity of θάνατος (the death of the body or destruction of the soul) really rises out of it.

d 1   ὑπ' αὐτοῦ . . . αὐτὸ . . . τοῦτο . . . πάνδεινον . . . θανάσιμον· Plato commonly uses the neuter even when referring to a strictly feminine noun when he wants to discuss it as a thing.

ἀποκτεινύντος. Plato prefers ἀποκτεινύναι to ἀποκτείνειν.

d 2   Beware of taking μάλιστα with θᾶττον or ἧττον with σχολαίτερον.

d 3   μή is found in association with ἀξιοῦν in Thuc. III 66, ἀξιοῦτε μὴ ἀντιδοῦναι δίκην, though οὐ is commoner. No doubt the complexity of the sentence has led Plato to a general feeling of remoteness.

ὥσπερ . . . ἀποθνήσκουσιν οἱ ἄδικοι. For the construction with μὴ ὥσπερ, cf. III 410 b. Tr. 'instead of the present situation where as an indirect result of it . . .' The argument is that if injustice automatically brought death in its train there would be no need for society to execute criminals. The confusion between the death of the body and the destruction of the soul is here obvious to all except Adam. There is an oblique reference to Socrates' own death. See *Apol.* 39 b, 'And now we are going to leave, I to suffer the judgement of death which you have imposed, they already under sentence of wickedness and immorality imposed by Truth. I am going through with my sentence, and they with theirs.'

d 6   ἀπαλλαγὴ γὰρ ἂν εἴη κακῶν. The thought of death as the end of the troubles of life is a commonplace, especially among those who speak of life pessimistically. So a character in Euripides (fr. 250) speaks of 'Death the Healer'. So too the late Greek poet Agathias (A.D. 536–582), here translated by George Croly, rector of St Stephen's Walbrook at the beginning of the nineteenth century:

> Why shrink at death, the end of all our woes—
> Life's healer—mighty mother or repose?
> If good, 'tis good for ever; but if ill,
> It wounds but once, and then the pang is still.
> Life's wan diseases strike us o'er and o'er;
> The traveller of death returns no more!

So Socrates' dying words were an injunction to sacrifice a cock to the god of healing (Plat., *Phaedo* 118a). So too A. E. Housman:

> Here, with one balm for many fevers found,
> Whole of an ancient evil, I sleep sound.

d 7 πᾶν τοὐναντίον, adverbial, 'on the contrary'.

e 2 καί, 'actually'.

πρός γ᾽ ἔτι τῷ ζωτικῷ, i.e. 'in addition to giving him vitality'.

e 3 ἐσκήνηται, military metaphor. Plato seems to prefer the form σκηνᾶν, Xenophon σκηνεῖν. The metaphor is pursued in τεταγμένον. For a remarkably sustained series of military metaphors, see *Phaedo* 102–4.

611 a 5 ἀεὶ ἂν εἶεν αἱ αὐταί. αἱ αὐταί is subject and εἶναι means 'to exist'. The fixed number of souls is to us a strange thought, but it often accompanies philosophies of reincarnation. The Greeks had great difficulty in envisaging creation out of nothing. The principle 'nothing out of nothing' was popularized by the Epicureans, but it is widely found among the Greek thinkers. Cf. Epicurus (*Ep. ad Her.* 38), οὐδὲν γίνεται ἐκ τοῦ μὴ ὄντος. Lucr. I 150, nullam rem e nilo gigni divinitus umquam, etc. Persius III 83, gigni/de nihilo nihilum. Democritus, μηδὲν ἐκ τοῦ μὴ ὄντος γίγνεσθαι (D.L. ix 44). The same view is attributed to Anaxagoras (Simplic. 156,9 = Diels 85). We cannot further trace the doctrine in quotation, but Aristotle (*Met.*, K 1062 b 24) tells us that it was an axiom of almost all the natural philosophers. It even passes to a professing Stoic like Marcus Aurelius (4,4), οὐδὲν ἐκ τοῦ μηδενὸς ἔρχεται. Plato's own δημιουργός is not a creator, but a craftsman working on pre-existing materials. Cf. also Tyndall, *Fragments of Science*, p. 91: 'One fundamental thought pervades all these statements, there is one tap root from which they all spring: this is the ancient maxim that out of nothing nothing comes, that neither in the organic world nor in the inorganic is power produced without the expenditure of other power.' Contrast the Christian view, as in Athanasius *De Inc. Verb.* 3, ἐξ οὐκ ὄντων καὶ μηδαμῶς ὑπάρχοντα τὰ ὅλα εἰς τὸ εἶναι πεποιηκέναι τὸν Θεόν.

a 7 ὁτιοῦν τῶν ἀθανάτων, 'any group of immortal beings'. What is Plato thinking of? Probably nothing very precise. The totality of immortal beings for him certainly includes the Forms as well as souls.

b 2 πολλῆς ποικιλίας. The gen. after γέμειν is a partitive gen. of the material or stock drawn upon. Cf. Verg., *Aen.* I 215, implentur veteris Bacchi pinguisque ferinae.

b 3 αὐτὸ πρὸς αὐτό, to be taken closely with ἀνομοιότητος and διαφορᾶς, 'disagreement with itself'. Plato has earlier given an acute analysis of the divided soul (IV 438 d ff., cf. 595 a 7 and note). He is now saying that this is perhaps not the true nature of the soul, and returning to the argument of the *Phaedo* (78 b–80 e), where he has put the case for the immortality of the soul on the grounds that it is not composite. There is an obvious contradiction here. Some have supposed that what Plato is saying is that the real essence of the soul is Reason, and Temper and Desire are incidental to the association of soul with body. On the other hand the *Phaedrus* (246 a ff.) asserts clearly that the soul in its ultimate nature is tripartite. Orthodox Christian readers ought not to boggle at a trinity within an essential unity! The truth is that Plato at this point is not clear in his own mind, and his words are cautious—εἴτε πολυειδὴς εἴτε μονοειδής (612 a 4). By the time he came to write the *Timaeus* he was prepared to assert that the intellect alone is immortal, and that there are temporal elements implanted in the soul (69 c). Thus we can trace the development of Plato's thinking, from the unity of the soul in the *Phaedo*, through the psychological analysis of the divided soul in *Rep.* IV, taken up in the *Phaedrus*, the problem posed by his uncertainty in *Rep.* **X**, and its resolution in the *Timaeus*. Those who forget that Plato's thought was living and developing land themselves in all sorts of difficulty.

b 6 μὴ τῇ καλλίστῃ κεχρημένον συνθέσει. He leaves the door open to the idea of a compound that is perfect and may be indestructible. This groping for the idea of what we would think of as chemical fusion is perhaps first found in Anaxagoras, who appears to say both that there are particles of everything in everything else and that you can never get at them however small you cut.

ὡς . . . ἡ ψυχή, with ἀΐδιον εἶναι not κεχρημένον.

b 9 καὶ οἱ ἄλλοι. One of the small pegs on which the dating of the dialogues hangs. The reference must be to the *Meno* and *Phaedo*. These therefore precede the *Republic*. The main evidence is provided by considerations of style. See Introduction.

c 4 εὑρήσει. sc. τις.

c 5 δικαιοσύνας τε καὶ ἀδικίας, 'different examples of justice and injustice'.

διόψεται, almost literally 'he will see through them', i.e. to the Form which they imperfectly exemplify.

d 1 τὸν θαλάττιον Γλαῦκον. A fisherman of Anthedon in Boeotia who ate some of the sacred grass which Cronus had sown, or (so the scholiast) bathed in a sacred spring, and became immortal. At some point, and for no very clear reason, he jumped into the sea and became a sea-god. He was specially worshipped by fishermen and sailors, and was noted for his oracles and his love-affairs. Various suggestions have been made as to his origin, from a Samothracian mystery to a personification of Cretan sea-power. He becomes assimilated to the more famous sea-god Proteus. Philostratus (*Imag.* ii 15) describes a representation of him—a man, with hair and beard dripping with water, bristly eye-brows, breast covered with sea-weed, and his lower limbs ending in the tail of a fish. The most familiar form of the legend is in Ovid, *Met.* XIII 904 ff. Lionel Johnson uses him as a symbol

> Ah, Glaucus, soul of man!
> Encrusted by each tide
> That since the seas began
> Hath surged against the side.

There is a striking Italian play *Glauco* by Ercole Luigi Morselli. The name is here chosen because of its resemblances to Glaucon. 'Glaucon, you don't want to be like Glaucus.'

d 2 Complex. ὑπό is followed by a series of infinitives. Of these the first subject is τὰ παλαιὰ μέρη, again subdivided, with the infinitives (a) ἐκκεκλάσθαι (b) συντετρῖφθαι καὶ λελωβῆσθαι. The second subject is ἄλλα picked up by the nouns in apposition, and the infinitive with it προσπεφυκέναι. τε in τά τε παλαιά is picked up in ἄλλα δέ; this is not uncommon in Plato.

e 1 εἰς τὴν φιλοσοφίαν αὐτῆς. Plato is feeling his way towards the view of the soul as intellect. φιλοσοφία must be taken literally. The sentence which follows, though complex, is not difficult, and care will work it out. ἐννοεῖν is followed by (a) ὧν ἅπτεται καὶ οἵων ἐφίετα ὁμιλιῶν (b) οἵα ἂν γένοιτο. The structure of the rest is based on participles referring to the soul.

ὧν ... οἶων, partitive gens. as usual with verbs of grasping or aiming.

περικρουσθεῖσα πέτρας τε καὶ ὄστρεα. The acc. (the normal direct obj. of the active) is retained with the passive. So VII 519 a (in a similar context) περιεκόπη τὰς τῆς γενέσεως συγγενεῖς ὥσπερ μολυβδίδας. Verg., Ecl. III 106, flores inscripti nomina regum. Cf. our 'He was given a book.' The real irregularity is not in the retained accusative, but in making the intransitive object the subject of the passive verb

612 a 1 In the *Phaedo* 81c Plato has described how the soul can become weighed down with corporeality, ἐμβριθὲς δέ γε, ὦ φίλε, τοῦτο οἴεσθαι χρὴ εἶναι καὶ βαρὺ καὶ γεῶδες καὶ ὁρατόν. In *Rep*. VII 519 a (just after the simile of the Cave) he describes physical pleasures as leaden weights hanging round the soul's neck so that it cannot look up. So Milton in *Comus*:

> When lust . . .
> Lets in defilement to the inward parts,
> The soul grows clotted with contagion,
> Imbodies and imbrutes, till she quite lose
> The divine property of her first being.

a 4 εἴτε ὅπῃ ἔχει. Rather as we say 'whether it is complex or simple or what'.

a 8 ἀπελυσάμεθα. ἀπολύεσθαι in the middle means 'to free oneself from' false charges, 'to refute them'. 'Have we succeeded in (a) refuting the other charges brought against justice (b) in particular in praising justice in itself rather than its fruits?' Cornford's rendering is impossible.

b 2 ὥσπερ Ἡσίοδόν τε καὶ Ὅμηρον ὑμεῖς ἔφατε. The plural refers to Glaucon and Adimantus. The reference is in fact to Adimantus' opening speech (II 363 a–d). Both challenged Socrates to praise justice irrespective of its consequences.

αὐτὸ δικαιοσύνην. Cf. II 363 a 1 and often, 'justice as a thing in itself'. So *Prot*. 361 a with the article αὐτὸ ἡ ἀρετή. The Christian Platonists make a single term of it, ἡ αὐτοδικαιοσύνη.

ἄριστον, 'to be the best thing'.

b 4 Γύγου. A historical figure, king of Lydia, c. 685–657, who assassinated his predecessor Candaules and married his widow.

The story is told in Hdt. I 8–12, and is the theme of a tragedy, unknown till recently; the discovery of a fragment of it has caused something of a storm in the classical tea-cup. Later legend told how he achieved power by using a magic ring which conferred invisibility (*Rep.* II 359 c ff., cf. Cic., *De Off.* III 9). Glaucon has argued that equipped with such a ring, and certain to evade detection, the so-called just man would behave as badly as anyone else. H. G. Wells's story *The Invisible Man* is a modern commentary on the same theme.

b 5 τὴν Ἄιδος κυνῆν. Hades, Poseidon and Zeus were the three male children of Cronos and Rhea. They battled with their father, and to strengthen them in the battle were given by the Cyclopes (the one-eyed smiths) respectively a helmet of invisibility, a trident, and a thunderbolt. Unseen through the helmet Hades stole Cronus' weapons, Poseidon threatened him with the trident to divert his attention, and Zeus struck him down with the thunderbolt. Then the brothers cast lots to decide their realms, and Zeus received the sky, Poseidon the sea, and Hades the underworld. 'ΑϜίδης means originally 'invisible'. For references to the helmet, see Hom., *Il.* V 845; Hes., *Scut. Her.* 227; Ar., *Ach.* 390. Such caps of darkness are commonplaces of the fairy story and folk tale.

b 8 πρὸς ἐκείνοις, 'in addition'. ἐκείνοις is used loosely in general references to the ideas of his previous sentence.

d 3 ἐπειδὴ τοίνυν κ.τ.λ. The text is uncertain; but the general meaning clear. In Book II Glaucon and Adimantus suggested that people are only good because 'honesty is the best policy'. The maxim may be true, but the man who lives by it is not truly honest. But why should we be honest if honesty is not the best policy? This is the question Socrates has been trying to answer.

d 4 δόξης, called by the older grammarians 'genitivus modi', regular with ἔχειν + adv. Cf. Hdt. V 20, καλῶς ἔχειν τῆς μέθης, 'to be pretty well drunk'. The field within which the state occurs.

d 5 καὶ ἡμᾶς, 'we too', like all the others who judge by consequences. Cornford's 'you' is based on no authority.

d 6 τοῦ δοκεῖν . . . τοῦ εἶναι, both used absolutely, 'from the appearance of living uprightly', 'from the actuality'.

e 6 κατ' ἀρχάς, in the discussion with Thrasymachus I 352 b 1.

613 a 2 ἐκ προτέρας ἁμαρτίας ὑπῆρχεν, i.e. in the former life: the phrase prepares the way for the myth. Hence the imperfect 'was his from birth'.

a 7 ἢ καί, 'or at any rate'.

b 1 ὁμοιοῦσθαι θεῷ. This whole conception of the ὁμοίωσις τῆς ψυχῆς τῷ θεῷ is of great importance in religious mysticism, and is found in the Hermetic writings, among the neo-Platonists, and in Greek Christianity. Athanasius (*De Inc. Verb.* 54 and elsewhere) can even write αὐτὸς γὰρ ἐνηνθρώπησεν, ἵνα ἡμεῖς θεοποιηθῶμεν. Similar expressions are found in Gregory of Nyssa, Basil, and Cyril, and (modified to meet Latin prejudices) in Tertullian and Cyprian. It perhaps springs from the dominant Greek doctrine of perception, that like knows like, used by Plato in the *Phaedo* as an argument for the immortality of the soul, which knows the immortal and immutable Forms. So the Hermetists (*Corp. Herm.* XI 20), 'Unless you make yourself equal to God, you cannot apprehend God, for like is known by like'. εἰς ὅσον δυνατὸν ἀνθρώπῳ qualifies the idea for Plato.

b 9 So the Quakers prospered when they set new standards of integrity in trade and business, e.g. in introducing fixed and marked prices. Their immediate losses were offset by the fact that they won the public confidence. But their motive was the integrity not the prosperity. Plato is right in first 'praising justice for its own sake' and only then proceeding to speak of its consequences.

b 11 οἱ δρομῆς κ.τ.λ. The race was the δίαυλος, to the end of the course and back, and the runners were evidently spoken of as running 'up' and then 'down' again, though this is not elsewhere mentioned, and the course was in fact flat. Such phrases are common. Those of us who live in the suburbs go 'up' to London, however elevated our residence, and an undergraduate who lives in the Scottish highlands still goes 'up' to Cambridge. The immoralists may have their flashy successes, but they cannot stay the course.

c 1 τὰ ὦτα ἐπὶ τῶν ὤμων ἔχοντες. Gray (quoted by Adam) calls this 'a metaphor taken from horses and other animals, which let their ears drop when they are tired and overdriven'. But surely it is an admirable direct description of the lolling head of the beaten runner.

c 2 ἀποτρέχοντες. However tired they are, they get away in a hurry to avoid the ridicule.

c 3 τὰ ἆθλα. At Olympia there were no prizes except the wreath—officially—but the cities rewarded victors generously and Solon had to regulate such expenditure at Athens. In *Il.* xxiii Achilles offers various prizes for Patroclus' funeral games. In the wrestling the winner is to receive a three-legged cauldron, worth twelve oxen, and the runner-up a woman trained in domestic work, worth four oxen.

c 8 ἔλεγες, II 362 b.

d 3 ὁπόθεν, 'someone from whatever family'. The implication is that the family is more important than the person.

d 8 γέροντες. As Macbeth (a good example of the character Plato had in mind) saw:

> And that which should accompany old age,
> As honour, love, obedience, troops of friends,
> I must not look to have, but in their stead
> Curses, not loud but deep.

e 1 ἄγροικα ἔφησθα, II 361 e. The word ἀγροικοτέρως is there used. These are not talked about in polite society.

e 2 εἶτα . . . ἐκκαυθήσονται. Some editors bracket these words, but they are in all manuscripts. We find it difficult to imagine branding, or gouging of eyes with a hot iron (so II 361 e which is here in reference) being thus casually referred to, but at *Gorg.* 473 c it is clearly the sort of fate an unsuccessful revolutionary might expect. Barbarism was not far away from Greek civilization, and a generation which has known Buchenwald and Hiroshima is in no state to throw stones.

e 3 καὶ ἐμοῦ, 'imagine that you have in fact heard from my lips of their suffering all these'.

614 a 2 οἷς for ἅ by easy attraction. Cf. Thuc. vii 21, ἀπὸ τῶν πόλεων ὧν ἔπεισε.

a 5 ταῦτα, subject, with οὐδέν predicate.

b 2 For Plato's use of myth in general, and this myth in particular, see Appendix 4. Ἀλκίνου γε ἀπόλογον, proverbial for a long story. Cf. Arist., *Rhet.* III 16, 1417 a 13; *Poet.* 16, 1455 a 2; Ael., *V.H.* xiii 14; Suidas, s.v. ἀπόλογος Ἀλκίνου. This is the story which Odysseus told to Alcinous, king of Phaeacia—the genitive is objective, not subjective—which occupies four books of the *Odyssey* (ix–xii) and includes Odysseus' visit to Hades, a further reason for its reference here.

'Αλκίνου . . . ἀλκίμου. Plato loves such play on names and other words. Cf. *Apol.* 25 c, Μέλητος and ἀμέλεια; *Symp.* 174 b, 'Αγάθων and ἀγαθῶν; *ib.* 185 c, Παυσανίου δὲ παυσαμένου. See also Denniston, *Greek Prose Style*, pp. 136-8.

b 3 ἀλλὰ . . . μέν. The μέν is never taken up. Cf. Ar., *Ach.* 428. μέν is originally the same as μήν, and ἀλλὰ . . . μέν may mean 'all the same'.

'Ηρὸς τοῦ 'Αρμενίου, τὸ γένος Παμφύλου. Suidas makes Er a Hebrew name, and indeed it appears among Joseph's ancestors (Lk. 3, 28). Some writers, including Clement of Alexandria, identified Er with Zoroaster. The pattern of thought is not typically Hebrew or Zoroastrian. Platt (*C.R.* 1911, 13-14) ingeniously identifies Er with Ara son of Aram, an Armenian, who is said in Moses of Chorene's *Armenian History* I 14, 15, to have been killed in battle and brought to life again. Pamphylia is part of the southern coast-line of Asia Minor, scene of Cimon's victory over Persia at the battle of the Eurymedon (*c.* 467). It was colonized by the Greeks in early days, but remained under Persian rule until Alexander. The name means 'every tribe', and if Platt is right, this is a typical Platonic pun, as he calls Diotima the μάντις a Mantinean. Armenius (not Harmonius, as Plutarch and Thomas Gray thought) may represent a derivation from Aram or from Armenia.

b 5 τῶν νεκρῶν ἤδη διεφθαρμένων. Cf. Martha at the raising of Lazarus in Jn. 2, 39, 'Lord, by this time he stinketh: for he hath been dead four days'. But Lazarus did not record his experiences.

b 7 ἐκεῖ of the after-life, ἐνθάδε of life on earth. Cf. 619 d 8. So οἱ ἐκεῖ is a euphemism for the dead. This represents normal Greek practice. It is delightfully inverted in Aristophanes' *Frogs* where the scene is set in Hades.

b 8 ἐπειδὴ οὗ ἐκβῆναι. οὗ gen. of the reflexive ἔ, not common in Attic. The inf. is found in subordinate clauses in o.o. by an easy attraction. Cf. 620 d 6.

c 1 ἀφικνεῖσθαι. In *Phaedo* 107 d, 113 d guided by its attendant spirit.

τόπον τινὰ δαιμόνιον. See 614 e 2 note.

c 2 δύ' εἶναι χάσματα . . . καὶ . . . ἄλλα καταντικρύ. These are quite separate from the roads to and from the earth. These communicate with the places of punishment and reward respectively. In relation to each there is a 'dual carriageway'; hence the four apertures, all for 'one-way traffic', two marked 'no entry: exit only'. The soul in fact journeys up to the right, or down to the left. Here the decision is imposed on the soul by judges. Its symbolism is, however, important. Hesiod, *Works and Days* 287, first speaks of the two roads of life. Pindar's 'way of Zeus' which the righteous follow (*Ol.* II 70) implies that they eschew other roads. Prodicus' fable of the Choice of Heracles (Xen. *Mem.* II i 21) represented him standing at a fork in the road. Sophocles in his greatest play makes splendid symbolical use of the fact that Oedipus stood at the parting of the ways when he killed his father. To the Pythagoreans this symbolism was especially significant. For them right and good fell under one head, left and evil under another, and they used the letter Υ to represent the choice. It is found on a remarkable relief from Philadelphia where the choice between Virtue and Vice is graphically represented on the tomb of a man who has chosen well. The Orphic gold plates which give instructions to the soul enjoin it to take the right fork. Vergil uses the same imagery for Aeneas' descent to the lower regions (*Aen.* VI 540), 'Hic locus est partes ubi se via findit in ambas.' [Seneca] ridicules it in his satire on Claudius when he says that the emperors go to heaven by the Appian Way. We may remember too that Hecate, the goddess of the Underworld, was worshipped at cross-roads, which all the world over seem associated with departed spirits. The Christians took up the same theme. Jeremiah 21, 8 had contrasted the way of life and the way of death, and Jesus picked up his words in the famous passage in the Sermon on the Mount (Mt. 7, 13) about the broad road which leads to destruction and the narrow road which leads to life. Christianity was early called 'The Way' and 'The Two Ways' is among the oldest Christian documents. Lactantius, *Inst.* VI 3 likens these two roads to the Pythagorean Υ. Plato maintains the imagery in his myths with some consistency; no doubt it derives from the Pythagoreans.

ἐχομένω ἀλλήλοιν, 'adjoining one another'.

c 3 δικαστάς. In *Gorg.* 523 e these are Minos, Rhadamanthys, and Aeacus.

c 4 Cf. Mt. 25, 31 ff. '. . . And he shall set the sheep on his right hand and the goats on his left. . . . And these shall go into everlasting punishment, but the righteous into life eternal.'

c 6 σημεῖα περιάψαντας, rather as customs officers mark one's baggage. Indeed in later accounts of the ascent of the soul the soul has to pass officials called τελῶναι.

d 2 ἄγγελον. Dives asks for such a messenger in Jesus' parable (Lk. 16, 27–31). διακελεύοιντο, still after ὅτι. They used the actual words 'we command'. οἱ dat. of ἕ.

d 5 δικασθείη, impersonal passive, 'judgement was passed'. So Thuc. I 28, ὁποτέρων ἂν δικασθῇ εἶναι τὴν ἀποικίαν.

d 6 ἐκ μὲν τοῦ, demonstrative, 'out of the one'.

ἐκ τῆς γῆς, 'out of the earth' (Cornford), not 'from earth' (Davies and Vaughan).

e 1 τὰς ἀεὶ ἀφικνουμένας, a common idiom 'each as it arrived', ἀεί meaning 'from time to time'.

e 2 ἀσμένας. O.C.T. ἀσμένας (as from ἁνδάνειν), but there is no justification for the rough breathing. The derivation is uncertain.

τὸν λειμῶνα. The image is Orphic or Pythagorean; that it is familiar is shown by the article. It probably derives from Homer's ἀσφόδελος λειμών, and can be glimpsed in Orphic fragments, in Empedocles and in Plutarch, as well as elsewhere in Plato's myths. In none of these is it a court of justice, but this is called the Plain of Truth in the pseudo-Platonic *Axiochus* 371 b. Adam is doubtless right in thinking that it lies on the surface of 'the True Earth' of the *Phaedo*; we live in misty hollows therein. Cf. also Lucian, *De Luctu* 9.

615 a 3 χιλιέτη. The magic of the number is still held in our 'millennium'. Verg., *Aen.* VI 748 has the same figure.

> has omnes ubi mille rotam volvere per annos
> Lethaeum ad fluvium deus evocat agmine magno.

It sounds as if it comes out of Pythagorean number-speculation. There is a slight discrepancy with *Phaedrus* 249a where 1,000 years is the span from birth to birth, not death to birth; he is speaking in round figures.

a 4 θέας, note the accent.

ἀμηχάνους τὸ κάλλος, acc. of respect. The accusative basically limits the action of verbs, and by an obvious extension may sometimes limit the scope of adjectives, often in Greek, poetically in Latin. So Tibullus I 6, 49, stat saucia pectus.

a 5 πολλοῦ χρόνου, sc. ἐστί. Cf. *Laws* IV 708d, χρόνου πολλοῦ καὶ παγχάλεπον, 'It is a matter of a long time', i.e. 'It would be a long business'.

a 6 ὅσα πώποτέ τινα ἠδίκησαν. Note the emphasis on not wronging others. The Socratic paradox, 'It is better to be wronged than to wrong another', is found also in Democritus 45.

a 8 δεκάκις ... ἑκατονταετηρίδα. The Pythagorean perfect number 10 (1 + 2 + 3 + 4), and its square and cube are at the root of this passage. A high proportion of number magic is associated with either 3 or 7 or 10. Plato has a more extended view of the duration of life than the Psalmist.

b 3 ἢ πόλεις προδόντες κ.τ.λ.

> One to destroy is murder by the law;
> And gibbets keep the lifted hand in awe,
> To murder thousands takes a specious name,
> War's glorious art, and gives immortal fame.
>   Young, *Love of Fame*

So in the famous story, the pirate told Alexander that they were in the same trade, but Alexander got away with it by practising it on a large enough scale. Plato does not go as far as this, but he is well aware of the personal responsibility of public men—a responsibility doubly important because they are so seldom confronted with the results. These specific references, not found elsewhere in the myths, are occasioned by the theme of the dialogue.

c 1 τῶν δὲ εὐθὺς γενομένων κ.τ.λ., lit. 'about the as-soon-as-they-were-borns and the short-lived'. Presumably the terms were familiar—the former being short for 'those who died as soon as they were born'. The implication is of some sort of doctrine of limbo, found among the Orphics, as also in Vergil, *Aen.* VI 426 and Dante, *Inferno* IV 30. Cf. Cumont, *After-Life in Roman Paganism* 128 ff.

c 2 εἰς δὲ θεούς κ.τ.λ., a clumsy sentence. The gens. depend on μισθούς which stands for both rewards and punishments. There are two categories (*a*) behaviour (good or bad) towards gods and parents (the Latin 'pietas') (*b*) murder. αὐτόχειρ φόνος means not suicide, but any killing done with your own hand. Cf. Soph., *Ant.* 1175–6 where the statement αὐτόχειρ αἱμάσσεται is met with the question 'By his own hand or his father's?'

c 6 Ἀρδιαῖος. Not otherwise known, and perhaps fictitious.

d 3 φάναι, pleonastic as often.

οὐδ' ἂν ἥξει. ἄν + fut. is sometimes used in Attic Greek, though editors tend to emend it when they find it. It is typical of Plato's semi-poetical style, and expresses a shade of meaning between the plain future and ἄν + opt.—more grandiose than the one, less remote than the other. Homer uses ἄν or κέν as freely with the fut. ind. as with the opt., e.g. *Il.* iv 176, καί κέ τις ὧδ' ἐρέει.

ἐθεασάμεθα γάρ κ.τ.λ. Cornford gets the emphasis well. 'This was one of the terrible sights we saw.'

d 7 τῶν μεγάλα ἡμαρτηκότων, partitive genitive.

e 2 ἐμυκᾶτο. Cf. Verg., *Georg.* IV 493, the 'fragor' which echoes round the lower world when Orpheus turns round too soon and loses Eurydice. Cf. also Milton, *P.L.* IX 782:

> Earth felt the wound and Nature from her seat
> Sighing through all her works gave signs of woe.

and *ib.* 1000:

> Earth trembled from her entrails as again
> In pangs and Nature gave a second groan.

Aristotle, *An. Post.* II 94 b 32, tells us that the Pythagoreans regarded thunder as a threat of terror to those in Tartarus.

e 4 διάπυροι ἰδεῖν. L. and S. quite wrongly ignore the epexegetic ἰδεῖν and cite this as metaphorical. It is of course literal.

616 a 1 χεῖράς τε καὶ πόδας καὶ κεφαλήν, acc. of respect—natural, since if the people were not named, this would be the normal object. κεφαλήν is difficult: presumably they were gagged.

a 2 ἐκτός with εἷλκον.

a 3 κνάμπτοντες, lit. 'carding wool' used of tortures on a similar basis.

τοῖς ἀεὶ παριοῦσι. Cf. 614 e 1 note.

ὧν ἕνεκά τε καὶ ὅτι. We more easily reverse them, 'the fact that . . . and the reason for it'.

a 7 σιγήσαντος, gen. abs.

b 1 For this difficult passage I follow Cornford and append his comment:

'A new feature, interpolated by Plato, is the vision of the structure of the universe, in which the "pattern set up in the heavens" (592 b) is revealed to the souls before they choose a new life. Plato's universe is spherical. At the circumference the fixed stars revolve in 24 hours from East to West, with a motion which carries with it all the contents of the world. Within the sphere are (1) the seven planets, including Sun and Moon, which all have also a contrary motion from West to East along the Zodiac. Their speeds differ. The Moon finishes its course in a month; the Sun, Venus, and Mercury in a year: while Mars, Jupiter, and Saturn have an additional motion ("counter revolution", 617 b) which slows them down so that Mars takes nearly 2 years, Jupiter about 12, and Saturn nearly 30. (2) The Earth at the centre rotates daily on its axis (which is also the axis of the universe) so as exactly to counteract the daily rotation in the opposite sense of the whole universe, with the result that the earth is at rest in absolute space, while the heavenly bodies revolve round it.

'What the souls actually see in their vision is not the universe itself, but a model, a primitive orrery in a form roughly resembling a spindle, with its shaft round which at the lower end is fastened a solid hemispherical whorl. In the orrery the shaft represents the axis of the universe and the whorl consists of 8 hollow concentric hemispheres, fitted into one another "like a nest of bowls", and capable of moving separately. It is as if the upper halves of 8 concentric spheres had been cut away so that the internal 'works' might be seen. The rims of the bowls appear as forming a continuous flat surface; they represent the equator of the sphere of fixed stars and, inside that, the orbits of the 7 planets.' See also his book, *Plato's Cosmology*. Cornford overstates his case when he says dogmatically that the souls are looking at a model. The spindle is after all attached to the actual heavens and part of the system of the universe. Equally plainly there is some confusion. Necessity cannot both be sitting upon the Earth, and bearing on her knees a system of which the Earth is a part. I fear that there is an irreconcilable contradiction, as Plato would have realized had he been practical enough to make a model of his whole description. For a noble attempt at a consistent explanation, see J. S. Morrison in *J.H.S.* LXXV (1955), p. 59 ff. (esp. pp. 66-8).

b 4 τεταρταίους. The Greeks often use an adj. where we prefer an adv.

ἄνωθεν with τεταμένον, despite *Phaedo* 100 b, where it is used of a bird's eye view.

b 5 It is not easy to see how something can be straight like a pillar and also like a rainbow, but the picture of the Milky Way may help. It is like a bow, and yet pillar-like in quality.

c 1 αὐτοῦ, probably the light (subjective gen.), possibly the heaven (objective gen.).

c 3 τὰ ὑποζώματά τῶν τριήρων. Ships were undergirded (cf. Acts 27, 17), sometimes permanently, sometimes temporarily. For the former there were ropes running horizontally round the outside of the ship, for the latter ropes were passed under the keel and ran in a vertical plane, presumably having ends bound together somewhere on deck. Even the horizontal ropes appear to have been joined inside to produce tension. (Ap. Rhod. I 367). Surely Plato takes his picture from this: light encircles the universe, and the shaft through the middle binds the ends firm: indeed in the middle of the column of light you can trace the two ends of the chain which holds the world together· This bond around the outside is visible through the crystalline sphere as the Milky Way.

c 4 'Ανάγκης ἄτρακτον. The spindle appears to lie in the middle of the shaft of light, with one end of the binding chain attached to its top and the other to its foot. But the two parts of the picture are difficult to reconcile, and the spindle is before long seen on the knees of Necessity.

The undergirding and the spindle are examples of the way the Greeks used verbal illustrations where we should more easily use diagrams. So the kneading-trough of *Phaedo* 99 b or the fish-trap of *Timaeus* 78 b. The Ionian natural philosophers had used the same sort of illustration, and have won thereby from Marxist commentators a praise which they less freely accord to Plato. For the shape of a Greek spindle, see diagram.

Necessity has taken the spindle of Moira. Professor George Thomson sees here a reflection of social changes, believing that the concept of Moira (a share) arises out of primitive communism, that of Necessity (compulsion) out of a slave society. If so,—and our expressions are affected by our environment—the change is unconscious not deliberate.

Empedocles personifies Necessity as lying at the root of his system. Parmenides' Way of Seeming also has a central Necessity, though this is not to be taken as representative of Parmenides' thought. No

FIG. 2 (616 c 4).—A GREEK SPINDLE

The spindle would hang freely. The wool, drawn from the distaff, passed under the hook (to keep the spindle upright) and was wound round the shaft. The whorl helped rotation.

doubt all three derive from the Pythagoreans. In *Laws* VII 81-8 b 2 Plato asserts the subordination of God to necessity. Necessity comes in Greek speculation to stand for those parts of life where free will does not operate. Sometimes this field is further analysed—Gorgias distinguished between the purposes of the gods, of Chance, and of Necessity. Later Chance becomes herself a goddess, or alternatively almost equated with Necessity.

d 2 ἔλεγεν, i.e. Er.

d 4 διαμπερές. It is difficult to know whether to take this with ἐγκέοιτο (Shorey) or ἐξεγλυμμένῳ (Cornford), but comparison with **e** 3 below suggests the former, though the sense is a little harder.

e 1 κύκλους κ.τ.λ., 'showing their lips on the surface as circles, and

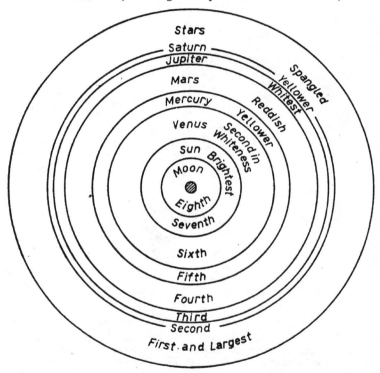

FIG. 3 (616 e 3).—THE WHORL

producing a continuous plane of a single whorl surrounding the shaft'. Davies and Vaughan mistranslate.

e 3 See diagram. Cornford's rendering, by naming the circles, clarifies the text considerably. The names are taken from *Epinomis*, possibly a late work of Plato, more probably written by one of his immediate disciples. According to *Epinomis* the association of the planetary spheres with gods was borrowed from the Syrians: no doubt it emanated from Babylon. The breadth of the rims represents the distances of each orbit from its neighbour.

'The circle forming the rim of the first and outermost whorl (Fixed Stars) is the broadest, next in breadth is the sixth (Venus); then the fourth (Mars); then the eighth (Moon); then the seventh (Sun); then the fifth (Mercury); then the third (Jupiter); and the second (Saturn) is narrowest of all. The rim of the largest whorl (Fixed Stars) was spangled, the seventh (Sun) brightest; the eighth (Moon) coloured by the reflected light of the seventh; the second and fifth (Saturn, Mercury) like each other and yellower; the third (Jupiter) whitest; the fourth (Mars) somewhat ruddy; the sixth (Venus) second in whiteness. The Spindle revolved as a whole with one motion; but, within the whole as it turned, the seven inner circles revolved slowly in the opposite direction; and of these the eighth (Moon) moved most swiftly; second in speed and all moving together, the seventh, sixth, and fifth (Sun, Venus, Mercury); next in speed moved the fourth (Mars) with what appeared to them to be a counter-revolution; next the third (Jupiter), and slowest of all the second (Saturn).'

617 a 1 ἀπὸ τοῦ ἑβδόμου . . . προσλάμποντος. That the Moon shines with reflected light was known to Anaximenes in the sixth century.

a 3 ξανθότερα. To Plato yellow was a mixture of white and red (*Tim.* 68 b). Saturn and Mercury were sometimes called Φαίνων and Στίλβων because of their colour. The colours are based on observation. The reddish colour of Mars, and the pallor of Venus and Jupiter are well known.

a 5 τὴν αὐτὴν φοράν adverbial accusative with κυκλεῖσθαι στρεφόμενον, clearly limiting the action of the verb. φοράν Cornford 'motion'. Better 'in the same direction'. Cf. τὴν ἐναντίαν, below. φορά is a sense of movement from one place to another. At b 2 it is properly translated 'speed'.

a 8 ἅμα ἀλλήλοις. The Sun, Venus, and Mercury all complete their circuit in a year. They are not moving at the same speed, because their orbits are of different lengths, but their rates of revolution are the same.

b 2 ἐπανακυκλούμενον. The spindle is rotating in one direction.

The seven inner spheres have a rotatory movement in the other direction. This appears to mean that the Moon, the Sun, Venus, and Mercury are all moving faster than the spindle, but Mars, and presumably Jupiter and Saturn, are moving slower, and therefore are being carried in fact back again with the motion of the spindle. This is not apparent in the sky, because in relation to the fixed stars they still move 'forwards' not 'backwards'.

b 4 Necessity sits at the centre of the universe.

b 5 The name of Siren has taken on a more sinister sound in the twentieth century. In Greek legend they were in fact rapacious monsters, bird-women, who lured sailors to their doom by their singing; cf. the German Lorelei. They are probably pre-Olympian spirits of death; cf. the Welsh Birds of Rhiannon. By Hellenistic times they are virtually goddesses of music, and Apollonius of Rhodes IV 896 makes them daughters of a Muse.

b 7 μίαν ἁρμονίαν συμφωνεῖν. συμφωνία is our 'harmony' (the concord of two or more notes). ἁρμονία is a scale or mode. This is the celebrated music of the spheres. Cf. Shakespeare's *Merchant of Venice* V 1:

> There's not the smallest orb which thou behold'st
> But in his motion like an angel sings.

Milton, *Arcades* 63:

> the celestial Sirens' harmony
> That sit upon the nine infolded spheres.

(Plato has eight spheres only.) So *On the Morning of Christ's Nativity*, the stanza beginning 'Ring out, ye crystal spheres'. So too Thoreau, *Inspiration*:

> She with one breath attunes the spheres
> And also my poor human heart.

The phrase 'the music of the spheres' is found in Pope, *Essay on Man* I 202. Addison's familiar hymn, 'The spacious firmament on high', provides a magnificent rationalization of the concept; the universe cries to Reason's ear 'The hand that made us is divine.'

The Pythagoreans, whose system linked mathematics, music, mysticism, and morals, supposed that each of the planets as it moved issued a note, the whole producing the Heptachord. Later the circle of the fixed stars was also given a note, making a complete scale. Why do we not perceive the sound? Because it is with us from birth and has no contrasting silence to show it up. If you live with a pneumatic drill outside your window you soon cease to become conscious of it, until it stops. See Arist., *De Caelo* II 9. So Cowper:

> He who sits from day to day
>> Where the prison'd lark is hung,
> Heedless of his loudest lay,
>> Hardly knows that he has sung.

> Where the watchman in his round
>> Nightly lifts his voice on high,
> None, accustomed to the sound,
>> Wakes the sooner for his cry.

c 2 *Μοίρας.* μοῖρα (cf. μέρος) is originally a man's portion or destiny. Hence in the *Iliad* associated particularly with death. In Homer μοῖρα sometimes derives from the gods, but sometimes they seem to have their own destiny. She is sometimes, and easily, personified, but only once appears in the plural (*Il.* xxiv 49). The idea of the thread of life passes simply from a figure of speech into a divine construction, and the three aspects of a man's destiny, his birth, life, and death, lead to a tripling of the divine power behind. Hence emerge Lachesis (She who allots), Clotho (the Spinner) and Atropos (the Inflexible); their names are first given by Hesiod (*Theog.* 218, 905). They appear first as daughters of Night (*ib.* 217), later of Zeus and Themis (*ib.* 904). Here they are daughters of Necessity. The symbolism of each genealogy is clear. The Fates are finely depicted in Michelangelo's celebrated painting.

λευχειμονούσας, an Orphic detail.

c 7 διαλείπουσαν χρόνον, 'leaving a period in between', in which Lachesis takes over, as explained below. The first two sisters each simultaneously spin one part of the system. They then stand back, and Lachesis in her turn helps to keep both moving.

d 2 προφήτην, 'interpreter'. The prophet, whether in Greek or Hebrew, is not one who foretells the future, but one who proclaims the will of God.

d 7 ἐφήμεροι, cf. Ps. xc 4: 'A thousand years in thy sight are but as yesterday when it is past, and as a watch in the night.' Compared with the great Immortals we are but creatures of a day.

θνητοῦ γένους depends on ἄλλης περιόδου . . . θανατηγόρου.

e 1 δαίμων. In Homer synonymous with θεός; in Hesiod first appearing as a spiritual power intermediate between God and man, and throughout the story of Greek religion retaining this important function. Here an attendant spirit, rather as the Persian 'fravashi' or Roman 'genius'. The idea that the attendant spirit has a soul assigned to it is also found in the *Phaedo* myth 107 d. Cf. also Lys. II 78, ὁ δαίμων ὁ τὴν ἡμετέραν μοῖραν εἰληχώς.

Men. fr. 550:

> ἅπαντι δαίμων ἀνδρὶ συμπαρίσταται.
> εὐθὺς γενομένῳ μυσταγωγὸς τοῦ βίου
> ἀγαθός.

Theocr. IV 40:

> αἰαῖ τῷ σκληρῷ μάλα δαίμονος, ὅς με λελόγχει.

Later, by a curious reversion, the divine guide is once again endowed with full godhead in the person of Hermes, the leader of souls, who is prominent in the gnostic and Hermetic literature. Plato perhaps took the term from Empedocles, but he completely transformed it, and in *Timaeus* 90 a–c the δαίμων appears as pure reason. Its resemblance with the Freudian super-ego has often been pointed out. This is still more marked in its later development at the hands of the Stoics where it clearly represents 'the ideal, as contrasted with the empirical, personality' (Bonhöffer, *Epiktet* 84).

e 2 ἐξ ἀνάγκης. The choice is free but irrevocable. This is Plato's masterly reconciliation of free-will and determinism. Once the choice is made the destiny is fixed. But choice lies at the root of life; there Plato is at one with the Existentialists. Maurice Hare wrote a well-known limerick on Predestination:

> There was a young man who said 'Damn!
> It appears to me now that I am
> Just a being that moves
> In predestinate grooves—
> Not a bus, not a bus, but a tram.'

'True', replies Plato, 'but you choose your route.'

e 3 ἀρετὴ δὲ ἀδέσποτον. Cf. Milton, *Comus* 1018:

> Mortals that would follow me,
> Love Virtue, she alone is free.

For the neuter, cf. ἄριστον at 612 b 2, and often.

e 4   αἰτία ἑλομένου · θεὸς ἀναίτιος. These magnificent words with their concision and chiasmus of thought form the real climax to the *Republic*. So the climactic phrase in the *Phaedo* (114 c) is καλὸν γὰρ τὸ ἆθλον καὶ ἡ ἐλπὶς μεγάλη. Because Plato does not habitually use chiasmus, the device is more effective when it does occur. The words are frequently quoted later, and appear on a first-century bust of Plato found at Tibur.

e 6   τοὺς κλήρους is object of ῥίψοι and not connected with ἐπὶ πάντας.

e 8   ἐᾶν, the subject is τὸν προφήτην.

618 a 2   θεῖναι. The subject is still τὸν προφήτην.

πολὺ πλείω so that the last in the lot has a fair choice. But the lot helps to account for some of the inequalities of this life.

a 3   ζῴων. So Empedocles declares that he has been before his present existence a boy, a girl, a bush, a bird, and a voiceless fish in salty flood. For similar views in Pythagoras, see 600 b 2 note. So too Don Marquis's delightful cat Mehitabel recounts her experiences in human incarnations. In the *Phaedrus* 249 b only a soul which has seen the truth is permitted to take human form. This is another aspect of Platonic philosophy which must derive ultimately from India. The Neo-Platonists were much exercised to know how far these theories of transmigration were to be taken seriously. Plotinus interpreted them literally. Proclus, Syrianus, and Olympiodorus thought that they were to be taken literally in part only; they believed that the corrupt soul would company with wild beasts. Iamblichus and Porphyry sought an allegorical interpretation; and Augustine commends Porphyry for preferring truth to Plato (*De C.D.* X 30).

a 5   διατελεῖς, a very rare word, 'lasting'.

a 8   ἐπὶ εἴδεσιν, 'for what they looked like'—not here used technically.

b 2   ψυχῆς δὲ τάξιν κ.τ.λ., 'the lives contained no pre-ordained pattern of character, seeing that character must change through the choice of one life rather than another'. The thought is not wholly clear. What Plato is saying is that the act of choice, not the life chosen, determines the character; therefore the character cannot simply 'go with' the life. Beyond this he does not explicitly put, but might well sympathize with, the view held later by the Stoics, that though the external events of our lives are determined the spirit in which we accept them is not. Indeed this is almost implied by συντόνως ζῶντι (619 b 4). Only to the Stoics our destiny is given us by God, to Plato we bring it on ourselves.

b 4 τὰ δ' ἄλλα, i.e. everything except character. δ', 'but'; we might expect an anticipatory μέν, but the style is conversational.

b 6 μεσοῦν, pres. inf.

c 3 τίς αὐτὸν ποιήσει δυνατὸν καὶ ἐπιστήμονα κ.τ.λ. Socrates' criticism of the people of Athens is that they do not bother about the right things. Cf. Jesus, 'Seek ye first the Kingdom of God and His righteousness and all these things shall be added unto you' (Mt. 6, 33). Socrates' criticism of the sophists is that they profess to teach the right way of life, but do not themselves know what it is. They teach men how to 'get on' in this life. This passage argues that there is something far more important than that. The *Apology* as a whole forms an admirable commentary on this text. In fact the passage is self-contradictory, for if the destiny is determined with the choice of life we are not free to decide what master we shall attend or what lessons we shall learn. This is the weakness of determinism as a philosophy. If it is true, the man who holds it holds it not because it is true but because it is determined that he shall. The determinist who argues his case (except that, poor fellow, he cannot help it) is like Bertrand Russell's friend who declared that she was a solipsist and could not understand why there were not more solipsists.

c 5 ἐκ τῶν δυνατῶν. This is realism. Progress in the spiritual life is slow; we learn gradually, and take one step at a time; our effective choice is limited.

c 7 πρὸς ἀρετὴν βίου πῶς ἔχει, 'what relation they bear to . . .' In English we say 'the relationship of . . . to . . .'

c 8 τί κάλλος κ.τ.λ. There are two questions, each twofold: 'What power has beauty in combination with wealth or poverty?' 'What character goes with beauty to enable it to produce good or evil results?'

d 6 αἱρεῖσθαι for διαιρεῖσθαι, with τόν τε χείρω καὶ τὸν ἀμείνω βίον as obj.

619 a 4 ἔτι δὲ αὐτὸς μείζω πάθῃ. This is the 'thrice ancient law' of the *Phaedo*: 'What you have done you must suffer'. Cf. 615 a.

a 5 τὸν μέσον . . . βίον. This exemplifies the Delphic precept μηδὲν ἄγαν. As a philosophy of life it is represented for us by Horace's 'golden mean' ('auream mediocritatem') and the advice given to Phaethon in Ovid 'medio tutissimus ibis'. In Plato's disciple Aristotle it became a principle of ethical analysis. It is found in Phocylides, Theognis, Pythagoras, Heraclitus, Aeschylus, Sophocles, Euripides, Isocrates, and often elsewhere in Greek literature, and is paralleled in the philosophy of Confucius, whose grandson K'ung Chi wrote *The Doctrine of the Mean* in the fifth century B.C., and more recently in Herbert Spencer, Mannheim, and Jung.

b 3 ξὺν νῷ ἑλομένῳ, 'if he makes a prudent choice'. The asyndeton in this sentence is noteworthy.

b 4 συντόνως, 'earnestly', 'straining every nerve'.

b 7 εἰπόντος, gen. abs.

c 1 εἱμαρμένην, sc. μοῖραν. βρώσεις καὶ ἄλλα κακά are in apposition.

c 7 ἔθει ἄνευ φιλοσοφίας. In *Phaedo* 82 a there is similar reference to those who practise the civilized and social virtues, but from right habits, not from rational intellectual conviction. There it is said that some of them may be reincarnated as humans, the rest become socially organized insects such as bees, wasps, or ants. It is interesting to note that here they are admitted to Plato's heaven, although they lack a truly philosophical virtue. It is also sobering to reflect how much of one's own socially commendable behaviour emerges from habit and environment rather than from the deep springs of personality.

d 1 ὡς δὲ καὶ εἰπεῖν, 'so to say'. We use almost the same idiom. Hence with numbers often 'about'.

d 3 ἅτε πόνων ἀγυμνάστους . . . ἅτε αὐτοὺς . . . πεπονηκότας. There is much wisdom here.

d 5 ἐξ ἐπιδρομῆς, 'in a rush'.

d 8 ἐνθάδε. Cf. 614 b 7 note.

620 a 1 ἰδεῖν, epexegetic.

a 3 τὰ πολλά, almost adverbial, 'for the most part they choose'.

a 4 Ὀρφέως. The legendary musician who was torn to pieces by the Maenads, women-worshippers of Dionysus, for his failure to honour the god. The Orphic ritual was involved with the cult of

Dionysus, and Proclus has an unusually intelligent comment: 'Orpheus, because he was the principal in the Dionysiac rites, is said to have suffered the same fate as the god' (*Comm. in Remp.* 398). Graves (*Greek Myths* 28.1) compares him with the Welsh tree-god Bran. The story of Eurydice, immortalized by Vergil at the end of the *Georgics*, is a late addition. Plato's explicit references to Orpheus and the mysteries associated with him seem curiously detached from the undoubted influence their content exercised upon his thought.

a 6 Θαμύρου. Thamyras or Thamyris was a singer who challenged the Muses, and was deprived of both his eyes and of his art. He was, like Orpheus, a pupil of the musician Linus. Milton takes him with Homer as the type of his own blindness. (*P.L.* III 35).   .

b 2 Αἴαντος. Ajax, son of Telamon, 'the bulwark of the Achaeans' in the *Iliad*, who stands for the power of brute strength, and can hold his own with Hector in battle, or with Odysseus in wrestling. The story here alluded to is the competition between Ajax and Odysseus for the arms of Achilles. Ajax lost, and this led to insanity and suicide. The story was told in the *Little Iliad*; it is referred to in *Od.* xi 543 where the soul of Ajax refuses to speak to Odysseus; it forms the theme of a surviving play by Sophocles.

b 4 Ἀγαμέμνονος, Commander of the Greeks at Troy, murdered on his return home by his wife Clytemnestra and her lover Aegisthus. Aeschylus' play recounts the story with terrifying dramatic atmosphere.

b 6 Ἀταλάντης. Atalanta was a huntress who tried to avoid marriage. She raced with her suitors, spearing them if she could catch up with them (a reminiscence of some religious rite). Milanion, however, won her hand by means of three golden apples given him by Aphrodite. As Atalanta caught up he would drop one of these, and use the delay while she picked it up to get clear again. Here she appears as the type of female athleticism. Plato has earlier pleaded for equal opportunities for men and women in physical education; he has a final thrust at masculine exclusiveness.

c 1 Ἐπειοῦ. Epeius, a coward in battle, though not in the boxing-ring, devised the Wooden Horse by which Troy was captured. The exclusiveness (as often) worked both ways, and there cannot have been many openings for the free-born Greek man with leanings towards craftsmanship without degrading himself in the eyes of his fellow-citizens. But a woman might easily be an expert in some craft.

c 3 Θερσίτου. Thersites appears in Homer as a critic of the High Command, an ugly foul-mouthed fellow, who is beaten into silence by Odysseus. There he is, it' seems, not Achaean by blood. Later stories of his death at the hands of Achilles imply high birth: this scene is vividly portrayed on a vase in Boston.

c 4 'Οδυσσέως. Odysseus is the cunning schemer of the Greeks before Troy; the *Odyssey* tells the story of his trials and wanderings on his return journey. There is no agreement about the origin of these. Probably they contain some historical fact, a deal of folk-lore, an element of allegory, and some reminiscences of religious conflict and practice. See W. B. Stanford, *The Ulysses Theme*. But, treating the myth on its merits, one can well believe that he would feel 'anything for a quiet life'.

d 5 πάσας μείξεις μείγνυσθαι, an excellent example of the true cognate accusative.

d 6 The symbolism of this passage needs no explanation.

ἡρῆσθαι. For the infinitive in a subordinate clause in o.o., cf. 614 b 8 note.

d 8 δαίμονα. Cf. 617 e 1 note.

e 1 ὅν, subject of ἄγειν.

621 a 2 τῆς Λήθης. The spring of forgetfulness appears (though it is not actually named, it is contrasted with Memory) in the gold plates found buried in South Italy and giving directions to the soul how to proceed in the underworld according to the beliefs of the Orphic religion. Plato borrows it from there to create by a typical word-play a contrast to the plain of Truth πεδίον 'Αληθείας. Λήθης πεδίον appears in Ar., *Frogs* 186 as an idea likely to be familiar to his audience. It is difficult to hold together the passage through Forgetfulness with the moral implications of reincarnation. In Milton, as here and in Vergil, Lethe is a river:

> Lethe, the river of oblivion, rolls
> Her wat'ry labyrinth, whereof who drinks
> Forthwith his former state and being forgets.

a 5 τὸν 'Αμέλητα ποταμόν. So Verg., *Aen.* VI 715 'securos latices'. The name is reminiscent of Bunyan.

a 8 τὸν ἀεὶ πιόντα. Cf. 614 e 1 note.

b 1 ἐπιλανθάνεσθαι. In Plato's epistemology knowledge consists in the recollection of the eternal and perfect Forms which have been perceived before birth. The Forms do not enter into this myth, but the behaviour of the souls is the same. Those who are saved by φρόνησις preserve a clearer recollection of the Forms.

b 3 ἄνω. It appears from the *Phaedo* that the souls are in the Antipodes.

c 2 τὴν ψυχήν, acc. of respect.

c 5 δικαιοσύνην. He returns to the overt theme of the dialogue.

c 6 ἡμῖν αὐτοῖς φίλοι. Wordsworth, 'Hence lives he to his inner self endeared'.

c 7 τὰ ἆθλα. Cf. *Phaedo* 114c (quoted above 617 e 4 note) and Paul's use of the same metaphor at 1 Cor. 9, 24, 'So run that ye may obtain' and 2 Tim. 4, 7–8, 'I have finished my course. . . . Henceforth there is laid up for me the crown of righteousness.'

d 1 αὐτῆς, i.e. δικαιοσύνης.

περιαγειρόμενοι. In league cricket in the North Country the hat is taken round for batsmen who make 50 or bowlers who take 5 wickets. Plato implies that successful athletes would 'take round their own hats'.

d 2 εὖ πράττωμεν. In *Ep.* III 315 b, Plato says that this is his favourite greeting to his friends. It makes a happily personal end to his greatest work.

APPENDIX 1

THE THEORY OF FORMS

What do I mean when I use the word 'horse'? When I first see a horse and am told what it is I acquire a visual memory of that individual horse which springs to mind by association when the word is mentioned. Other individual visual memories begin to accumulate, until at some point I acquire a mental concept, not just of a horse, or of several horses, but of Horse. It is this which Plato calls the Form of Horse. (The term Idea is misleading, while Universal, though accurate, is technical; εἶδος means basically 'what a thing looks like'.) It is arguable that I may arrive at this by a process of abstracting the common qualities of all the horses I have seen and constructing out of those my mental concept of the essence of Horse, or 'horseness' as one might call it. But consider next some simple geometrical concepts, that of a circle, for instance. A circle is by definition a line every point of which is equidistant from a given point. A line by definition has length and no breadth and is therefore invisible.[1] I have never seen a circle. Yet I can proffer a number of facts about circles. The angle subtended by a diameter at any point on the circumference is a right angle. This is never more than approximately true of any visible circle. It cannot be said to be abstracted as a common property of the circles I have seen, because it is not strictly true

[1] I cannot follow R. I. Aaron, *Theory of Universals*, p. 94. He suggests that we do see 'straight' lines as straight. Only subsequent measurement shows our sight to be defective. Presumably, however, he would not argue that we see the breadthlessness of the line.

of any of them; besides I arrived at the truth by reason not observation. Yet it is undoubtedly true of circularity. Geometrical propositions are not, as Mill thought, approximate generalizations about visible objects; they are, as Protagoras saw, truths about invisible objects.[1] I may define a horse in such a way that every material, visible, sensible horse fulfils my definition; but no visible circle fulfils the definition of circularity. This distinction is not made by Plato. He treated the essential Horse like the essential Circle as a perfection which was not in fact fulfilled by any particular horse we see. So too with the moral and aesthetic qualities, such as justice and beauty, with which he was at first predominantly concerned. Just acts and beautiful objects in this world are never more than imperfect reflections of true Justice and Beauty.

In short, underlying each mass of sensible particulars is a single, transcendent Form, common to all of them, but more perfect than any of them. Single, because otherwise we should have to postulate another Form to account for the resemblance between the several similar forms. Transcendent, because it is independent alike of minds which perceive and objects which are perceived, having an objective existence of its own and being more perfect than any of its particular manifestations. Common, because if it were different for different people, or if there were no common feature of particular objects, conversation would become impossible, for common names imply such common qualities. The result of this is to set against the imperfections of this world the vision of an ultimate and permanent perfection which is to be apprehended not with the senses but with the soul. When the evangelist John speaks of the 'true light' (or 'true vine' or 'true bread') he is using this conception of the archetypal light, αὐτὸ τὸ φῶς, of which all light in this world is a μίμημα or symbol.

[1] J. S. Mill, *System of Logic*, II 5, 1; Arist., *Met.* B 997 b 35.

In this way Plato reconciled the conflicting philosophies of Heraclitus and Parmenides. Heraclitus maintained that the whole world is in a state of flux.[1] Everything is on the move, altering daily, hourly, minutely, momently. 'Alles endet; was entstehet?' Even the everlasting hills are not everlasting. You cannot step into the same river twice, for it is not the same river. So John Donne in *The Second Anniversarie*:

> And what essentiall joy can'st thou expect
> Here upon earth? what permanent effect
> Of transitory causes? Dost thou love
> Beauty? (And beauty worthy'st is to move)
> Poor cousened cousenor, *that* she, and *that* thou,
> Which did begin to love, are neither now;
> You are both fluid, chang'd since yesterday;
> Next day repaires, (but ill) last dayes decay.
> Nor are, (although the river keepe the name)
> Yesterdaies waters, and to daies the same.
> So flowes her face, and thine eyes, neither now
> That Saint, nor Pilgrime, which your loving vow
> Concern'd, remaines; but whil'st you thinke you bee
> Constant, you are hourely in inconstancie.

Parmenides, on the other side, demonstrated with irrefragable logic that true reality is one single continuous perfect static whole which did not come into being, does not change, and will not pass away. His disciple and associate Zeno buttressed his position with paradoxes of 'immeasureable subtlety', of which the most familiar is 'Achilles and the tortoise', showing the impossibility of change or motion. Plato was conscious of the cogency of both these positions. He had studied with disciples of both thinkers,[2] and the

[1] I cannot accept G. S. Kirk's rejection of this in his generally admirable *Heraclitus, The Cosmic Fragments*.

[2] D.L. III 6; *ib.* 12.

I

points of view are strongly represented in the dialogues. His solution was to integrate the two approaches. True reality lay in the world of the Forms, stable, unchanging and permanent. The material world which we inhabit is indeed ever in flux, but it is not the real world. The senses are not to be trusted; all truth comes from the intellect.

Plato also was able to solve another problem which had exercised Greek thought in the latter part of the fifth century, the opposition between νόμος and φύσις. νόμος is a law or custom, φύσις originally means the way a thing grows, and there was at first no clash. But as knowledge of the world beyond Greece spread, there came the realization that different customs prevailed in different parts of the world. Consequently it was asserted that all laws, including the laws of morality, are relative. We find such amoralism in an important fragment of Antiphon discovered at Oxyrhynchus; the laws of the state are unnatural, and to obey them except where compelled is abject folly; the laws of nature cannot be broken. We find it in the satyric drama *Sisyphus* written by Plato's relative Critias. We find it put by Plato into the mouth of Callicles in the *Gorgias*. Countering these views were references to unwritten divine laws which we find in Sophocles' *Antigone*, in Pericles' funeral oration, and in the Xenophontic Socrates. It was the great merit of the Theory of Forms to give this counter-attack a metaphysical foundation. The moral laws of our life here are seen to derive their sanction from the unalterable constitution of the universe, where absolute good, absolute justice, perfect courage exist unchanging. The moral order is based on nature, not convention.

It will be obvious that Socrates' concern with ethical truths and definition by generalization forms the starting-point of much of this speculation. In this sense Plato could say that there were no writings of Plato, only Socrates made new and young. He is building on his master's founda-

tions, rejuvenating the older man and making him relevant
to the problems of a new generation.

We know that later in the Academy five arguments were
current to demonstrate the Theory of Forms. The first
derives from the conception of science. In its simplest form
it asserts that every science has one single object and if it is
the object of knowledge it must be unchanging and eternal.
There are unchanging and eternal Forms therefore as the
objects of scientific knowledge. The second argument is
known as 'the one over the many'. Socrates is *a* man and
Plato is *a* man. But neither Socrates nor Plato is *Man*. What
is Man? The Psalmist's question takes on a new meaning.
Man is, in technical language, the unity of the multiplicity,
the single Form behind the many particulars. The third
argument is short and straightforward. It is based on our
knowledge of what no longer exists. Our knowledge of the
dodo is not affected by its extinction, because it is not
knowledge of any particular dodo, but of the Form of
dodoity. The fourth argument is concerned with the imperfections of the material world. Particular examples of
equal objects are not in fact perfectly equal. They aspire
towards perfect equality; they 'imitate' equality, which
exists in its own right. The fifth argument picks up the
second, and indeed is little more than a restatement of it.
It is the so-called 'third man' argument. Socrates is a man,
and Plato is a man. We must postulate a third man, the
form of Man, to account for their common quality. The
general expression of this argument is that when things are
called by the same name, but are not identical with that
name, they are so by relation to one universal.

It is interesting to watch the gradual unfolding of this
in the mind of Plato. The early dialogues go little if at all
beyond the thought of Socrates, and the distinction between
definition and example. In the *Meno* we encounter the
doctrine of Recollection. Socrates elicits from a slave by a

series of leading questions the solution to a geometrical problem. He had not acquired the knowledge involved in his
lifetime; it must therefore have been in the strict sense innate
and acquired before birth.

Our birth is but a sleep and a forgetting.

But the Forms are not specifically mentioned. In the
Cratylus, which is fashionable in approaching metaphysical
problems linguistically, the metaphysical questions become
so insistent that they have to be answered. The context is
the making of a shuttle for a weaver. The carpenter in so
doing looks at the form or pattern, at the 'very shuttle', not
at its broken exemplar. It is curious, and relevant to
Republic X, that we here deal with the Form of an artefact.

The *Phaedo* provides the first systematic exposition of the
theory which answers these emergent questions. Whatever
the precise relation of Form to object τῷ καλῷ τὰ καλὰ
καλά; it is by beauty that beautiful things are beautiful. The
theory once expounded is assumed in the *Republic*. There the
mystical conception of the Form of the Good 'beyond
reality' is presented; it creates the power of knowledge in the
mind and truth in the object of knowledge. 'Good' here is
not a moral term; it embraces all that we might call good.
Here we are beyond the depths of intellect. Two famous
images, of the Line and Cave, elucidate the general theory
further. The first depicts the objects of perception and
knowledge by a line AB, divided at points D, C, and E so
that AC : CB : : AD : DC : : CE : EB (See Fig. 4). The sec-
tion AC of the line represents objects of physical perception,
not properly to be called objects of knowledge; this is subdivided between images and reflections on the one hand
and material objects on the other. The mental reactions
appropriate to these are εἰκασία (conjecture) and πίστις
(belief) together comprising δόξα (opinion, as opposed to
knowledge). The other part represents objects of intellectual

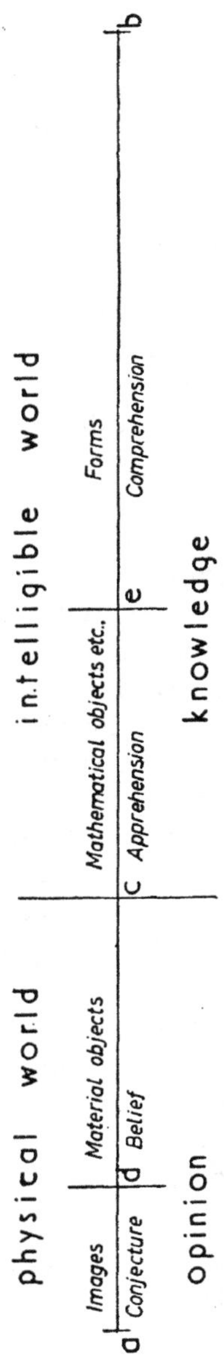

apprehension, which are again subdivided according to whether we start from undemonstrated assumptions and use visible illustrations (e.g. geometrical diagrams) in our approach to them or not. Their respective approaches are διάνοια (apprehension) and νόησις (comprehension). This illuminates the passage in the tenth book where the artist is described as being at two removes from truth. In the image of the Cave Mankind is depicted as chained in an underground chamber facing a rocky wall. Behind them is a parapet, behind the parapet a path, and on the far side of the path a fire. Along the path pass people who hold aloft different shaped images above parapet-level so that their shadows fall on the wall opposite. The parallel of a cinema will serve, except that there the celluloid exists to produce the shadow, not in its own right, and the patrons ought to be aware that they are looking at an illusion. If one of the prisoners is released and taken into the open he will at first have great difficulty in seeing. But he will gradually come to realize that he is now in the true world. If he goes back he will stumble in the darkness and no one will believe the story he has to tell. So it is with the philosopher. Yet go back he must.

physical world | intelligible world

Images	Material objects	Mathematical objects etc.	Forms
Conjecture	Belief	Apprehension	Comprehension

opinion | knowledge

a — d — c — e — b

FIG. 4

The vision of the world is given mystical and semi-poetical expression in the *Phaedrus* and *Symposium*, 'He will see a Beauty eternal, not growing or decaying, waxing or waning. . . . Beauty absolute, separate, simple and ever-lasting; which lending of its virtue to all beautiful things which we see born to decay, itself suffers neither increase nor diminution, nor any other change.' 'There the soul beholds true justice, true moderation, and knowledge—not the knowledge that comes to be, or that exists in another thing of those we call real, but that which is truly knowledge in that which truly is. And feasting on the contemplation of the other things that likewise truly are, diving back into the inner heaven, the soul goes homeward.'

Later the theory underwent criticism, modification and development. In the *Timaeus*, and implicitly in the *Philebus*, we see the cosmological importance of the Forms. They are the blue-print which the Almighty Craftsman uses in con-structing the universe; the stamp, so to speak, impressed upon the receptacle of matter. In the *Sophist* a new dynamic conception enters the world of Forms; there are some sorts of κίνησις which are not incompatible with the permanence with which Plato invests the Forms as ultimate reality and the objects of true knowledge. Further we know from Aristotle that Plato came to identify the Forms with numbers.[1] This was due to Pythagorean influence; numbers have all the clarity which Plato attributes to the knowledge of true reality and their apprehension is intellectual. Perhaps he regarded material objects as constructed out of points, and moral and aesthetic qualities as dependent upon pro-portion, and therefore expressible mathematically. We know too that at this stage he rejected the existence of Forms of manufactured objects which he had accepted in the

---

[1] W. D. Ross, *Plato's Theory of Ideas*, pp. 216-20, rejects this, perhaps on inadequate grounds. Aristotle's evidence is weighty. The identifica-tion was certainly made by Plato's successor Speusippus.

Cratylus and *Republic*. Finally, in the *Parmenides* he is radical in self-questioning. Of what are there Forms? How can the Form be in many objects and remain óne? Must we not postulate a Form behind the Form, to explain the resemblance, for example, between a particular man and the Form Man, and so involve ourselves in an infinite regress? How can Forms which are separate from our world affect it? The answers are inconclusive, and show that the problem of its relation of Form to object in particular had not been fully thought out. But Plato never felt that the questions shook the foundations of his belief.

The issues which Plato's doctrine raises became through Porphyry's commentary on Aristotle a dominant issue in the philosophy of the Middle Ages. In British philosophy the brilliant Cambridge Platonists Cudworth, More and Whichcote brought them to life again. More recently A. E. Taylor has based an argument for the existence of God on the fact that moral values point to a transcendent good (the Platonic Form), and this in its turn points to a Person in whose being this transcendent good is embodied.[1] But it is on the poets as much as the philosophers that the theory has made its impact. Here is Ronsard:

> Si notre vie est moins qu'une journée
> En l'éternel; si l'an qui fait le tour
> Chasse nos jours sans espoir de retour;
> Si périssable est toute chose née;
> Que songes-tu, mon âme emprisonnée?
> Pourquoi te plaît l'obscur de notre jour,
> Si pour voler en un plus clair séjour,
> Tu as au dos l'aile bien empennée!

So much for this world. Now the contrast.

> Là est le bien que tout esprit désire,
> Là le repos où tout le monde aspire,

[1] *Essays Catholic and Critical*, 'The Vindication of Religion'.

Là est l'amour, là le plaisir encore!
Là, O mon âme, au plus haut ciel guidée,
Tu y pourras reconnaître l'idée
De la beauté qu'en ce monde j'adore.

That, of course, is deliberately Platonic, even to the language. The next witness is the Elizabethan philosopher-poet Sir John Davies:

And thou, my soul, which turn'st thy curious eye,
 To view the beams of thine own form divine;
Know, that thou canst know nothing perfectly,
 While thou art clouded with this flesh of mine.

Donne turns his beloved into a kind of Platonic archetype:

If ever any beauty I did see
Which I desir'd, and got, 'twas but a dreame of thee.

Milton makes Raphael ask of Adam:

What if Earth
Be but the shaddow of Heav'n, and things therein
Each to other like, more than on Earth is thought?

Elizabeth Barrett Browning had Plato mediated to her through Swedenborg:

Every natural flower which grows on earth
Implies a flower upon the spiritual side
Substantial, archetypal, all aglow
With blossoming cause.

Her husband concludes *Abt Vogler* with a Platonic thought:

On the earth the broken arcs; in the heaven, a perfect round.

Finally,—though this is but summary and selective—a witness from the twentieth century, Alfred Noyes:

The outer world is but the pictured scroll
  Of worlds within the soul,
A coloured chart, a blazoned Missal-book
  Whereon who rightly look
May spell the splendour with their mortal eyes
  And steer to Paradise.

APPENDIX 2

PLATO'S THEORY OF ART

In estimating Plato's aesthetic philosophy it is necessary
to remember three things. Firstly, Greek philosophy paid
little attention to aesthetics, for the most part. They produced no Croce, still less a Bosanquet. Furthermore we can
trace no fundamental thinking in this field before Plato
himself. The Ionians had been predominantly concerned
with questions of physical theory and cosmology, the
sophists with epistemology, and Socrates with ethics. Plato
was a pioneer, and he directed his attention principally to
the literary arts.

Secondly, the conflict between philosophy and poetry of
which he speaks was genuine and deep. Cornford has traced
its roots back to the figure of the shaman, in whom all
wisdom was to be found. The philosopher and the poet each
represent different aspects of the ancient shaman, and each
claims to hold the position which the shaman once occupied.
When Nicias made his son Niceratus learn the whole of
Homer off by heart he did it not out of any love for literature
per se, but because he regarded the knowledge thus acquired
as having practical value as a guide through life. Against
this claim the philosophers in general and Plato in particular stood firm.

Thirdly, the conflict is internal to Plato as well as
external to him. When Patin coined his celebrated phrase
about Lucretius 'l'anti-Lucrèce chez Lucrèce', his words
had a much wider application. Plato had been a writer of
tragedy; this way his course was set when he met Socrates.

He remained all his life a master of poetic prose, dramatic situation, and character study. When he ejects Homer and his successors from his ideal commonwealth (as Milton saw in *De Idea Platonica*) he is ejecting a part of himself. Hence no doubt the intensity with which he writes.

With these points in mind we may proceed to examine Plato's actual views. He reconciled the obvious beauty and attraction of art with his repudiation of the artist's claim to knowledge, by means of a view which may authentically have originated with Socrates. When Socrates in the *Apology* described his assaying of the poets, he found them incapable of explaining their own works and came to the conclusion that they wrote not by wisdom, but by natural endowment, being inspired like oracles and prophets. The same theme is taken up in the *Ion*, important for all its slightness. As soon as Ion lays claim to expertise in any subject Socrates is swift to refute his claims; as long as he rests on divine inspiration and abdicates all intellectual pretensions he is secure. In the *Phaedrus* the noble myth is an encomium of madness, and we read that 'the man who approaches the door of poetry without the Muses' madness, convinced that by his skill he will make a good enough poet, is imperfect in himself, and the poetry of the sensible man will be set at nothing by that of those who are mad'.[1] But there are different kinds of madness.

> The lunatic, the lover, and the poet
> Are of imagination all compact.

We soon find that the philosopher, the lover of wisdom, is the true artist, and the poet is far inferior, placed in order of precedence just above the artisan. His is the lowest type of inspiration.

Plato's general view of art is contained in the term μίμησις, a term which he passed on to Aristotle. Unfortunately the

[1] 245 a.

term itself is ambiguous.[1] Conventionally translated 'imitation', it does sometimes convey what we should today call
photographic copying. But this does not exhaust its content,
as Aristotle is at some pains to make clear, and it is best
rendered 'representation'. The painter copies the bed he is
depicting; the dramatic or epic poet impersonates his
characters. Music in some sense represents a life of enerva-
tion, say, or of virile courage. Boswell remarked that some
music made him want to rush into battle. 'Sir,' said Dr
Johnson, 'if it made me feel such a fool I should not listen
to it.' Plato's objection to such representational art is three-
fold. He criticizes the representation of undesirable objects.
He feels that representation is not based upon genuine
understanding or critical judgement; it is, in short, unintelligent, and merely perpetuates the errors of sense-perception. He believes it to be undesirable for a man to
engage in such impersonations instead of living his own
life; this is based on the economic principle 'one man one
job' which has now become a moral dogma.

Plato does not however confine art to representation. His
words in the tenth book that they have rejected all poetry
that is representational implies that there is a sort of poetry
which is not representational.[2] Earlier he has spoken of
the three types of poetry—narrative, representational (i.e.
dramatic), and a mixture of the two (epic, which employs
direct and indirect speech).[3] His criticisms have been
directed to representational or mimetic verse. He is aware
of the power of beauty in art, and is willing to use that to a
good end. Hence he does not rule out narrative verse, still
less exhortatory. Similarly he speaks incidentally but apprais-
ingly of the painter who paints not the likeness of an actual
man, but the vision of what the beautiful man would be.[4]

[1] Cf. J. Tate, 'Imitation in Plato's *Republic*' in *C.Q.* 1928 and 1932, two
important articles, with which I do not however always agree.
[2] X 595 a.   [3] III 392 d.   [4] V 472 d, cf. VI 484 c.

Plato's judgement of art is in short ethical. In a political context the clear conclusion of this is censorship, and this is in fact what emerges. Dramatic poetry is out; so is epic in so far as it employs direct speech; so are all enervating or orgiastic modes in music. Representational art is not wholly eliminated. The poet may represent the words of a good man; the musician may represent the life of heroes in war or gentlemen in peace.[1] The painter may hold the ideal of beauty before the public. Apart from these, writers will be encouraged to tell stories for the good of the citizens. Plato once touches on, but does not develop, the conception of art as relaxation.[2] In the *Laws* he speaks more clearly of the positive value of art. Art has two functions, the education of the young and the relaxation of the adult.[3] It may be judged by three criteria, the pleasure it gives, its technical competence, and its social utility,[4] but the first two subserve the third. Technical competence is at any time only a means to an end, and the object in which we take pleasure varies according to our character. Popularity is not to be taken as the standard of the value. Hence censorship remains, in not markedly different terms from those of the *Republic*.

It is interesting to observe Aristotle's implicit criticisms of Plato in the *Poetics*. In his discussion of tragedy he accepts the view that art is μίμησις. He negates Plato at four points.

1. He insists throughout on the broadest possible conception of 'representation'; at no time is it confined to crude copying, as it tends to be in Plato.

2. He argues that the object of representation in tragedy is worthwhile, and Plato has only protested at the representation of undesirable objects. This is subtly done by substituting for strictly ethical language the ambiguous σπουδαῖος, 'significant'.

3. By his theory of κάθαρσις ('purgation') he gives tragedy

[1] III 399 a–b.   [2] III 396 e.   [3] *Laws* II 653 d.
[4] II 667 b.

a social justification. He suggests that tragedy excites in us
pity and fear, and by exciting them works these undesirable
emotions out of our system. We go for the specious pleasure
of having our emotions titillated; the process is justified by
its social consequences.

4. The word κάθαρσις, though clearly here a medical
term, carries with it overtones of religious significance,
associated with Apollo. Indeed it was long assumed that it
meant 'purification' here. This is not so, but the overtones
remain. Plato turned art into a sort of Dionysiac frenzy.
Aristotle is reasserting the Apolline element which is associated with moderation and control.

Three final comments remain to be made. We tend to be
righteously shocked at Plato's rigid imposition of censorship.
We profess freedom of speech and publication. Yet we have
a Lord Chamberlain's office determining what may or may
not be put on the stage. We classify films into 'U', 'A', 'H',
and 'X'. We agonize over the influence of horror comics.
Here, as so often, the *Republic* is the great question-raiser. It
may not give us the answer which satisfies us, but it forces
us to examine our own practice, and its basis.

Secondly, the *Republic* challenges us equally to work out
what we believe to be the purpose and social function of
art, and the uneasiness most of us feel about Plato's ex-
clusively utilitarian answer warns us against over-simplifica-
tion. In his useful little book *European Painting and Sculpture*,
Eric Newton makes this point strikingly. 'If the artist tells
me a story I shall exclaim "how interesting!"; if he wishes
to overawe me with mystical conceptions of the Godhead I
am ready to be impressed; if he wants to construct a purely
formal pattern of line and colour or mass or sound, I will
say "how beautiful!"; if he preaches I am ready to be con-
verted; if he wants to be of use to me I shall say "thank
you". Art has done all these things at various times in the
history of civilization.'

Finally, it is a little curious that Plato did not develop a more constructive theory of art along his own lines. For it was always open to him to say that the artist at his highest could represent the Forms directly, that he has glimpsed the vision of the ultimate beauty of the *Symposium*. Why then did he not do so? No doubt Grube is right in suggesting that it was because of his own inner conflict and psychological development.[1] In all his aesthetic theorizing the horses of his personality were tugging against the charioteer Reason— and who shall say that for once they were not right to do so?

[1] G. M. A. Grube, 'Plato's Theory of Beauty' in *Monist*, 1927.

APPENDIX 3

THE IMMORTALITY OF THE SOUL

There are few more surprising passages in Greek literature than an exchange between Socrates and Glaucon in *Republic* X 608. Socrates says, 'Have you not realized that our soul is immortal and never subject to death?' And Glaucon gazes at him in astonishment and exclaims, 'Good heavens, no!' The conversation is a healthy reminder not to read back into other times and other places ideas which we take for granted. Here is an ordinary, well-educated, thoughtful young Athenian, to whom the idea of the immortality of the soul comes as a paradoxical novelty. We can here discern something of the revolution Socrates and Plato achieved in European thought. To understand this better it will be well briefly to survey Greek beliefs upon the survival of the soul.

The chthonic element in primitive Greek religion is well-attested; in such religions the dead man is regarded as being in the direct care of the gods and in some sense as surviving. The Homeric story of the funeral of Patroclus shows the residuum of vigorous belief along these lines. The body of the dead hero is placed on the pyre (this is of course an alien practice), locks of hair are laid upon it, sheep and oxen are slaughtered. Jars of oil and wine are set around, and four horses, two dogs, and twelve Trojans killed. All are burnt with the body, and wine, no doubt representing blood, is poured out upon the earth. The dead man's needs are well provided for. He has food and refreshment, slaves to serve him, horses and dogs with which to go hunting. The great chamber-tombs at Mycenae tell the same story, with their vaulted main-chamber for sacrifice, and the furniture, ornaments, and pottery left in them for the dead man's use. No doubt the classical festivals of the dead, such as Nemesia and Anthesteria at Athens, for all the association of the latter with Dionysus, are survivals of this primitive stage.

But this is by no means the characteristic outlook of the Homeric poems. There, as exemplified in the eleventh book of the *Odyssey*, the dead appear as strengthless, witless wraiths. Tennyson had them in mind when he wrote the line

Thin as the bat-like shrillings of the dead.

So did Aldous Huxley when he contrasted the squeak-and-gibber school of thought with the harp-and-scream. All their faculties are gone for ever. οὐ γὰρ ἔτι σάρκας τε καὶ ὀστέα ἶνες ἔχουσι. 'In the murky underworld they float unconscious or with a twilight half-consciousness wailing in shrill diminutive voice, helpless, indifferent.' The Psalmist says, 'I had rather be a doorkeeper in the house of my God than dwell in the tents of wickedness.' Achilles makes a similar contrast between life and death: he had rather be a poor man's serf on earth than ruler of the dead.

The change is associated with the waves of invaders from the north whose virility drives them to live this life to the full, and look no further. It is associated also with the point at which belief in life as something physical becomes articulate. Onians, in his careful examination of the early language of the Greeks, in speaking of life and the soul has shown the material nature of the concepts. Thus, he suggests, φρένες are the lungs, θυμός the breath, αἰών (the stuff of life) is the liquid which flows from the eyes in tears, and ψυχή (the life-soul) is associated with the head and linked with the seed which is supposed to emanate from that source. It follows that what is left after death is insubstantial and ineffective if it has lost these physical attributes.

The eagerness with which the ghosts in the *Odyssey* lap up
the blood shows how they lack the very stuff of life. No
rational mind working upon a heritage of this kind can be
expected to arrive at ideas of immortality, or even any real
survival, without fresh stimulus to transform the direction
of man's beliefs and thoughts.

The consequence is that in the public pronouncements of
the classical and later ages, outside the philosophical schools,
we have very little indication of belief in immortality. The
tombstones, where one might expect to find it, lack it almost
entirely. Their characteristic sentiments are: 'I was not.
I was born. I am not. It is nothing to me. Traveller, fare
you well.' Love you may find on the sculptured reliefs of
husband and wife, but not faith or hope. When the poets
offer immortality it is only the spurious and vicarious immortality of fame. Even the orators, who might be expected
to attempt consolation by reference to an eternal life of
conscious blessedness never seem to do so; witness Pericles
in the funeral speech. Jebb writes, 'The continued existence
of the Soul after death is not questioned by the orators; but
its consciousness of what happens in this world is only
affirmed with deliberate uncertainty. Such qualifications as
εἴ τινες τῶν τετελευτηκότων λάβοιεν τρόπῳ τινὶ τοῦ νῦν
γιγνομένου πράγματος αἴσθησιν ["if any of the dead could
in any way apprehend what is happening now"] are fre-
quent.' The sum of the picture is not so much to assert the
denial of any immortality of the soul in Athenian society,
as to imply that it simply was not an idea present to the
minds of the majority of the community. There were sur-
prisingly few immortal longings about the Greeks. We see
this more markedly in the interchangeability of the words
'immortal' and 'God'. The two are normally synonymous.
The result is that strange terminology creeps into some
Christian writings of the Greek tradition, and Athanasius
and others can say freely that Christ became human that

he might make us divine, meaning that he became mortal that he might make us immortal. In the normal Greek usage for a human to aspire to immortality would be ὕβρις. That was the prerogative only of the gods, and to know your own place was the central rule of human life.

The exceptions to this general picture are for the most part more apparent than real. Translation, for example, is not the same as survival after death, but the removal of a privileged individual out of the clutches of death. In fact, the occasional stories of translation only confirm the above picture, for the existence of such instances of translation as an especial boon bestowed by the gods implies that the fate of those who suffer death is extinction or virtual extinction. Such translation is attested in Homer of Menelaus, Ino Leucothea and Ganymede; Calypso offers to make Odysseus 'immortal and ageless for all time'. Mythology adds such figures as Amphiaraus, Trophonius, Iphigenia, and Achilles. Other exceptions are associated with hero-worship, deriving probably from ancestor-worship, and in later times associated principally with the founders of cities. Hero-worship affected the religious practices of the individual, but it afforded him no hope that a like destiny might be granted to him. It is doubtful even whether the founder of a city would suppose that that action would transform his fate, though he might be vaguely pleased that his memory would be kept warm. The man in the street was untouched by all this.

There was, however, what one is tempted to call a nonconformist tradition which spoke in vastly different terms, which offered a personal religion almost wholly alien to the state-worship of the Olympians, and with it the hope of immortality. This lay in the mystery religions. The most famous of these were the Eleusinian mysteries. They were a survival and revival of the ancient chthonic practices; traditionally they dated back to the fifteenth century, and the

archaeologists have produced a temple of that era in confirmation. In the Homeric Hymn to Demeter the mysteries
appear as the secret cult of a close corporation. To those who
share in it, and to them alone, it promised a blessed fate
after death, 'Blessed is the man who has beheld these holy
acts; but he that is uninitiated and has no share in the holy
ceremonies shall not enjoy a like fate after his death, in the
gloomy darkness of Hades.' In the seventh century this
exclusiveness was broken down, and admission was extended first to Athens, and later to all Greece generally.
All Greeks might enter—men and women (both the respectable and the less respectable), children and slaves. Murderers and foreigners were excluded. We know little about
the mysteries. The association with Demeter shows that the
origin is agricultural. The mystery which was disclosed was
in some way thus the mystery of life. It is reasonable to see
some kind of parallel between the corn being buried in the
earth and rising to new life and the new life to be experienced by the worshipper who has assimilated himself
to the spirit of life which animates the corn. We know that
the worshippers bathed in the sea. θάλασσα κλύζει πάντα
τἀνθρώπων κακά.[1] They then proceeded ceremonially from
Athens to Eleusis. But about the rites there can be only conjecture. We hear of 'things recited', 'things revealed', and
'things performed', and we know that the highest rite was
called the 'spectacle' and presumably consisted of something
that the worshippers saw. There appears to have been a
ritual meal; there may also have been a ritual marriage.
Christian writers on the offensive (in more senses of the
word than one) tell us of the use of sexual symbols, which
may have been involved; we are also told that the highest
mystery was a corn-ear, and in this there may be truth.
It is probable that there was no verbal mystery, but that
some dramatic representation was seen, and could be pro-

[1] Eur. *I.T.* 1193.

faned only by action. Such a religious pantomime might well represent the rape of Kore, the wanderings of Demeter, and the final reunion of the goddesses. In all this we are in the realm of guesswork, but such guesses are at least plausible. The life that is promised to the blessed initiates may be seen portrayed in Aristophanes' *Frogs*; the happiness consists in the continued celebration of the mysteries in the Underworld. But the German scholar Erwin Rohde goes too far when he says that Eleusis taught not *that* the soul will live, but *how* it will live. It is true that the same underworld seems to serve both for the pure and for the uninitiated. But the latter know merely the gloomy darkness of Hades; they have nothing that can rightly be called life. The secret of the corn-goddess must be the secret of life and death. 'Except a corn of wheat fall into the ground and die, it abideth alone; but if it die, it bringest forth much fruit.' So is it with the life of men. The importance of the Eleusinian mysteries is that through them the possibility of this first becomes relevant to life of the people.

A greater innovation was provided by the Orphic mysteries. Their introduction must be set in the sixth century, when we are told that Onomacritus, a giver of oracles in Pisistratus' court, founded the secret worship of Dionysus at Athens. Their ultimate origin was undoubtedly Thrace, but there was some link with Pythagoras, and individual authors to whom the Orphic poems are attributed are connected with the Pythagoreans of Italy and Sicily. According to Orphic mythology Dionysus Zagreus is the son of Zeus and Kore. The wicked Titans, urged on by Hera, slay and devour him. Athene rescues the heart and takes it to Zeus, who swallows it. From Zeus and Semele now springs a new Dionysus in whom Zagreus comes to life again. The Titans are destroyed by Zeus' lightning, and from their ashes arises the race of men, a race compounded of good and evil, the evil from the Titans, the good from Dionysus Zagreus whom

the Titans swallowed. Man's task, then, is to free himself
from the Titanic element in his nature, that is his body.
σῶμα σῆμα says the punning phrase; the body is a
tomb. In the circle of necessity the soul becomes succes-
sively the life-companion of many men and of many animals.
The soul is by its nature immortal; it is the Dionysiac element in man, and being immortal is held for ever in the
cycle of death and rebirth—unless it can be withdrawn.
Further we are faced with the 'sacred doctrine' of the
judgement of the soul, and the reality of penalties for ancient
guilt in former lives. There is a 'thrice-ancient law', 'What
you have done, you must suffer.' How then is it possible to
escape from the wheel of birth with its gloomy inevita-
bility, to fly out from the circle of death and punishment
and rebirth? Through Orpheus and his mysteries. The
initiate enjoys a milder fate. His is the συμπόσιον τῶν ὁσίων,
the banquet of the blessed. He spends his time in μέθη
αἰώνιος, uninterrupted intoxication, the night before without the morning after. 'When a man dies', runs a fragment
of Plutarch, 'he is like those who are initiated into the
mysteries. Our whole life is a journey by tortuous ways
without outlet. At the moment of quitting it come terrors,
shuddering fear, amazement. Then a light that moves to
meet you, pure meadows that receive you, song and dances
and holy apparitions.' [1] The gold tablets found at Petelia
and Thurii, of high interest in many ways, contained buried
instructions for the soul in the world beyond the grave.
Eventually the initiate is withdrawn from the cycle of
becoming and perishing, and thereafter lives for ever as a
god. *Nulla salus extra ecclesiam* is a hard saying and will always
have its critics. Diogenes the Cynic was one such. 'Is
Pataecion the thief to have a better fate than the gallant
Epaminondas', he is recorded as saying, 'merely because
he has been initiated?' No doubt there were many who,

---

[1] Plut., *De Anima* 2.

like Trygaeus,[1] with death before their eyes, went to borrow three drachmae for a pig to sacrifice at the initiation ceremony. But it would be unfair not to speak also of the moral demands of the faith. When Plutarch wrote to his wife Timoxena to console her upon the death of their infant daughter he said, 'Because of those sacred and faithful promises given in the mysteries of Bacchus, we hold it firmly for an undoubted truth that our soul is incorruptible and immortal. Let us behave ourselves accordingly, outwardly ordering our lives, while within all should be purer, wiser, incorruptible.'

Plato regarded the Orphics of his own day as charlatans and nuisances, but his picture of the destiny of the soul is closely based on Orphic imagery, presumably mediated through the Italian communities. Pythagoras and Empedocles both believed in transmigration. 'Remain thou still in darkness,' says Feste in *Twelfth Night* to the incarcerated Malvolio. 'Thou shalt hold the opinion of Pythagoras, ere I will allow of thy wits; and fear to kill a woodcock, lest thou dispossess the soul of thy grandam.' Socrates was an influence of equal importance. We need not believe that the detailed philosophical exposition of the *Phaedo* belongs to Socrates, but that he spent his last hours in discussing the immortality of the soul and went to his death in calm hope is certain. If we want additional confirmation it is found in Xenophon. In his account of the education of Cyrus there is a defence of the soul's immortality on four grounds.[2] One is the terror which murderers still feel their victims to inspire in them. The second is the fact of honours being paid to the dead. The third is that the soul is the source of motion and intelligence. On death the body is resolved into its natural elements—dust to dust and ashes to ashes. But the soul is not involved in the dispersal of the body: it is independent. Finally there is the resemblance of sleep and

[1] Ar., *Pax* 372.   [2] Xen., *Cyr.* VIII 7, 17.

death, and in sleep the soul is free from the constraint of the body. It has frequently been noted that the principles which Xenophon is trying to establish in the *Cyropaedia* are those found in his account of Socrates. I do not think there is any question but that Xenophon derived his belief in the immortality of the soul from Socrates. Equally certainly the arguments by which he defends it are not Plato's. It is noteworthy that there is no trace of belief in transmigration. Pythagorean influence on Socrates is dubious in the extreme.

Plato in the *Phaedo* brings forward four arguments for the soul's immortality, two of them being presented together. The first is based upon the concept of rebirth. The general principle is laid down that everything comes out of its opposite. If a thing becomes greater it must first have been smaller; if smaller, greater. So we may suppose that life comes out of death, as death out of life. The fallacy which leaps from comparative terms to absolute is obvious, though the argument is not questioned. The second argument is based on the Theory of Recollection which seems to demonstrate the soul's pre-existence, since knowledge is acquired before birth; it has to be combined with the first to demonstrate post-existence. The third argument is based upon the affinity between the subject and object. There are two kinds of existence, the eternal unchanging Forms, and the mutable particulars of the sensible world. The body perceives the latter, and like them is mutable and impermanent. The soul's nature is to apprehend the Forms, and like them it is eternal—though the weakness of the argument is immediately seen if we insist that the soul must also be unchanging. The final argument arises out of a discussion of properties and accidents. Each particular has its essential Forms. The number three contains not merely threeness but oddness and cannot admit evenness. Just so, whatever has soul has life. Life is the invariable concomitant of soul. It follows that the soul cannot admit death into its being.

To these arguments Plato adds a fifth in the last book of the *Republic*. Everything has its own peculiar good and its own peculiar evil. Thus, ophthalmia is the appropriate evil of the eye, disease of the body in general, blight of corn. The evil of the soul is sin—injustice, intemperance, cowardice, ignorance. But the soul is not destroyed by sin. A bad man continues to live. Therefore the soul is immortal, because disease, which is the appropriate evil of the body, can only kill the body, not the soul. The fallacy here is the uncritical assumption of the identity of the moral personality and the principle of life in a man. A sixth argument appears in the *Phaedrus*. It is derived from an earlier thinker, Alcmaeon.[1] The soul is immortal because it is always in motion. It is in fact self-moved, and Plato implies that souls are the only things that are self-moved, and hence ultimately the only possible source of movement in other objects. If souls were not immortal the universe would run down, which Plato regards as a *reductio ad absurdum*. This argument contains more arbitrary assumptions than any of the others —the self-moving of the soul, the uniqueness of that quality, the necessary origin of motion in the self-moved, the consequential running-down of the universe if individual souls cease to be, indeed the absurdity of such a consequence, all these are gratuitously assumed. Finally in the *Timaeus* the creation of souls by God leads to the conclusion that He would not wish, and nothing else would have the power, to destroy His handiwork.

Plato produces these arguments with an air of conviction, but I cannot feel that he was happy about them. Grote has an ironical passage in which he writes, 'Nemesius, the Christian bishop of Emesa, declares that the proofs given by Plato of the immortality of the soul are knotty and difficult to understand, such as even adepts in philosophical study can hardly follow. His own belief in it rests upon the

[1] Arist., *De Anima* 405 a 30.

inspiration of the Christian Scriptures.' So put, we may smile at the simple faith of the worthy bishop. But in *Phaedo* and *Republic* alike when Plato has presented his intellectual case he soars beyond it, in what can only be called a great act of faith, into his majestic myths of judgement. His use of myth, as we shall see, means that he is in the realm of the Great Unprovable. It is his conviction that matters, not the arguments used in its defence. It points forward to what is perhaps the greatest vision of eternity that the human personality has ever conceived. 'A pleasant life is theirs in heaven; they have truth for mother, nurse, real being and nutriment. They see all things, not the things that are born and die, but those which have real being; and they see themselves in others. For them all things are transparent, and there is nothing dark or impenetrable, but every one is manifest to every one internally; for light is manifest to light. For everyone has all things in himself and sees all things in one another; so that all things are everywhere, and all is all, and each is all, and the glory is infinite.' [1] Plotinus had an 'amor intellectualis Dei' but he is first and foremost a great mystic. That mystical vision of heavenly immortality he caught from Plato, and that is not the least of our debts to the master.

[1] Plotinus, *Enn.* 5, 8, 4.

APPENDIX 4

MYTH IN PLATO

It used to be fashionable in German scholarship, to which Platonic studies owe so much, to put an exclusive emphasis upon the intellectual and rational element in Plato's philosophy and to ignore the imaginative and poetical.[1] It is now generally recognized that the two elements exist side by side: 'Alongside the scientific element, or as we might say *above* it, there is another.'[2] Mythos is accepted in partnership with Logos. The change was striking enough to call for a comment in the second edition of Natorp's great study,[3] a fact more significant when we realize that Natorp's first edition was one of those preoccupied with the other side.

The importance of the myths is now almost universally acknowledged. But what is a myth, and why does Plato use them? To those questions a bewildering multitude and variety of answers have been given. It is well to observe at the beginning that Plato himself admits the basic meaning to be the stories which nurses tell to children,[4] what we should call 'bedtime stories', and there are occasions when the contrast between λόγος and μῦθος is very nearly that between fact and fiction. Unfortunately this in itself does not

[1] E.g. H. Cohen, *Platons Ideenlehre und die Mathematik* (1878); N. Hartmann, *Platons Logik des Seins* (1909); O. Wichmann, *Platon und Kant* (1920).

[2] L. Ziegler, *Der abendländische Rationalismus und der Eros* (1905); Preface, p. vii.

[3] P. Natorp, *Platons Ideenlehre* (1921²), p. 467.

[4] Plat., *Prot.* 320 c, *Gorg.* 527 a. See also *Rep.* X 621 b, *Theaet.* 164 d, *Phil.* 14 a, *Laws* I 645 b and cf. Photius 279, 1.

carry us very far. The myths are too prominent in Plato's work for us to write them off as 'bedtime stories', and, whatever their function, this is obviously a typical example of the irony he inherited from Socrates.

We may begin by asking why Plato used them. We can at once dismiss a number of answers. Thus Weber's view that they provided a mask for his heresies is too cynical to need refutation. Schleiermacher thought Plato had an eye on their pedagogic utility. This depends on his theory that Plato's dialogues are a planned exposition in series of the Theory of Forms. But in any case the myths are on the whole by far the most difficult part of Plato, and this runs counter to his view. Hirzel, Teichmüller and Couturat dismissed them as moralizing rhetoric, perorations for show. This is unduly unflattering to Plato, who was never a popular preacher. Field tried to cut through the whole discussion by saying that Plato wrote myths because he enjoyed doing so. This is no doubt true, but hardly adequate; the myths bear a more purposive look than this implies. Deuschle, Susemihl, Fischer and Forster were nearer the mark when they suggested that the myths existed to assert the reality of a future life about which it was not possible to possess scientific knowledge. Their frame of reference was too narrow, for the *Timaeus* myth deals with cosmology, and not just the destiny of the human soul. But they were thinking along the right lines. So too were Baur and Windelband in saying that the myths provided the religious foundations for Plato's philosophy. 'His method is to assimilate the intellectual content of that doctrine of the soul to his dialectic, and to interpret it in terms of the conception of the two worlds that goes with his doctrine of Ideas. When in this way the essential elements of his religious view appear to have been scientifically established, Plato is at liberty to add to them, in his myths, the graphically living form which the thoughts had assumed either in the religious society and its culture or in the free play of his own imagination with this material.' [1] Plato in fact used the myth to fill in gaps in his world-picture, his *Weltanschauung*, which science could not fill, but which were needed to complete the life of the spirit which all his other work subserved. As Wilamowitz puts it, 'Plato is conscious that the Ultimate and highest is never scientifically demonstrable.' [2]

The cognate question as to what in fact constitutes a myth has received some peculiar answers. Thus Couturat, starting from the popular use of the word to denote tales for children, moral fables, superstitious beliefs and legends about rites, gods, or city foundations, went on to declare that the characteristics of the Platonic myth were personification, analogy, invocation to the gods, citations from the poets, etymologies and jokes, and thus put the whole of the *Phaedo*, *Republic* and *Laws* except for the exposition of the Theory of Forms into this category. This proves too much and ignores Plato's particular use of the word, which is more discriminating. Croiset and Hirzel tried to find a criterion in the nature of the prose, dialectic writing being marked by dialogue, mythic by continuous prose. This would turn into myths Socrates' account of Simonides' poem in the *Protagoras*, Callicles' defence of might in the *Gorgias*, and Glaucon's of injustice in the *Republic*, and the whole of the *Laws*. Some critics have defined myth in terms of allegory, and Frutiger's theory of symbolic interpretation falls under this head. But on the whole the myths are not symbolical, and Plato more than once deplores allegorical interpretation. [3] Bishop Westcott usefully drew the distinction between allegory and myth. In allegory the thought is grasped first and then arranged in a particular dress. In myth the thought and form come into being together; the thought is the vital

[1] W. Windelband, *Platon*, 1920[6], p. 123.
[2] U. von Wilamowitz-Moellendorf, *Platon*, p. 1.
[3] Plat., *Rep.* II 378 d; *Phaedr.* 229 b–e.

principle which shapes the form, and the form is the sensible image which displays the thought. The parable is again distinct from both. In the gospels the Sower is an allegory, the Prodigal Son a parable, and the Sheep and Goats a myth. Prodicus' famous fable of the choice of Heracles is an excellent example of allegory.[1] Renan declared that every expression applied to an infinite object was a myth, and that myths were accounts of supernatural events. The difficulty here is that there is more than one approach to the infinite and the supernatural, and Plato clearly contrasts the rational approach of the Theory of Forms with the mythic approach. But it is equally wrong to regard, as some continental scholars have done, the rational element as lacking from the myth. Thus when Bréhier defines myth as 'l'expression d'une pensée encore enfantine qui n'a pas encore su s'élever de l'image au concept, qui sait déjà raconter, et qui ne sait pas encore expliquer', when we find myth described as 'unreflective popular fable in which impersonal forces, generally those of nature, are represented under the guise of persons whose actions and adventures have a symbolic sense', when we find it said that myth differs from fable or parable in being direct and spontaneous, having in it no elements of reflection or external design, when Wundt describes its characteristic as personification that is taken for an immediate reality, and when Ribot defines its function as 'd'animer les objets inanimés et de concevoir toute la nature à l'image de l'homme', one wonders whether they really thought Plato so naïve, unreflective and deluded as their words imply.

In his important book, *The Myths of Plato*, J. A. Stewart interpreted the myths in terms of Kant's philosophy: 'The myth', he said, 'appeals to the inarticulate and non-logical in man.' Their purpose is to arouse Transcendental Feeling. Their substance is twofold. On the one hand they contain

[1] Xen., *Mem.* II i, 21.

the imaginative representation of the Ideas of Reason, ideals, a soul that is immortal, an intelligible cosmos, a wise and good God, and the like. On the other, they include the imaginative deduction of the categories of understanding and moral virtue, by tracing to their origin in the wisdom and goodness of God and in the constitution of the cosmos certain habitudes and faculties belonging to man's moral nature. For example, the answer to the question 'Why do I go on?' is 'Because I am a soul, created with these faculties by a wise and good God, under whose government I live in a universe which is His own finished work.' If the question be asked 'Where are these ideas and categories?', science either can give no answer or answers 'Nowhere'. Myth provides an answer. This is Plato's counter to materialist science. In it he sets forth the *a priori* condition of conduct and knowledge.

Couched in abominable jargon and grandiose in expression though it is, it is a fair statement. μῦθος or εἰκὼς μῦθος is a likely tale. It is an imaginative presentation of an imagined reality. It provides an alternative approach to Reason, it goes beyond Reason, but it does not run counter to Reason. ὁ φιλόμυθος φιλόσοφός πώς ἐστιν, said Aristotle [1] —'the mythologist is in some sense a philosopher', 'the love of myth overlaps the love of wisdom'. Are we then to take the myths seriously? To believe as dogmas such things as Plato's picture of the fate and nature of the soul, with pre-existence, recollection, retribution, reincarnation, final purification, and never-ending disembodied existence? Zeller said 'Yes', Hegel 'No'. Zeller is the more nearly right, but the assent should not be given without qualifications. The truth has been well put in a popular book by W. K. C. Guthrie. 'But these conclusions themselves necessitated a belief in regions of truth into which the methods of dialectical reasoning could not follow. The value of the myth is that

[1] Arist., *Met.* A 2, 982 b 18.

it provides a way into these regions, opened for us by poets and other men of religious genius. We take account of myth not because we believe it to be literally true, but as a means of presenting a possible account of truths which we must admit to be too mysterious for exact demonstration.' [1] This could hardly be better put. Later Platonists saw this as one of three approaches to God. The way of wisdom was the way of analysis or elimination. It started from physical attributes and stripped them away until it reached the pure monad. The way of philosophy or synthesis worked inductively from the creation to God. The way of the inspired poet or the way of analogy worked by myth. [2]

In the *Republic* Plato prepares the way for that 'admirable yarn' which is to keep his classes distinct and content by some examination of the occasions when such inventiveness is justified. [3] The myths or stories we tell to children are inventions of this kind and are not expected to be the literal truth. We do not abide by the strictest canons of veracity in dealing with madmen, in war, and in the devising of myths *in which we can only approximate to the truth.* Here is this same view of the myth in a different setting. The subject-matter of the myths is always something on which we have no concrete evidence, the making of the world, our notions of morality and free-will, the nature of the soul's existence before birth and after death. In the *Phaedo* Plato uses the Orphic term for faith, ἐλπίς, but we also find the more characteristic word for probability, εἰκός, and this precisely indicates his aim. A fragment of the comic dramatist Cratinus shows the same strain. [4] 'It's obvious,' says one character, 'that you are a man and have a soul.' 'As Plato

[1] W. K. C. Guthrie, *The Greek Philosophers from Thales to Aristotle,* p. 99.
[2] Origen *c. Cels.* vii 42, 44; Alcinous, *Epit.* 10.
[3] Plat., *Rep.* II 377 a, 382 c, III 414 c.
[4] D.L. III 28.

would put it,' says the other, 'I don't know it, but I suppose
so.' This simple jest provides a true understanding of the
myths, links them with Plato's use of the postulate (ὑπονοῶ
and ὑπόθεσις) and offers some explanation of how it was
possible for a later school of scepticism to derive from a
thinker so rational and so dogmatic.

It is of some significance that not merely has contemporary scholarship come to emphasize the myths in Plato,
but contemporary religious thought has come to value the
whole concept and use of myth for its own sake. To some
extent this arises from the study of the thought-processes of
primitive man. Thus W. F. Jackson Knight, commenting on
a book of Hocat's, has pointed out that in primitive societies
many myths concern new birth by entry again into earth,
the universal mother. The Frankforts in *The Intellectual
Adventure of Ancient Man* contributed a masterly survey of the
myths of the Ancient Near East. They pointed out that
little which could be called pure thought emerges from the
written records; they were always clothed in imagination.
To the modern mind, nature is impersonal; to the ancient
it consists in life confronting life. Myth perpetuates a knowledge of the objective world which is neither fantastic nor
allegorical. It reveals an aspect of metaphysical truth valid
only to the faithful. This analysis of ancient practice is
closely parallel to Plato's usage. At the same time the
Frankforts are too sanguine about the rationality of modern
man. There is a streak of atavism which has come to the
fore, a cult of the primitive in art and music, which may
account for the return to myth on the part of Christian
thinkers.

Whatever the reason, the fact is there, even though the
use of the term is not precisely Platonic. In two thinkers
especially myth features prominently. Reinhold Niebuhr
insists upon the myth as a symbol, to be taken seriously but
not literally. Just as a poet's evocation of the battle of

Waterloo may convey the significance of the event more truly than the most careful and laborious catalogue of equipment and chronology and all the other minutiae, so myth gets at a truth which history in the narrow sense cannot apprehend. In this category Niebuhr includes the account of the Fall in Genesis, the doctrine of the Trinity, the sinlessness and Godhead of Christ, the two natures, the atonement, the Second Coming, and the resurrection of the body. Berdyaeff writes similarly: 'Myth is a reality immeasurably greater than concept. It is high time that we stopped identifying myth with invention, with the illusions of primitive mentality. . . . Behind the myth are concealed the greatest realities, the original phenomena of the spiritual life. The creation of myths among peoples denotes a real spiritual life, more real indeed than that of abstract concepts and of rational thought. Myth is always concrete and expresses life better than abstract thought can do; its nature is bound up with that of symbol. Myth is the concrete recital of events and original phenomena of the spiritual life symbolized in the material world. . . . Myth presents to us the supernatural in the natural, the suprasensible in the sensible, the spiritual life in the life of the flesh. . . . Myth always represents a reality, but its reality is symbolic.' [1] And again: 'The whole meaning, importance and value of life are determined by the mystery behind it, by an infinity which cannot be rationalized but can only be expressed in myths and symbols.' As interpretations of Plato these statements bear no value either rational or mythical, for the insistence that symbol is the essence of myth is not his. But as significant contemporary acknowledgements of the place of imagination working in accord with reason and going beyond reason they are of great importance. For this is what Plato was asserting. It is the more notable that Niebuhr is one of those who has consistently deplored the Greek

[1] N. Berdyaeff, *Freedom and the Spirit*, p. 70.

influence upon Christian thinking and sought to replace it
by unsullied Hebraism. It should be added that recent theo-
logical trends favour 'demythologizing'.

We may perhaps attempt some sort of integration of
Plato's eschatological myths, noting in passing that in none
of them do the Forms appear. The soul is given a free choice
of the sort of life he will live on earth, though the choice is
influenced at each new birth, without being determined, by
the soul's previous experience. This choice attaches to the
soul a δαίμων. Once the decision is made the external
circumstances of the life are determined, but not the spirit
in which they are accepted. This is Plato's resolution of the
ancient conflict between free will and determinism. As the
Stoics were later to maintain, freedom consists not in what
you do but in what you are, it belongs to *esse* not *operari*.
After death the soul, stripped of everything extraneous, is
led by its δαίμων to the place of judgement, which lies in a
meadow by a cross-roads. From there the left-hand road
leads down to Tartarus, the right up to the Isles of the
Blest. There are also two roads leading back from earth and
heaven. The former is the route by which the souls arrive,
the latter is used by those punished and purified, and coming
to rebirth. A fifth transverse road leads to the plain of Lethe,
which lies above the ground. After judgement the soul may
be cast for ever into Tartarus, or suffer the same fate for one
year and proceed to the cleansing of the Acherusian lake,
or be immersed directly in that lake, or pass in a state of
holiness to the Pure Mansions above, or, when a truly
philosophic spirit is found, to even fairer mansions for ever.
The first and last of these are permanent, and some souls
remain eternally in the Pure Mansions. The rest return after
a thousand years to the meadow. There they spend seven
days. Then they enter upon a four days' journey till they
reach the Pillar of Light which spans from heaven to earth,
and by it the spindle of necessity. They there make their

choice of lives. Then they pass under the spindle, make their way through a dry plain to Lethe, drink the waters of forgetfulness, and sink into sleep. At midnight with a crash of thunder they fly up to the earth like meteors.

VOCABULARY

ἀγαθός, adj., good
ἀγανακτεῖν, v., grouse
ἀγανακτικός, adj., to do with grief
ἀγαπᾶν, v., love
ἀγαπητός, adj., desirable
ἀγγεῖον, n.n., bucket
ἀγγέλλειν, v., report
ἄγγελος, n.m., messenger, reporter
ἄγειν, v., lead, drag, practise
ἄγκιστρον, n.n., hook
ἄγριος, adj., monstrous, savage
ἀγροικία, n.f., crudity
ἄγροικος, adj., crude, unmention-
able
ἄγρυπνος, adj., alert
ἀγύμναστος, adj., unpractised
ἀγωγή, n.f., impulse
ἀγών, n.m., test
ἀγωνία, n.f., physical fitness
ἀδαμαντίνως, adv., inflexibly
ἀδάμας, n.m., steel
ᾄδειν, v., sing
ἀδελφός, n.m., brother
ἀδέσποτος, adj., not subject
ἀδικεῖν, v., do wrong
ἀδίκημα, n.n., crime, sin
ἀδικία, n.f., wrongdoing
ἄδικος, adj., unjust, criminal
ἀδόκιμος, adj., undistinguished
ἀδύνατος, adj., impossible
ἀεί, adv., always, from time to time
ἀετός, n.m., eagle
ἀηδών, n.f., nightingale
ἀθάνατος, adj., immortal
ἀθλητής, n.m., athlete

ἄθλιος, adj., miserable
ἆθλον, n.n., prize
ἀθρεῖν, v., look at, consider
ἀθυμεῖν, v., grow disheartened
ἀΐδιος, adj., everlasting
αἰδώς, n.f., sense of shame or respect
αἱρεῖν, v., take, direct: (mid.),
choose
αἵρεσις, n.f., choice
αἰσθάνεσθαι, v., perceive, realize
αἰσχρός, adj., dishonourable
αἰσχύνεσθαι, v., feel shame
αἰτεῖν, v., request: (mid.), claim
αἰτία, n.f., responsibility
αἰτιᾶσθαι, v., hold responsible
αἴτιος, adj., responsible
ἀκαιρῶς, adv., unfittingly
ἀκοή, n.f., faculty of hearing
ἀκολασία, n.f., intemperance
ἀκούειν, v., hear
ἀκριβής, adj., precise, exact
ἀκροᾶσθαι, v., listen to
ἄκρος, adj., highest; ἄκρον, n.n., end
ἀλγηδών, n.f., pain
ἀλήθεια, n.f., truth
ἀληθής, adj., true, genuine
ἀλίσκεσθαι, v., be caught
ἄλκιμος, adj., valiant
ἀλλά, conj., but; ἀλλὰ γάρ, but really
ἀλλήλους, pron. (acc.), one another
ἀλλοῖος, adj., different
ἄλλος, adj., other; οἱ ἄλλοι, the rest;
ἄλλως, adv., otherwise; ἄλλως τε
καί, especially

165

ἀλλότριος, adj., unfamiliar, relating to someone else
ἀλόγιστος, adj., irrational
ἅμα, adv., at the same time
ἀμαθία, n.f., ignorance
ἁμαρτάνειν, v., sin
ἁμαρτία, n.f., sin
ἀμβλύς, adj., shortsighted
ἀμείνων, adj., better
ἀμέλεια, n.f., neglect
ἀμελεῖν, v. + gen., be indifferent to, neglect
ἀμέλης, adj., heedless
ἀμεταστρεπτί, adv., irrevocably
ἀμετάστροφος, adj., irrevocable
ἀμήχανος, adj., unmanageable, inconceivable
ἀμυδρός, adj., dim
ἀμφότερος, adj., both
ἄν, part. indicating a condition whether expressed or latent
ἀναβαίνειν, v., go up
ἀναβιοῦν, v., return to life
ἀναβλέπειν, v., open one's eyes
ἀναγκάζειν, v., compel
ἀναγκαῖος, adj., necessary; ἀναγκαίως, adv., necessarily
ἀνάγκη, n.f., necessity, compulsion
ἀναιρεῖν, v., take up: (mid.), pick up for oneself
ἀναίτιος, adj., not responsible
ἀναλαμβάνειν, v., pick up
ἀναλογίζεσθαι, v., take into account
ἀναμιμνήσκειν, v., remind: (mid.), remember
ἀνάμνησις, n.f., recollection
ἀνασκοπεῖν, v., survey
ἀναφαίνεσθαι, v., come to light
ἀνδάνειν, v., please
ἀνέκπληκτος, adj., unshaken
ἀνεξέλεγκτος, adj., unrefuted
ἀνεπιστημοσύνη, n.f., ignorance
ἀνεπίφθονος, adj., unexceptionable

ἄνευ, prep. + gen., without
ἀνέχειν, v., sustain: (mid.), bear with, endure
ἀνήκεστος, adj., irremediable
ἀνήρ, n.m., man
ἄνθος, n.n., bloom
ἀνθρώπειος, adj., human
ἀνθρώπινος, adj., human
ἄνθρωπος, n.m., man, person
ἀνιατῶς, adv., incurably
ἀνιέναι (ἰέναι), v., come up
ἀνιέναι (ἰέναι) v., relax
ἀνιστάναι, v., set up: (pass. and intr.), stand up
ἀνόητος, adj., unintelligent
ἀνομοιότης, n.f., irregularity
ἀνόσιος, adj., impure, ungodly
ἀντέχειν, v., withstand: (mid.), get firm hold of
ἀντίστροφος, adj., counterpart
ἀντιτείνειν, v., resist
ἄνω, adv., at the top, above: (of a running track), at the turn
ἄνωθεν, adv., from above
ἄξιος, adj., worthy
ἀξιοῦν, v., think it right
ἀπαγγέλλειν, v., report back, tell
ἀπαιτεῖν, v., demand, ask in return
ἀπαλλαγή, n.f., release
ἅπας, adj., all, every
ἀπεργάζεσθαι, v., produce
ἀπέχειν, v., keep apart: (mid.), refrain
ἀπιέναι, v., depart
ἀπιστεῖν, v., be sceptical
ἀπλήστως, adv., in an unsatisfied condition
ἀπό, prep. + gen., away from
ἀποβλέπειν, v., turn attention to
ἀποδεικνύναι, v., demonstrate
ἀποδιδόναι, v., present, give back
ἀποδύρεσθαι, v., shed tears
ἀποθνήσκειν, v., die

ἀποκρίνεσθαι, v., answer
ἀποκτεινύναι, v., kill
ἀποκωλύειν, v., prevent
ἀπολαμβάνειν, v., receive as a right
ἀπολαύειν, v., reap the fruits
ἀπολείπειν, v., fall short of, omit
ἀπολλύναι, v., lose
ἀπολογεῖσθαι, v., make a defence
ἀπόλογος, n.m., story
ἀπολύειν, v., free from: (mid.), refute
ἀποπηδᾶν, v., sprint away
ἀποπιμπλάναι, v., satisfy thoroughly
ἀποπληρωτής, n.m., executor
ἀποστέλλειν, v., dismiss
ἀποτείνειν, v., deliver at length
ἀποτρέχειν, v., run away
ἀπράγμων, adj., quietistic
ἅπτειν, v., join: (mid.), grasp, take part in
ἄρα, part., after all
ἆρα, interrog. part. ἆρ' οὐ, Lat., nonne
ἀργός, adj., lazy
ἄρδειν, v., water
ἀρέσκειν, v., please
ἀρετή, n.f., excellence, virtue
ἀριθμεῖν, v., count
ἀριστερός, adj., left; ἀριστερά, n.f., left hand
ἁρμονία, n.f., scale, mode, musical setting, tunefulness
ἁρμόττειν, v., fit
ἄρτι, adv., a little while ago
ἀρχαῖος, adj., old, original
ἄρχειν, v., be in command (of): (mid.), begin
ἀρχή, n.f., office
ἀσεβεία, n.f., disrespect
ἀσθένεια, n.f., weakness
ἄσμενος, adj., glad
ἀσπάζεσθαι, v., welcome
ἀσπάλαθος, n.m., thorn
ἀστεφάνωτος, adj., ungarlanded

ἀστήρ, n.m., star, meteor
ἀστός, n.m., citizen, fellow-countryman
ἅτε, adv., inasmuch as
ἀτιμάζειν, v., dishonour
ἄτοπος, adj., out of place, surprising
ἄτρακτος, n.m., spindle
ἄττα = τινά, certain things
ᾄττειν, v., shoot, dart
αὖ, adv., again
αὖθις, adv., again
αὐλεῖν, v., play the flute or recorder
αὐλητής, n.m., player of the flute or recorder
αὐλοποιός, n.m., one who makes flutes or recorders
αὐλός, n.m., flute, recorder
αὐτόθι, adv., there
αὐτός, ή, όν, pron., he, she, it: sometimes emphasizing noun or pronoun, himself, in person; ὁ αὐτός, the same
αὐτόχειρ, adj., with one's own hand
αὐχμεῖν, v., dry up (tr.)
αὐχμός, n.m., dirt
ἀφανίζειν, v., remove
ἀφιέναι, v., abandon
ἀφικνεῖσθαι, v., arrive
ἀφιστάναι, v., set apart from
ἀφροδίσια, n.n.pl., love affairs
ἀφροσύνη, n.f., heedlessness
ἄφρων, adj., uneducated, unthinking
ἄχθεσθαι, v., feel sorrow

βαίνειν, v., go
βαρύς, adj., heavy
βασιλεύειν, v., be king
βασιλεύς n.m., king
βδελύττεσθαι, v., feel disgust at
βέβαιος, adj., guaranteed

βελτίων, βέλτιστος, adj., better, best
βῆμα, n.n., platform
βία, n.f., force
βίαιος, adj., involuntary
βίος, n.m., life, means of livelihood
βιοῦν, v., live
βλέπειν, v., see, look
βοᾶν, v., scream
βοήθεια, n.f., help
βούλεσθαι, v., want; βούλεσθαι εἶναι, mean
βουλεύειν, v., plan: (mid.), deliberate
βροντή, n.f., thunder
βρῶσις, n.f., eating
βωμολοχία, n.f., stupid foolery

γαμεῖν, v., marry
γάρ, part., for: in conversation sometimes to be rendered yes; or no
γε, part. used to emphasize the preceding word
γεηρός, adj., earthy
γέλοιος, adj., humorous, ridiculous
γελωτοποιεῖν, v., raise a laugh
γελωτοποιός, n.m., buffoon
γέμειν, v., to be weighed down
γένεσις, n.f., birth
γεννᾶν, v., bring to birth
γέννημα, n.n., product
γένος, n.n., race, sort
γέρων, n.m., old man
γῆ, n.f., earth
γίγνειν, v., bring to birth: (mid.), become, be; τὰ γεγονότα, the past
γιγνώσκειν, v., recognize, know
γόης, n.m., magician
γοητεία, n.f., wizardry
γονεύς, n.m., parent
γόνυ, n.n., knee
γοῦν, part., certainly
γραφεύς, n.m., painter

γραφική, n.f., painting
γράφειν, v., draw
γυμνοῦν, v., strip
γυναικεῖος, adj., of woman
γυνή, n.f., woman

δαιμόνιος, adj., mysterious
δαίμων, n.m., attendant spirit, god
δακρύειν, v., cry
δακτύλιος, n.m., ring
δανείζειν, v., lend: (mid.), borrow
δέ, part., and, but
δείδειν, v., fear
δεικνύναι, v., demonstrate
δειλία, n.f., cowardice
δεῖν, v., bind; δεῖ, it is necessary; εἰς δέον, opportunely
δεινός, adj., formidable
δεκάκις, adv., ten times over
δεκαπλάσιος, adj., ten times as great
δεκαταῖος, adj., ten days' old, after ten days
δένδρον, n.n., tree
δεξιός, adj., right; δεξιά, n.f., right hand
δεσμός, n.m., fastening
δεσπότης, n.m., master
δεῦρο, adv., (to) here
δεύτερος, adj., second
δέχεσθαι, v., receive, allow
δή, part., in fact
δῆλος, adj., obvious
δημιουργεῖν, v., produce
δημιουργία, n.f., professional skill
δημιουργός, n.m., craftsman
δημοσίᾳ, adv., in public life
διά, prep. + acc., owing to: + gen., by means of, at an interval of, through
διαβαίνειν, v., cross
διαγιγνώσκειν, v., distinguish
διαδικάζειν, v., finish the trial

διαθεᾶσθαι, v., examine thoroughly
διαιρεῖν, v., dissociate, distinguish
διακεῖσθαι, v., am disposed
διακελεύεσθαι, v., direct, impel
διαλαμβάνειν, v., seize
διαλείπειν, v., leave
διαλλάττειν, v., take in exchange
διαλύειν, v., disintegrate
διαμπερές, adv., right through
διανοεῖσθαι, v., have in mind
διάνοια, n.f., intelligence
διάπυρος, adj., fiery
διάσοφος, adj., professorial
διατελής, adj., lasting
διατιθέναι, v., dispose
διατρίβειν, v., spend time
διαφανής, adj., conspicuous
διαφέρειν, v., differ, act differently,
  carry through to the end
διαφερόντως, adv., exceptionally
διαφθείρειν, v., decompose
διαφορά, n.f., disagreement
διδασκαλός, n.m., teacher
διδόναι, v., give
διεξέρχεσθαι, v., pass right through,
  go through in minute detail
διέρχεσθαι, v., pass through, go
  through in detail
διηγεῖσθαι, v., recount
διιέναι, v., run through
διιστάναι, v., dispose
δικάζειν, v., pass judgement on
δίκαιος, adj., right, upright: δικαίως,
  adv., rightly, justifiably
δικαστής, n.m., judge
δίκη, n.f., right
δίνη, n.f., whirling motion
διό, adv., for this reason
διοικεῖν, v., govern, organize
διοίκησις, n.f., government
διομολογεῖν, v., reach a firm agreement about
διορᾶν, v., discern, see through

δοκεῖν, v., seem
δόκιμος, adj., distinguished
δόξα, n.f., reputation, opinion
δοξάζειν, v., opine, judge
δουλεία, n.f., slavery
δρᾶν, v., do
δρομεύς, n.m., runner
δρομικός, adj., expert in running
δρόμος, n.m., race, course
δύναμις, n.f., power
δύνασθαι, v., be able
δυνατός, adj., competent, possible
δύο, adj., two
δυσγένεια, n.f., low birth
δυσμαθία, n.f., slowness to learn
δωδεκαταῖος, adj., on the twelfth
  day
δῶρον, n.n., present

ἑ (αυτόν), pron. refl., himself
ἐάν, conj., if
ἐᾶν, v., let, let be; χαίρειν ἐᾶν, let go
ἕβδομος, adj., seventh
ἐγγίγνεσθαι, v., be present in, be
  innate
ἐγγύθεν, adv., from nearby
ἐγγύς, prep. + gen., near
ἐγείρειν, v., arouse
ἐγκεῖσθαι, v., nestle in
ἐγκρατής, adj., powerful, in control
ἐγκωμιάζειν, v., sing the praises
  of
ἐγκώμιον, n.n., complimentary address
ἐγώ, pron., I
ἔθειν, v., be accustomed, used mostly
  in pf. εἴωθα with pres. meaning;
  εἴωθα, + inf., I generally
ἐθέλειν, v., wish, like
ἐθίζειν, v., accustom
ἔθος, n.n., habit
εἰ (περ), conj., if

εἴδειν, v. obsolete, see, found in aorist εἶδον. Pf. οἶδα, know

εἶδος, n.n., form, aspect

εἴδωλον, n.n., image, phantom

εἰδωλοποιεῖν, v., produce phantasies

εἴκειν, v., yield

εἴκειν, v. obsolete, be like, found in pf. ἔοικα with pres. meaning

εἰκός, n.n., probability, analogy

εἰκοστός, adj., twentieth

εἰκότως, adv., justifiably

εἱμαρμένη, see μείρεσθαι

εἶναι, v., be: pres. part., ὤν; τὰ ὄντα, the present; τῷ ὄντι, in reality

εἴρειν, v., say, common in pf. εἴρηκα

εἰς, prep. + acc., to, into, in relation to

εἷς, μία, ἕν, adj., one

εἶτα, adv., then, next

ἐκ, prep. + gen., from, out of

ἕκαστος, adj., each

ἑκάτερος, adj., each (of two)

ἑκατέρωσε, adv., in either direction

ἑκατονταετηρίς, n.f., century

ἐκβαίνειν, v., leave

ἐκγλύπτειν, v., scoop out

ἔκγονος, n.m., descendant

ἐκδέρειν, v., flay

ἐκδιδόναι, v., give in marriage

ἐκεῖ, adv., there, in the other world

ἐκεῖθεν, adv., from there, from the other world

ἐκεῖνος, pron., that, the former

ἐκεῖσε, adv., in that direction

ἐκκάειν, v., burn out

ἐκκλάειν, v., break off

ἐκκομίζειν, v., draw out

ἑκούσιος, adj., voluntary

ἔκτεισμα, n.n., penalty

ἐκτίνειν, v., pay off

ἐκτός, adv., out: prep. + gen., apart from

ἕκτος, adj., sixth

ἐκφέρειν, v., sweep on

ἐλάττων, adj., smaller

ἐλαύνειν, v., drive

ἐλεεῖν, v., pity

ἐλεινός, adj., pitiable, pitiful

ἔλεος, n., pity, pathos

ἐληλάσθαι, pf. pass. of ἐλαύνειν

ἕλκειν, v., pull

ἐμβάλλειν, v., throw into

ἐμβλέπειν, v., look at

ἐμμένειν, v., abide by

ἔμπειρος, adj., experienced

ἐμπίπτειν, v., fall in, be thrown in

ἐμποδών, adv., in the way

ἐμποιεῖν, v., implant

ἔμφυτος, adj., natural

ἐν, prep. + dat., in

ἐναντίος, adj., opposite

ἐναντιοῦσθαι, v., oppose, contradict

ἐναντίωμα, n.n., contradiction

ἐναντίωσις, n.f., opposition

ἐναργής, adj., clear

ἐνδιδόναι, v., surrender

ἐνδύειν, v. (act. and mid.), put on

ἐνεῖναι, v., be in

ἕνεκα, prep. + gen., by reason of

ἔνθα, adv., then

ἐνθάδε, adv., here, in this world

ἐνθένδε, adv., from here, from this world

ἐνθυμεῖσθαι, v., consider, reflect

ἐννοεῖν, v., think, realize

ἐνταῦθα, adv., at this point

ἐντεῦθεν, adv., from there

ἐντός, adv., inside

ἐντυγχάνειν, v. + dat., meet

ἐξαγγέλλειν, v., report

ἐξαίφνης, adv., suddenly

ἐξαπατᾶν, v., fool, deceive

ἐξαπίνης, adv., suddenly

ἐξελέγχειν, v., disprove

ἐξετάζειν, v., scrutinize, identify

ἐξευρίσκειν, v., discover
ἐξέχειν, v., project
ἐξηγεῖσθαι, v., lead, prescribe
ἕξις, n.f., disposition
ἔξω, adv., outside: sup., ἐξωτάτω
ἐπᾴδειν, v., weave a spell
ἐπαινεῖν, v., approve of
ἐπαινέτης, n.m., admirer
ἔπαινος, n.m., approval
ἐπαίρειν, v., exalt, induce
ἐπαίειν, v., be knowledgeable
ἐπανακυκλεῖν, v., bring right round:
    (pass.), move round in the oppo-
    site direction
ἐπεί, conj., when, since
ἐπειδάν, conj., whenever
ἐπειδή (περ), conj., since
ἔπειν, v. obsolete, say, found in aorist
    εἶπον
ἐπεῖναι, v., be incumbent on
ἔπειτα, adv., then
ἕπεσθαι, v. + dat., follow
ἐπί, prep. + acc., to: + gen., in the
    light of, in the time of: + dat.,
    to, with a view to, by reason of,
    on, for
ἐπιδεικνύναι, v., exhibit
ἐπιδρομή, n.f., hurry
ἐπιεικής, adj., reasonable; ἐπιεικῶς,
    adv., pretty well
ἐπιέναι, v., come forward
ἐπιθυμεῖν, v., desire
ἐπιθυμητικός, adj., relating to desire
ἐπικλώθειν, v., spin one's fate
ἐπίκτητος, adj., acquired
ἐπιλαμβάνειν, v., seize: (mid.), arrest
ἐπιλανθάνεσθαι, v. + gen., forget
ἐπιμέλεσθαι, v., take care
ἐπίνοια, n.f., invention
ἐπισκέπτεσθαι, v., investigate, found
    mostly in other tenses than pres. for
    ἐπισκοπεῖν
ἐπισκοπεῖν, v., investigate

ἐπίστασθαι, v., understand
ἐπιστατεῖν, v. + gen., superintend
ἐπιστάτης, n.m., superintendent
ἐπιστήμη, n.f., knowledge
ἐπιστήμων, adj., knowledgeable
ἐπιστρέφειν, v., turn: (mid.), revolve
ἐπιστροφή, n.f., turning
ἐπιτάττειν, v., give instructions
ἐπιτηδεύειν, v., practise
ἐπιτήδευμα, n.n., activity
ἐπιτιθέναι, v., attach to, inflict
ἐπιφέρειν, v., introduce
ἐπίχειρα, n.n.pl., wages
ἐπιχειρεῖν, v., try
ἐπιχρωματίζειν, v., lay on colour
ἐπονομάζειν, v., call
ἐπορθοῦν, v., set on its feet again
ἔπος, n.n., word, line of epic
    poetry
ἑπτά, adj., seven
ἐπῳδή, n.f., spell, charm
ἔρασθαι, v., be in love
ἐργάζεσθαι, v., produce, fashion,
    perform
ἔργον, n.n., work, function
ἐρημία, n.f., isolation
ἐρυσίβη, n.f., mildew
ἔρχεσθαι, v., come
ἔρως, n.m., love, passion
ἐρωτᾶν, v., ask
ἑσπέρα, n.f., evening
ἑστιᾶσθαι, v., dine off
ἑστίασις, n.f., banquet
ἑταίρα, n.f., associate
ἑταῖρος, n.m., associate
ἕτερος, adj., one, other
ἔτι, adv., further, still
ἕτοιμος, adj., ready
ἔτος, n.n., year
εὖ, adv., well
εὐγένεια, n.f., high birth
εὐδαιμονεῖν, v., enjoy happiness
εὐδαίμων, adj., felicitous

εὐδοκιμεῖν, v., have a good name
εὐεργεσία, n.f., good deed
εὐεργετεῖν, v., do a good deed
εὐήθης, adj., simple-minded
εὐθύς, adj., straight: adv., straight away
εὐλαβεῖσθαι, v., take good care
εὔλογος, adj., reasonable
εὐμαθία, n.f., quickness to learn
εὐμενῶς, adv., sympathetically
εὐμήχανος, adj., ingenious
εὐμίμητός, adj., easily represented
εὐνομεῖσθαι, v., be well governed
εὔνους, adj., well-disposed, delighted
εὐπάθεια, n.f., glorious experience
εὐπετής, adj., easy
εὑρίσκειν, v., find
εὐσέβεια, n.f., respect
ἐφάπτειν, v., fix: (mid.), grasp, touch
ἐφέπειν, v. (act. and mid.), pursue
ἐφήμερος, adj., of a day
ἐφιέναι, v., incite to: (mid.), long for
ἔχθρα, n.f., distaste
ἔχειν, v., have, hold, possess, be able: + adv., be: (mid.), clutch, adjoin
ἕως, conj., until

ζῆν, v., live
ζητεῖν, v., look for
ζητητής, n.m., student
ζωγραφεῖν, v., paint
ζωγραφός, n.m., painter
ζῷον, n.n., living thing
ζωτικός, adj., alive

ἤ, part., or
ἤ, part., surely
ἡγεῖσθαι, v., lead, think

ἡγεμών, n.m., leader
ἤδη, adv., now
ἡδονή, n.f., pleasure
ἡδύνειν, v., sweeten, make ornate
ἡδύς, adj., enjoyable
ἦθος, n.n., character
ἥκειν, v., have come
ἥκιστα, adv., least
ἠλακατή, n.f., shaft
ἥλιος, n.m., sun
ἡμεῖς, pron., we
ἡμέρα, n.f., day
ἡμερήσιος, adj., lasting a day
ἥμερος, adj., tame
ἦμι, obsolete form of φημί, whence impf. ἦν, ἦ
ἥμισυς, adj., half
ἦν, (1) impf. of εἶναι, was; (2) impf. of ἦμι, said
ἡνία, n.f., reins (mostly in plural)
ἠρέμα, adv., gently
ἥρως, n.m., legendary hero
ἡσυχία, n.f., tranquillity
ἡσύχιος, adj., tranquil
ἧττον, adv., less

θαλάττιος, adj., from the sea
θανάσιμος, adj., fatal
θανατηφόρος, adj., involving death
θάνατος, n.m., death
θάπτειν, v., bury
θᾶττον, adv., more quickly
θαυμάζειν, v., be surprised
θαυμαστός, adj., remarkable
θαυματοποιία, n.f., creation of illusions
θέα, n.f., spectacle
θέαμα, n.n., spectacle
θεᾶσθαι, v., look at, consider
θέατρον, n.n., theatre
θέειν, v., run
θεῖος, adj., divine

θεομισής, adj., in the gods' disfavour

θεός, n.m., god

θεοφιλής, adj., favoured by the gods

θεωρεῖν, v., be spectator of, make a judgement

θηρίον, n.m., animal, monster

θνητός, adj., mortal

θρέψας, aorist part. act. of τρέφειν

θρηνώδης, adj., querulous

θρηνῳδία, n.f., wailing

θρόνος, n.m., seat, throne

θυγάτηρ, n.f., daughter

θυμός, n.m., anger

ἰαμβεῖον, n.n., iambic line

ἰᾶσθαι, v., cure

ἰατρικός, adj., to do with medicine; ἰατρική, n.f., medical science

ἰδέα, n.f., form

ἴδιος, adj., private; ἰδίᾳ, adv., in private life

ἰδιωτεία, n.f., private status

ἰδιώτης, n.m., ordinary citizen, private individual

ἰέναι, v., come, go (generally used as fut. to ἔρχεσθαι)

ἰέναι, v., let out

ἱκανῶς, adv., adequately

ἰός, n.m., rust

ἱππικός, n.m., jockey, rider

ἶρις, n.f., rainbow

ἴσος, adj., equal; ἴσως, adv., equally, perhaps

ἱστάναι, v., cause to stand up, weigh: (mid. and intr. tenses), stand

ἰσχυρός, adj., strong

ἰσχύς, n.f., physical strength

κάδος, n.m., box

καθάπερ, adv., like

καθαρός, adj., pure, clean

καθῆσθαι, v., sit, sit in judgement

καθιστάναι, v., set up

καθορᾶν, v., look down on, spot

καί, conj., and, actually, even, also; sometimes announces first term of a sequence followed by καί, and

καίτοι, part., yet

κακία, n.f., defect, vice

κακός, adj., evil, bad

κακουχία, n.f., iniquity

καλεῖν, v., name

κάλλος, n.n., beauty

καλλωπίζεσθαι, v., pride oneself

καλός, adj., noble

καμπύλος, adj., bent

καρτερεῖν, v., hold out

κατά, prep. + acc., down, in accordance with, at

καταβαίνειν, v., come down

καταβάλλειν, v., throw down

καταγέλαστος, adj., preposterous

καταδέχεσθαι, v., readmit

καταλείπειν, v., leave behind

καταμανθάνειν, v., understand

καταντικρύ, adv., full face

κατασκευάζειν, v., organize

κατασκηνᾶσθαι, v., encamp

κατατέμνειν, v., cut up

καταφαίνειν, v., make clear: (mid.), become clear

καταφρονεῖν, v., look down on

κατείρειν, v., denounce; found in fut. κατερῶ

κατέχειν, v., hold back

κατηγορεῖν, v., bring a charge

κατιέναι, v., return from exile

κάτοπτρον, n.n., mirror

κάτω, adv., at the bottom: (on a running track), at the start

καῦμα, n.n., heat

κεῖσθαι, v., lie, lie in store

κενεαγορία, n.f., babbling
κενός, adj., empty, bare
κεραννύναι, v., mix
κερδαίνειν, v., gain
κεφάλαιος, adj., principal; κεφάλαιον, n.n., chief point
κεφαλή, n.f., head
κῆδος, n.n., trouble
κηλεῖν, v., enchant
κήλησις, n.f., charm, attraction
κινδυνεύειν, v., run the risk, be
   likely to
κίνδυνος, n.m., danger
κίων, n.m. and f., pillar
κλᾶν, v., weep
κλῆρος, n.m., lot
κλίνη, n.f., bed
κλινοποιός, n.m., manufacturer of
   bed
κλινουργός, n.m. = κλινοποιός
κνάμπτειν, v., card
κοῖλος, adj., concave, hollow
κοιμᾶν, v., put to sleep
κοινωνία, n.f., partnership
κομίζειν, v., carry: (mid.), carry off,
   win, receive
κόνις, n.f., dust
κόπτειν, v., strike: (mid.), beat one's
   breast
κόρη, n.f., maiden
κράς, n. (gender unknown), head
κρατεῖν, v., be in authority
κράτιστος, adj., most important
κραυγάζειν, v., bark
κρίνειν, v., judge
κρίσις, n.f., decision
κτᾶσθαι, v., get
κύβος, n.m., cube: (pl.), dice
κυκλεῖν, v., turn in a circle: (mid.),
   move in a circle
κύκλος, n.m., circle
κύκνος, n.m., swan
κῦμα, n.n., wave

κυνῆ, n.f., helmet
κυροῦν, v., ratify
κύων, n.f., bitch
κωλύειν, v., prevent
κωμῳδικός, adj., comic
κωμῳδοποιός, n.m., comedian

λαγχάνειν, v., get by lot
λαιμαργία, n.f., greed
λακέρυζος, adj., yelping
λαμβάνειν, v., take, receive, accept,
   catch
λαμπρός, adj., brilliant
λανθάνειν, v., escape detection:
   + part., do without realizing
λέγειν, v., speak
λειμών, n.m., meadow, field
λεῖος, adj., smooth
λεπτῶς, adv., subtly
λευκός, adj., white
λευκότης, n.f., whiteness
λευχειμονεῖν, v., wear white
λέων, n.m., lion
λήθη, n.f., forgetfulness
λογίζεσθαι, v., calculate
λογισμός, n.m., reasoning, conclusion
λογιστικός, adj., to do with reasoning or calculation
λόγος, n.m., argument, account,
   mention, reason, word, speech
λύειν, v., break up
λυπεῖν, v., distress
λύπη, n.f., sorrow, distress
λυπηρός, adj., unenjoyable
λωβᾶσθαι, v., be detrimental to,
   ruin
λώβη, n.f., detriment
λωφᾶν, v. + gen., take a rest from

μὰ Δία, exclamation after a negative,
   Good God, no!

μάθημα, n.n., learning
μαθητής, n.m., pupil
μακρός, adj., long
μάλα, adv., much, very much so: comp., sup., μᾶλλον, μάλιστα
μανθάνειν, v., understand, learn
μαραίνειν, v., wither (tr.)
μαστιγοῦν, v., flog
μάχεσθαι, v., fight
μέγας, adj., great: comp., sup., μείζων, μέγιστος
μέγεθος, n.n., size
μεθόδος, n.f., doctrine
μειγνύναι, v., mix
μεικτός, adj., mixed
μεῖξις, n.f., combination
μείρεσθαι, v., receive by right: pf. pass, εἵμαρται, it is fated; εἱμαρμένη, n.f., destiny
μέλλειν, v., be going to; τὰ μέλλοντα, the future
μέλος, n.n., lyric
μέν, part. announcing the first term of a contrast, and normally followed by δέ
μέντοι, adv., however
μεριμνᾶν, v., reason out
μέρος, n.n., part
μέσος, adj., middle
μεσοῦν, v., be in the middle
μεστός, adj., full, covered
μετά, prep. + acc., after: + gen., with
μεταβάλλειν, v., change
μεταβολή, n.f., interchange
μεταίτιος, adj., party to
μεταλαμβάνειν, v., get a share of
μεταξύ, adv., in the middle: prep. + gen., between
μετεῖναι, v., be among; μέτεστι, (impers.), there is available
μετέχειν, v., share in
μετριάζειν, v., behave with moderation

μέτριος, adj., reasonable
μέτρον, n.n., measure, metre
μετροῦν, v., measure
μέχρι, prep. + gen., up till
μή, neg. part., not
μηδαμῇ, adv., not at all
μηδέ, part., nor, not even
μηδείς, μηδεμία, μηδέν, pron., no one, nothing
μήν, part., further, certainly, yet
μηχανή, n.f., device
μιαίνειν, v., defile
μιμεῖσθαι, v., represent
μίμημα, n.n., representation
μίμησις, n.f., representation
μιμητής, n.m., representational artist
μιμητικός, adj., associated with dramatic representation
μισεῖν, v., despise, hate
μισθός, n.m., reward
μῖσος, n.n., hatred
μνημεῖον, n.n., memorial
μνήμη, n.f., mention
μνημονεύειν, v., record, remember
μόγις, adv., with difficulty
μοῖρα, n.f., portion, destiny
μονοειδής, adj., simple, uniform
μόνος, adj., alone; μόνον, adv., only; μόνον οὐ, almost; ὅσον μόνον, so far and no farther
μονοῦν, v., isolate
μουσικός, adj., musical, cultured; μουσική, n.f., music, poetry, art
μοχθηρός, adj., rotten, corrupt
μῦθος, n.m., story
μυκᾶσθαι, v., bellow
μυρίος, adj., countless

ναί, part., yes
νεανικός, adj., impetuous, 'fresh'
νεκρός, n.m., dead body

νέος, *adj.*, young, recent
νῆσις, *n.f.*, spinning
νικητήριον, *n.n.*, prize
νικηφόρος, *adj.*, victorious
νοεῖν, *v.*, conceive, think
νομίζειν, *v.*, think
νομοθέτης, *n.m.*, law-giver, author
of constitution
νόμος, *n.m.*, law
νοσεῖν, *v.*, be diseased
νόσημα, *n.n.*, malady
νόσος, *n.f.*, disease
νοῦς, *n.m.*, intelligence
νῦν, *adv.*, now
νυνδή, *adv.*, just now
νύξ, *n.f.*, night
νῶτον, *n.n.*, back, surface

ξανθός, *adj.*, yellow
ξένος, *n.m.*, foreigner
ξύλον, *n.n.*, timber
ξύν, *prep.* + *dat.*, with

ὁ, ἡ, τό, *pron.*, he, she, it: *def. art.*,
the; ὁ μὲν . . . ὁ δέ, the first, the
second
ὄγδοος, *adj.*, eighth
ὅδε, ἥδε, τόδε, *pron.*, this, the following
ὁδός, *n.f.*, way, journey
ὀδύρεσθαι, *v.*, cry
ὀδυρμός, *n.m.*, lamentation
ὅθεν, *rel. adv.*, from where
οἱ, (1) *nom. pl. of* ὁ, (2) *dat. of* ἕ
οἴεσθαι, *v.*, think
οἴκαδε, *adv.*, homewards
οἰκεῖν, *v.*, be in a certain state, be
governed
οἰκεῖος, *adj.*, personal, particular
οἰκία, *n.f.*, home
οἰκίζειν, *v.*, found

οἴκοι, *adv.*, at home
οἷος, *rel. pron.*, such as; *interrog.
pron.*, of what sort?; οἷον, e.g.;
οἷός τ' εἶναι, *v.*, be able
οἴσω, *fut. ind. of* φέρειν
ὀκτώ, *adj.*, eight
ὄλεθρος, *n.m.*, destruction
ὀλίγος, *adj.*, few
ὅλος, *adj.*, complete; ὅλως, *adv.*,
completely, in general
ὁμιλεῖν, *v.*, go with
ὁμιλία, *n.f.*, company, association
ὅμοιος, *adj.*, like, fellow
ὁμοιοῦν, *v.*, make like: (*mid.*), become like
ὁμολογεῖν, *v.*, agree
ὁμονοητικῶς, *adv.*, consistently
ὅμοσε, *adv.*, to close quarters, to
grips
ὅμως, *adv.*, all the same
ὀνινάναι, *v.*, benefit
ὄνομα, *n.n.*, name, word, noun
ὄντως, *adv.*, genuinely
ὀξύς, *adj.*, keen, sharp
ὄπῃ, *rel. adv.*, where
ὀπῃοῦν, *adv.*, at any angle
ὄπισθεν, *adv.*, at the back
ὅπλον, *n.n.*, tool: *pl.*, arms
ὁπόθεν, *adv.*, from whatever source
ὁπόστος, *adj.*, at what number
ὁπότε, *conj.*, since
ὁρᾶν, *v.*, see
ὁρίζειν, *v.*, limit: (*mid.*), define
ὁρμή, *n.f.*, impulse
ὀρθός, *adj.*, correct; ὀρθῶς, *adv.*,
rightly
ὀρθότης, *n.f.*, correctness
ὅς, ἥ, ὅ, *rel. pron.*, who, which
ὅσιος, *adj.*, pious
ὅσος (περ), *rel. pron.*, as much as:
(*pl.*), as many as
ὅστις, ἥτις, ὅτι, *pron.*, who, what,
which

ὁστισοῦν, pron., anyone at all

ὄστρεον, n.n., shell

ὅταν, conj., whence

ὅτε, conj., when

οὐ(κ), neg. part.

οὗ, gen. of (1) ὅς, (2) ἕ

οὐδαμῶς, adv., not at all

οὐδέ, part., not even

οὐδείς, οὐδεμία, οὐδέν, pron., no one, nothing

οὐδέποτε, adv., never

οὐκοῦν, part., then; οὔκουν, then not

οὖν, part., so, therefore

οὔπω, adv., not yet

οὐράνιος, adj., through the heavens

οὐρανός, n.m., heaven, sky

οὖς, n.n., ear

οὗτος, αὕτη, τοῦτο, pron., this, the preceding; οὕτω(ς), adv., so, in this way

οὐχί, emphatic form of οὐ

ὀφείλειν, v., owe, ought

ὀφθαλμία, n.f., ophthalmia

ὀφθαλμός, n.m., eye

ὄχλος, n.m., gang

ὄψις, n.f., faculty of sight, vision

πάθημα, n.n., weakness

πάθος, n.n., sensation, suffering

παιδαγωγεῖν, v., escort, dance attendance on

παιδεία, n.f., education

παιδεύειν, v., educate

παιδία, n.f., pastime, amusement

παιδικός, adj., adolescent

παῖς, n.m., boy, child; ἐκ παιδός, from childhood

παλαιός, adj., old, bygone

παλαιότης, n.f., age, staleness, mouldiness

πάλιν, adv., again

πάμπολυς, adv., very much: (pl.), very many

πάνδεινος, adj., very shocking, very terrible

πανήγυρις, n.f., religious festival

παντάπασιν, adv., in every way

πανταχῇ, adv., everywhere

πανταχοῦ, adv., at every point

παντοδαπός, adj., of every kind, nondescript

πάνυ, adv., in every way, completely

παρά, prep. + acc., beside, along, contrary to: + gen., from

παραγίγνεσθαι, v. + dat., support, stand by

παράδειγμα, n.n., example

παραδέχεσθαι, v., let in

παραδιδόναι, v., hand over

παραμελεῖν, v., leave on one side

παραπλήσιος, adj., closely similar

παρεῖναι, v., be present

παρέρχεσθαι, v., pass by

παρέχειν, v., provide, render: (mid.), provide from one's own resources

παριέναι, v., come by

παριστάναι, v., set by, bring it home to: (pass. and intr.), stand by

πᾶς, adj., all, the whole, every; τὸ παράπαν, at all

πάσσοφος, adj., omniscient

πάσχειν, v., suffer

πεδίον, n.n., plain

πείθειν, v., persuade: (pass.), obey

πεινᾶν, v. + gen., be hungry for, long for

πειρᾶσθαι, v., try

πέμπτος, adj., fifth

πένεσθαι, v., be poor

πενθεῖν, v., show sorrow

πένθος, n.n., sorrow

πενία, n.f., poverty

περί, prep. + acc., about: + gen., about, at the value of

περιαγείρειν, v., take a collection: (mid.), take a collection for one-self

περιέναι, v., go about

περικρούειν, v., strip

περιμένειν, v., await

πέριξ, adv., round about

περίοδος, n.f., cycle

περιφέρειν, v., carry round

περιφορά, n.f., circumference, circle

περιφύειν, v., grow all round

πέτρα, n.f., rock

πετρώδης, adj., rocky

πῇ, interrog., how; πῃ, enclitic, in some way

πηγνύναι, v., fix: pf. used intr., have the fixed idea of

πίθηκος, n.m., monkey

πιμπλάναι, v., satisfy

πίνειν, v., drink

πίπτειν, v., fall, fall out, happen

πιστεύειν, v., believe, listen to

πίστις, n.f., belief

πλάγιος, adj., oblique; ἐκ πλαγίου, obliquely

πλάνη, n.f., error

πλατύς, adj., broad

πλῆθος, n.n., number

πλήττειν, v., hit

πλοῦτος, n.m., wealth

πνῖγος, n.n., suffocation

ποθεν, enclitic, from some source

ποιεῖν, v., produce, make: (mid.), value

ποίημα, n.n., composition

ποίησις, n.f., poetry

ποιητής, n.m., poet, producer

ποιητικός, adj., poetic

ποικιλία, n.f., variety

ποικίλος, adj., spangled, varied

ποῖος, interrog. pron., of what sort

πολεμεῖν, v., fight a war

πόλεμος, n.n., war

πόλις, n.f., city, state

πολιτεία, n.f., constitution

πολλάκις, adv., often

πολλαχῇ, adv., in many places

πολυειδής, adj., complex, multiform

πολύς, adj., much, many; οἱ πολλοί, the majority, the men in the street; comp., sup., πλέων, πλεῖστος

πονεῖν, v., labour, suffer

πονηρία, n.f., corruption, ineffi-ciency

πονηρός, adj., bad, immoral, un-worthy, inefficient

πόνος, n.m., labour, suffering

πόντος, n.m., ocean

πορεία, n.f., travel, journey

πορεύεσθαι, v., travel

πόρρω, adv., rather far

πόρρωθεν, adv., from a distance

ποταμός, n.m., river

ποτε, enclitic, ever

πότερος, interrog. adj., which; πότερον . . . ἤ, whether . . . or?; πότερον or πότερα, introducing question

που, enclitic, I think

πούς, n.m., foot

πρᾶγμα, n.n., affair, object

πρᾶξις, n.f., activity

πράττειν, v., act

πρεσβύτης, n.m., old man: comp. adj., πρεσβύτερος

πρίν, conj., before

πρό, prep. + gen., in advance of

προβαίνειν, v., turn out well

πρόγονος, n.m., ancestor

προδιδόναι, v., betray

προερεῖν, v., announce beforehand

προέρχεσθαι, v., go forward

προθυμεῖσθαι, v., be eager

προιστάναι, v. (act. and mid.), value higher than

προκεῖσθαι, v., be offered as prize

προλείπειν, v., leave all too soon
προπηλακίζειν, v., insult
προρρηθείς, see προερεῖν
πρός, prep. + acc., to, compared with, in relation to, against: + dat., in addition to
προσαγορεύειν, v., call
προσγίγνεσθαι, v., attach oneself to
προσέρχεσθαι, v., approach
πρόσθεν, adv., forward, in front
προσιέναι, v., go up to
προσκαθῆσθαι, v., settle in
προσλέγειν, v., say further
προσομιλεῖν, v., accompany
προσπταίειν, v., stumble
προστάτης, n.m., champion
προσφέρειν, v., bring towards: (mid.), behave towards
προσφερής, adj., resembling
προσφύειν, v., grow on
πρόσωπον, n.n., face
πρότερος, adj., earlier
προτιθέναι, v., present a case
προφήτης, n.m., interpreter
πρῶτος, adj., first
πτῶσις, n.f., fall
πτωχεία, n.f., beggary
πυνθάνεσθαι, v., inquire
πυρά, n.f., pyre
πυρετός, n.m., fever
πῶς, interrog., how; πως, enclitic, in some way

ῥᾴδιος, adj., easy: comp., sup., ῥᾴων, ῥᾷστος
ῥαψωδεῖν, v., string poems together
ῥεῖν, v. obsolete, say, found in v. adj., ῥητέος and part. ῥηθείς
ῥῆμα, n.n., phrase, verb
ῥῆσις, n.f., speech, address
ῥίπτειν, v., throw
ῥυθμός, n.m., time, rhythm

σαπρότης, n.f., rot
σεισμός, n.m., earthquake
σημαίνειν, v., indicate, point out
σημεῖον, n.n., evidence, mark
σηπεδών, n.f., rot
σιγᾶν, v., be silent
σίδηρος, n.m., iron
σιτία, n.n.pl., grain
σῖτος, n.m., corn
σκεῦος, n.n., article of furniture
σκηνᾶσθαι, v., be quartered, encamp
σκιαγραφία, n.f., scene-painting
σκληρότης, n.f., harshness
σκοπεῖν, v., look at
σκυτεύς, n.m., leather-worker
σκυτοτομία, n.f., cobbling
σκυτοτόμος, n.m., cobbler
σμικρός, adj., small
σοφία, n.f., wisdom
σοφιστής, n.m., expert, professor
σοφός, adj., wise
σπουδάζειν, v., be enthusiastic
σπουδαῖος, adj., important
σπουδή, n.f., serious matter
στασιάζειν, v., be in conflict
στέγειν, v., be watertight against
στέμμα, n.n., garland
στερεῖν, v., deprive
στεφανοῦν, v., garland
στόμιον, n.n., mouth
στρατηγία, n.f., military command
στρατόπεδον, n.n., army
στρεβλοῦν, v., rack
στρέφειν, v., turn: (mid.), revolve
σύ, pron. you (sing.)
συγγίγνεσθαι, v., be associated with, lecture to
συγγενής, adj., closely related
συγκεραννύναι, v., blend
συγχωρεῖν, v., agree
συλλογίζεσθαι, v., consider from all points of view

συμβουλεύειν, v., advise, be consulted

συμπάσχειν, v., share in the experience or suffering

συμπέμπειν, v., send with

συμπεριφέρειν, v., carry round as well

συμποδίζειν, v., fetter

συμφάναι, v., agree

συμφορά, n.f., misfortune

σύμφυτος, adj., congenital

συμφωνεῖν, v., sing in harmony

σύνδεσμος, n.m., complete fastening

συνειδέναι, v., realize

συνεῖναι, v., be with

συνεπιστρέφειν, v., help to turn

συνέχειν, v., hold together

συνεχής, adj., continuous

συνήθεια, n.f., habit

σύνθεσις, n.f., composition

σύνθετος, adj., composite

συννοεῖν, v., understand

συνουσία, n.f., company

συντιθέναι, v., bring together

συντόνως, adv., earnestly

συντρίβειν, v., crush

σφαγή, n.f., violent death

σφεῖς, pron., they, commonly reflexive in oblique cases

σφόδρα, adv., deeply, emphatically

σφόνδυλος, n.m., whorl

σχεδόν, adv., almost

σχῆμα, n.n., form, shape

σχολαῖος, adj., slow

σχολή, n.f., leisure; σχολῇ, slowly, hardly

σώζειν, v., keep safe

σῶμα, n.n., body

τάξις, n.f., order, disposition

ταραχή, n.f., confusion

τάττειν, v., design

τάχα, adv., soon

ταχύς, adj., quick

τε, part., announcing the first term of a sequence and normally followed by καί

τείνειν, v., stretch

τέκτων, n.m., carpenter

τελευταῖος, adj., last

τελευτᾶν, v., finish, die

τελέως, adv., completely, perfectly

τέλος, n.n., finish

τέταμαι, pf. pass. of, τείνειν

τεταρταῖος, adj., on the fourth day

τέταρτος, adj., fourth

τέτταρες, adj., four

τέχνη, n.f., skill, expertise, science

τεχνικός, adj., expert in craft

τήκειν, v., waste

τιθέναι, v., place, posit

τιμᾶν, v., honour, exalt

τιμή, n.f., honour, reputation

τιμωρία, n.f., punishment

τίς, τί, interrog., who, what; τις, τι, enclitic, a certain, someone, something

τοι, part., exactly, in fact

τοίνυν, part., then

τοιόσδε, adj., of this sort, of the following sort

τοιοῦτος, adj., such, of this sort

τολμᾶν, v., dare

τόνος, n.m., note

τόπος, n.m., place

τότε, adv., then

τραγικός, adj., to do with tragic drama

τραγωδία, n.f., tragic drama

τραγῳδοποιός, n.m., tragic dramatist

τράπεζα, n.f., table

τραχύς, adj., rough

τρεῖς, adj., three

τρέφειν, v., foster

τριήρης, n.f., warship
τρίτος, adj., third
τριττός, adj., of three kinds
τρόπος, n.m., way
τροφή, n.f., diet
τυγχάνειν, v., happen, (+ gen.) obtain; τυγχάνω ὤν, am actually, really am
τυραννίς, n.f., dictatorship
τύραννος, n.m., dictator
τύχη, n.f., occurrence, fortune, misfortune

ὑγίεια, n.f., health
ὑγιής, adj., healthy, unimpaired; ὑγιῶς, adv., soundly
ὕδωρ, n.n., water
ὑμεῖς, pron., you (pl.)
ὕμνος, n.m., hymn
υἱός, n.m., son
ὑπάρχειν, v., be from the beginning
ὑπέρ, prep. + gen., in behalf of, for
ὑπερβάλλειν, v., be excessive, be greatest
ὑπέρυθρος, adj., rather red
ὑπηρετεῖν, v., do service
ὑπό, prep. + acc., under: + gen., under, by the agency of
ὑπόζωμα, n.n., undergirding
ὑπολαμβάνειν, v., suppose
ὕστερος, adj., later; οἱ ὕστεροι, posterity
ὑψηλός, adj., high

φαίνειν, v., reveal: (mid.), appear, be clear
φάναι, v., say
φάντασμα, n.n., appearance
φάρμακον, n.n., remedy, antidote
φάσκειν, v., say
φαῦλος, adj., inferior
φέρειν, v., bear: (mid.), win

φεύγειν, v., avoid
φθέγγεσθαι, v., speak
φθέγμα, n.n., voice
φθείρειν, v., ruin
φιλεῖν, v., love
φιλία, n.f., friendship, affection
φιλοποιητής, n.m., lover of poetry
φίλος, adj., dear: n.m., friend
φιλοσοφεῖν, v., pursue wisdom
φιλοσοφία, n.f., philosophy, love of wisdom
φιλοτιμία, n.f., ambition
φοβεῖσθαι, v., fear
φόβος, n.m., terror
φόνος, n.m., murder
φορά, n.f., direction, speed
φρόνησις, n.f., intelligence
φρόνιμος, adj., intelligent
φυγή, n.f., banishment
φύειν, v., cause to grow; (intr.), grow
φυκίον, n.n., seaweed
φυλακή, n.f., guard
φύλαξ, n.m., supervisor
φύσις, n.f., nature
φυτεύειν, v., bring into being
φυτόν, n.n., plant, vegetable
φυτουργός, n.m., true maker, creator of the real
φωνή, n.f., voice, sound
φῶς, n.n., light

χαίρειν, v., find pleasure
χαλεπός, adj., difficult; χαλεπῶς, adv., with difficulty
χαλινός, n.m., bridle, bit
χαλκεύς, n.m., smith
χαλκός, n.m., copper
χαρίεις, adj., pretty, good
χαρίζεσθαι, v. -ι- dat., gratify
χάσμα, n.n., opening
χεῖλος, n.n., lip
χείρ, n.f., hand

χειροτέχνης, *n.m.*, workman
χείρων, *adj.*, worse
χθόνιος, *adj.*, underground
χιλιέτης, *adj.*, a thousand years long
χιλιοστός, *adj.*, thousandth
χρεία, *n.f.*, use
χρῆμα, *n.n.*, possession
χρῆναι, *v.*, be necessary
χρῆσθαι, *v.* + *dat.*, use
χρηστός, *adj.*, good, moral, efficient
χρόνος, *n.m.*, time, interval
χρυσός, *n.m.*, gold
χρῶμα, *n.n.*, colour
χωρίζειν, *v.*, separate
χωρίς, *adv.*, apart

ψυχή, *n.f.*, soul, life

ὦ, *introduces vocative*
ὧδε, *adv.*, as follows
ὦμος, *n.m.*, shoulder
ὡραῖος, *adj.*, with the bloom of youth
ὡς, *conj.*, as, that, because
ὡσαύτως, *adv.*, in the same way
ὥσπερ, *adv.*, like
ὥστε, *conj.*, with the result that
ὦτα, *pl. of* οὖς
ὠφελεῖν, *v.*, benefit
ὠφελία, *n.f.*, usefulness, profit

CPSIA information can be obtained
at www.ICGtesting.com
Printed in the USA
LVHW052155030321
680488LV00015B/162

9 781853 996825